For O'Brien —

on the apron of
The Runaway Theater —

best wishes,

Robert Dana
4. 20. 92

AGAINST THE GRAIN

Against the Grain

Interviews with
Maverick American Publishers

EDITED BY ROBERT DANA

University of Iowa Press  *Iowa City*

Library of Congress Cataloging-in-Publication Data
Against the grain.
    Contents: James Laughlin—Harry Duncan—Lawrence
Ferlinghetti—[etc.]
    1. Publishers and publishing—United States—
Interviews. 2. Underground press—United States.
I. Dana, Robert, 1929–
Z471.A35   1986   070.5′0973   86-1457
ISBN 0-87745-146-X

University of Iowa Press, Iowa City 52242
Copyright © 1986 by Robert Dana
All rights reserved
Printed in the United States of America
First edition, 1986

Book and jacket design by Patrick Hathcock
Typesetting by G&S Typesetters, Inc., Austin, Texas
Printing and binding by Kingsport Press, Kingsport, Tennessee

for Kim Merker, who suggested this book
for Peg Dana, who believed we could do it

Contents

Acknowledgments

In addition to my wife, Peg, for her unflagging support, and K. K. Merker, who launched the idea, thanks are due to Cornell College for half a dozen summers of faculty development grants, which supplied not only moral support but transcription, typing, typewriter ribbons, word-processing discs, gasoline, and plane tickets for interviewing trips; to my teaching colleagues at Cornell, who have allowed me to do my work; to Carol Brokel for this and all the other manuscripts she has typed and retyped over the course of twenty years; to Eric Houts and the Breakfast Club of Medicine Bow, Wyoming, for their tolerance and good humor on a 7,000-mile, month-long interviewing trip in the summer of 1981; to my son-in-law, Kevin Kriegel, for the sound enhancement of the very difficult David Godine tapes; to Prescott Barrows, who supplied the rare photograph of Harry Duncan and Paul Williams in the early days of the Cummington Press; to the *American Poetry Review* and its editors, Stephen Berg and David Bonanno, for first publishing the interview with James Laughlin; to Michael Heffernan at *Midwest Quarterly* for first publishing the interview with Lawrence Ferlinghetti; and finally, of course, to James Laughlin, Harry Duncan, Lawrence Ferlinghetti, John Martin, Daniel Halpern, Sam Hamill and Tree Swenson, Jonathan Williams, and David Godine for their time, their candor, and their enduring contributions to the world of American letters.

Introduction

"Rise like a rocket. Fall like a stick." Harry Duncan looked up at me from the composing stick in which he was arranging, one letter at a time, the words of a poem. I remember the frank look in his green eyes as he said this, the soft, aphoristic, absolutely certain, New England ring of his speech. It was probably the first, and the only, wisdom ever offered me by a publisher. I've carried it around ever since, in my pocket like a smooth stone, a charm against falling.

Harry Duncan had only recently brought the Cummington Press to Iowa City, but the fame of the press and the publisher were well known in American literary circles. Even in academic literary circles. Even in supposedly know-nothing, post–World War II, McCarthy era, middle western literary circles. There was no twenty-five-year-old contemporary of mine who didn't know that Harry Duncan had published Robert Lowell's first book, *The Land of Unlikeness*, that he had published Stevens and William Carlos Williams and Allen

Tate. And now, here he was somehow, inexplicably, set down by the gods of academe in the typographic lab of the University of Iowa. If there was in this something smacking of alchemy, there was no hint of the mountebank in the man himself.

On the contrary, as I stood there looking across the California typecase at this diminutive man in white shirt, bow tie, and suspendered trousers setting type with that meticulous, clean movement of a surgeon closing an incision, the mood was distinctly one of no nonsense. He had already established a reputation as a demanding teacher of typography and design. His poems had only a year or two before appeared in the first of Scribner's piggyback Poets of Today series. He had lived in Rome and was a formidable Catholic, once even appearing with somebody's splendid Persian cat as the spectacularly evil cardinal in a University of Iowa Theatre production of *The White Devil.*

I could continue developing this story while asking myself what relevance it has to a book of interviews with small, independent American publishers. Or say that the type Harry Duncan was setting that day was part of the first book of poetry issued by a small press ever to win the then-prestigious Lamont Prize for Poetry. Or say that one of my oldest friends, in the years immediately following my apprenticeship in Robert Lowell's workshop and later in the crazy brimstone of John Berryman's, became Harry's friend and protégé and successor, and my first publisher. K. K. Merker now runs both his own Stone Wall Press and the Windhover Press of the University of Iowa and teaches the craft of bookmaking to a new generation of aspiring students.

But important as such developments of plot may be, they have little to do with the indelible quality of that afternoon in 1959. The point lies—the measure seems clear to me now—in the personal nature of the experience. Small-press publishing is personal publishing. In essence, it's a matter of personal vision, personal taste and courage, and personal friendships—not a matter, at least in the beginning, of hype and bottom

lines. You hear it over and over in the stories of the publishers
themselves. How Paul Williams, as a young soldier, walked
in off a bitter winter road in backwoods Massachusetts to
become the designer for the Cummington Press and Harry
Duncan's friend and partner. How, in Rapallo, Italy, in 1936,
Ezra Pound told his young student and secretary, Harvard
dropout James Laughlin, to go home and "be a publisher."
Jonathan Williams, with David Ruff, launched Jargon Press in
1951 in San Francisco on the strength of three poems, one
"tiny" copperplate engraving, and their mutual friendship
with Kenneth Patchen. John Martin rescued Charles Bukowski from the Los Angeles post office, then later published
Robert Kelly, who "was pals with Diane Wakoski. And Wakoski
was pals with Clayton Eshleman. And Eshleman was pals
with Jerome Rothenberg. And Rothenberg was pals with
David Antin."

"Alternative publishing," the polite term developed and
now in use among both writers and academics for this and
other kinds of small-press activity, tells us that a profound
change has already taken place in the literary world, especially in that part of it in which these presses played, and continue to play, an important role. We are approaching the last
decade of the twentieth century. The modern impulse is spent,
the postmodern either spent or not quite ready for its quick
slouch toward Bethlehem. The literary center has not held.
The large publishing "houses"—a term going back, surely, to
the days of the family-owned enterprise in which "cultured"
men might lend the family name honor and light and influence by publishing books, or gentlemen might find reasonable,
rather than cutthroat, employment in publishing and selling
books—these houses have vanished as completely as the
Chrysler brothers and "American know-how." In their place,
the conglomerates, the bookkeepers, MTV, and megabucks.

But the unvarnished history of publishing in America tells
us that this is the nostalgic view: Max Perkins writing elo-
quent and perceptive letters to James Jones, Allen Tate, and
Scott Fitzgerald. Most commercial editors in New York pub-

lishing houses today don't even return phone calls, let alone
write their authors personal letters. And there is enough evidence in the biographies of T. S. Eliot, Henry Miller, James
Joyce, Anaïs Nin, and others to confirm an unsentimental perspective, to suggest that personal indifference to both the
plights and triumphs of writers has been all along the prevail-
ing editorial style. Moreover, the actual publishing record of
the commercial sector has been clear for more than a century.
As Sally Dennison points out in her recent study, *(Alternative) Literary Publishing*, "most of the nineteenth century
writers whom we now think of as important . . . published
their own works. . . . Poe's *Poems* of 1831, Hawthorne's early
fiction, Whitman's *Leaves of Grass*, Thoreau's *Walden*, Twain's
Huckleberry Finn, and Melville's later works . . . were all self-
published." The names of twentieth-century writers rejected
or ignored throw an equally harsh light.

So it has been the small presses, "little" presses, which
have kept before our attention fresh standards of quality and
the shape of the new, which is never anything more or less
than the shape of our own intentions, *in*-tensions, tendencies,
even where those tendencies are totally hidden from us. Even
where—perhaps especially where—the art itself creates the
life. Thus, those publishers chosen for inclusion in this first
collection of interviews earned their place by virtue of a certain recklessness. They insisted on cutting against the grain
of both business sense and received literary opinion. Their
first concern in almost every case was for the publication of
the unpublishable, of the not-yet-published, and for the shape
of what they believed to be the future. In some cases, the concern was as much for the craft of printing, the art of the book
as a *made* thing, as it was for the writing itself. So, in retro-
spect, the presses seem to divide into two basic types: the
small commercial press like New Directions or David R. Godine or Ecco on the one hand, and the small, fine-book presses
like Cummington or Copper Canyon on the other. But such a
classification, however useful, is elementary. Since small-press
publishing is personal publishing, each press reflects, more

richly and directly than any large commercial press could hope to, the character of its founder, its presiding spirit or spirits.

While the presses represented here do range from commercial to fine book, they also arrange themselves along other lines. New Directions is the oldest and most spectacularly successful; Copper Canyon and Ecco are the youngest, with the shortest track records. At Copper Canyon and Cummington, the talk is just as likely to be about the way different printing presses "bite" into paper, of the "character" or "personality" of a typeface and its suitability to a text, as it is about the text itself. Because neither Harry Duncan nor Sam Hamill and Tree Swenson have ever surrendered their conviction that a book is a work of "architecture" and that "we have to house literature in a way that does it *honor*." In fact, some of the more commercial of these presses, David R. Godine and John Martin's Black Sparrow, began on the letterpress side of publishing, often with a concern for hand-set types, hand-made papers, and hand-bound limited editions. The force of that concern can still be read in the visual design of their books, like rings inside a tree. Lawrence Ferlinghetti's City Lights, on the other hand, seems in part to take its impulse from the European tradition of bookseller as publisher. And Ferlinghetti's public utterances as a poet, as well as his willingness as a publisher to take up the cause of the poetic and political left, have created a vigor and an optimism for City Lights characteristically its own. Moreover, nearly every press under scrutiny here presents itself in an iconoclastic light, regardless of its actual character: New Directions for its Pound and Williams; City Lights for Allen Ginsberg. Black Sparrow has its Charles Bukowski, Copper Canyon its Thomas McGrath, and Jargon its Charles Olson and its proud list of "guys on the edges," "out there in left field, wacko, on their own."

These publishers may also be seen, to some extent, as expressions of certain geographical and historical qualities. New Directions, David R. Godine, and Ecco are East Coast in origin; Jargon comes out of North Carolina; Cummington is midwestern; Black Sparrow and City Lights are West Coast presses; and Copper Canyon, northwestern. And the long, neo-Romantic wave that is twentieth-century literary history has singularly favored three of these presses: New Directions, City Lights, and Jargon. It's useless to conjecture what dreamy mix of literary idealism, courage, and sharp business sense seeded the founding of City Lights and bloomed so richly in the _Howl_ obscenity trial of 1957. One can only guess what complex of occasions placed Lawrence Ferlinghetti in San Francisco at exactly that moment in the repressive history of the national psyche. And what would have happened to Charles Olson's work if a restless Jonathan Williams hadn't gone home to Black Mountain College in North Carolina in 1951? But no press is more remarkable with respect to its history than New Directions. James Laughlin is unique among the publishers whose voices are heard here and unique among his own contemporaries.

At the age of nineteen, Laughlin, with the advice and help of Ezra Pound, tapped into the deepest surge of the modernist movement. His first annual New Directions anthology, published in 1936, contained work by Pound, Henry Miller, William Carlos Williams, and e. e. cummings. The 1939 annual is characteristic: a play by Federico García Lorca; poems by Elizabeth Bishop, Dylan Thomas, Charles Henri Ford, John Berryman, Kenneth Patchen, Lawrence Durrell, and Kenneth Rexroth; and fiction by Dylan Thomas and William Carlos Williams. New Directions' program, as characterized by Hayden Carruth, one of its early editorial assistants, reads like the archetypal blueprint for small-press development:

> 1) to keep in print important works by the great men of the literary revolution, e.g., Pound and Williams; 2) to circulate English translations of important modern works in other languages . . . ; 3) to search out new writers, both experimentalists . . . and others, e.g., Ford and Schwartz; 4) to publish works from all literary camps, no

matter how contrary, and even to stir up controversy for the sake of the animating stimulus.

Thus, Laughlin had not only eastern cachet in the form of money (Jones and Laughlin Steel) and education (Choate and Harvard), but a direct line to Ezra Pound, the era's greatest literary mover and shaker. Although much has already been written and said of the importance of Pound's advice to the swift and brilliant development of New Directions, and of the proddings of Kenneth Rexroth in a similar role later, the fact remains that it was James Laughlin who had the uncommon good sense to listen to their advice. Not enough has been said of Laughlin's own literary acumen and intelligence. He was among the first American publishers to take an extensive interest in French literature, publishing Jean Cocteau, the surrealists, and even postmodern experimentalists like Raymond Queneau. New Directions also gave early audience to the work of important Latin American writers, including Pablo Neruda and Jorge Luis Borges. The iconoclasm that brought under the same roof Ezra Pound and Yvor Winters, Dylan Thomas and Tennessee Williams, Yukio Mishima and Pablo Neruda is surely Laughlin's alone, whatever advisors and editors he may have had. Thus gifted, New Directions rode the flood and chaos of modern letters like a Noah's Ark.

So the mark was set, and the fifty years of New Directions which ensued had an impact roughly equivalent to the publishing of *The Wasteland* or Joyce's *Ulysses*—a fresh wind constantly blowing. While some of the publishers represented here are openly aware of the magnitude and importance of the achievement of New Directions, none, wisely, has tried to duplicate history. Instead, each press has found or created its own particular ambience and shaped its own strong character. Each has earned its own place in the select group that makes up the first generation of important small presses on the American literary scene.

Now, in the late 1980s, the situation of the little press, the "alternative" publisher, has become nearly as congested, fragmented, and confused as the literary situation it serves. Or, given another perspective, as lively and complex. A recent edition of the *International Directory of Little Magazines and Small Presses* catalogued over thirty-five hundred English-language small presses (excluding university presses), more than half of which operate in the United States. R. R. Bowker's *Small Press* records the number of little presses, including self-publishers, at fourteen thousand! The causes of this massive inflation are many, but three seem paramount. First and still foremost, of course, is the continuing concern of the commercial sector with production and distribution costs, survival, and profit—a condition aggravated by the fact that these houses are now owned and operated largely by meglomerates in which, increasingly, the *only* language spoken is that of the abysmal bottom line. A second reason for the small-press revolution is the rapid proliferation during the fifties, sixties, and seventies of university writers' workshops. As Len Fulton, the founder of Dustbooks, has observed, "The single driving reason for the existence of new publishers is new writers." Thus, whatever criticisms may be leveled at the workshop phenomenon, and there are certainly enough, it has stimulated a rage for writing perhaps unparalleled in cultural history. Finally, there has been since 1965 the influence of the National Endowment for the Arts, with its financial support of specific projects by existing presses and seed money for the creation of new ones. And while it's not the express purpose of this book to evaluate such pressures, they inevitably, on occasion, make up an important part of the conversation.

Whatever the long-term effects of this escalation of writing and publishing may be—whether new bursts of literary brilliance or a leveling anemia and exhaustion—the fact is it continues. For every little press that fails, literally a dozen spring up in its place. The next generation of small presses likely to make a significant impact on contemporary literature is already in place, foremost among them perhaps Graywolf, North Point, Pushcart, Thunder's Mouth, and Alice James

Books. And just out of sight, of course, there's that press without name, still just a trip of electrons in the dreamer's head, poised for lift-off on the next historical light wave.

In the meantime, there's this record in the publishers' own words—no doubt mingling, like the writers they publish, fact with fiction—of how it all began for them, where it went, and what the future may hold for these eight small, maverick American presses.

AGAINST THE GRAIN

James Laughlin

Acting on the advice of Ezra Pound, who told him to "go back home to the States and do something useful," James Laughlin founded the publishing firm of New Directions in 1936 while still an undergraduate at Harvard University.

Dedicated to the work of the avant-garde, and with the help of his authors—mainly Pound, William Carlos Williams, and Kenneth Rexroth—New Directions built a broad list. It came to include many of the important writers of the twentieth century: Henry Miller, Nathanael West, Hermann Hesse, Dylan Thomas, Tennessee Williams, Jean Cocteau, and Jorge Luis Borges. Its younger writers include Denise Levertov, Gary Snyder, David Antin, John Hawkes, and Toby Olson.

In the fifty years of its publishing history, New Directions set the undisputed benchmark for small-press achievement.

Mr. Laughlin has been honored for his service to literature with degrees from Hamilton College, Brown University, and Colgate University, and awards for publishing from the American Academy of Arts and Letters, the New York Center for the Arts, P.E.N., and Publishers Weekly. *At seventy-two, he is still active as a publisher, in addition to lecturing on Pound and Williams, working on his "recollections," and acting as a consultant to the New York Center for Visual History, which is preparing a documentary film on William Carlos Williams.*

The following conversation took place in June 1980 in the Laughlins' Bank Street apartment in Greenwich Village.

DANA: You must have been very young when you went abroad, nineteen or so.

LAUGHLIN: Well, let's see. I finished school at Choate in '32. I did my freshman year at Harvard in '33 and half my sophomore year in '34. And that's when I went over to Europe. I got a leave of absence to go over because I found Harvard very dull. It was between faculty generations there. The great men—the old men like Kittredge, Lowes, and the rest of them—had retired, and the young lions like Matthiessen and Spencer hadn't come on yet. All we had, really, was Robert Hillyer, that mediocre poet. You couldn't mention Pound's or Eliot's name in Hillyer's class or you'd be sent out of the room.

DANA: Is that right?

LAUGHLIN: So I got leave to go abroad. I went to Europe to try to write, both poetry and stories, and to travel around.

DANA: Is it true that you fixed flat tires for Gertrude Stein?

LAUGHLIN: Yes indeed. It was summer, and I was at the Salzburg Music Festival. I used to go swimming every day in the public swimming pool, and I made there the acquaintance of a distinguished French professor with a limp, Bernard Fay, who evidently liked my looks—I had more hair than I have now.

We began talking. He spoke very good English, and I spoke enough French. It turned out that one of his best friends was

Gertrude Stein. I said, "Oh, I've been reading Gertrude Stein at home, and she sounds like a fascinating person." He said, "Would you like to meet her?" I said, "I surely would." So he wrote to her and said, "I've met this young American who might be useful to you. Can I bring him along to Bilignin?" That was her country place. I went there, I stayed about a month, and she put me to work. She was a utilitarian person.

And what I was doing for her—it was the summer before she was going to have her lecture tour in America and somebody had told her that she had to have press releases of her lectures to give to the press when she went to a city, so she gave me these lectures and said, "Now take these and produce a one-page press release for each one." Well, it nearly drove me crazy because the lectures, *Lectures in America*, are very philosophical and very interesting, but extremely diffuse. To try to identify the central theme of these lectures and to translate them from Steinese into American newspaperese was something of a task. Again and again I would whack something out and take it to her and she would read it and say, "No. You've missed the whole point. Go back and do it over." I stayed there about a month before I finally got those releases done to her satisfaction. I'd work in the mornings. She'd write in the morning, sitting out on the terrace. She had a beautiful place, what they call a *château ferme*—smaller than a château but better built than a farm—with a lovely view over the rolling hills down in the lower part of the Savoie.

Afternoons we would go out in her little Ford car with Alice B. Toklas and Gertrude sitting in the front, myself in the back with two hideous dogs—one named Basket, a white poodle, and one named Pepe, a nasty little black Mexican nipper. I was there in the back seat and could never get to see the view, because the dogs were constantly jumping around or trying to *lick* me.

In those days on the roads of the Savoie, there were many nails that came out of hikers' boots, so we'd get a lot of punctures. Some days we'd get *two* punctures. And when we got a puncture, Gertrude would pull off to the side of the road, and she and Alice would go over and spread out their picnic things in a nice, cozy spot in the field, and I had to change the tires, with the damned dogs leaping all over me. Then on our way home we would stop at the village *garagiste* in Bellay and give him the bad tires, which he would fix up for the next day's outing.

DANA: Was he the famous one who coined the phrase, "You are all a lost generation," or was that some other *garagiste*?

LAUGHLIN: I think that was somebody from Paris. Gertrude was a very dynamic, extraordinarily charismatic personality, and one couldn't help but be enormously impressed and influenced by her, except that some of her ideas were so crazy. She thought that Hitler was a great man. This was *before* the war. And she had a number of other similarly weird notions. Why a Jewess would think Hitler was a great man is a little hard to understand, but she did.

DANA: Someone once asked you why you stopped publishing Gertrude Stein, and you said, because you didn't think her work was that important at the time.

LAUGHLIN: Well, I've been proved wrong. Among the younger generation, particularly in California—people like Duncan and Antin and Rothenberg and others—she is now very much read.

DANA: Her work does seem to be beginning to revive. I noticed Haskell House has reissued *Tender Buttons*, for example, and William Gass has published a long essay about the technique of *Tender Buttons*.

LAUGHLIN: Uh-huh. But it was, of course, another thing that put me a little bit off. About the time I was there with her, I'm convinced she was doing automatic writing. I used to watch her from the room where I was typing out the bloody press releases. She would sit in a bath chair on the terrace with a big notebook, writing just as fast as she could without any pause whatever. No pause. No rewriting. And then poor Alice Toklas, sweet person—*not* all sweet, but sort of sweet—was given the notebooks to type out. It was pretty clear to me that at that particular phase . . . Now, I know very well that earlier, in the *Making of Americans* period and probably the *Tender Buttons* period, she was *not* doing automatic writing. You could tell it from the style. You could tell it in *Three Lives*. But at *that* moment she was doing, I think, automatic writing. Now, whether there was any influence in that from the Surrealists, I don't know. I think she would deny it. In fact, she said that *everyone* was influenced by *her*, and we had a big fight one day because I had been reading Proust. She said, "How can you read that junk? Don't you know, J, that Proust and Joyce both copied their works from *The Making of Americans*?"

DANA: That's remarkable.

LAUGHLIN: She was a megalomaniac. But she had great natural charm and, as I say, tremendous charisma. I mean, that marvelous head, and those wonderful flashing eyes. And the firmness of her deep voice. When she enunciated things, she took in a lot of people.

DANA: Of course.

LAUGHLIN: And she liked people. She really *did* like people. She loved to have people come around. During and after the war, she had her house full of wandering GIs, you know, who just came around to see her and, I suppose, get a free cookie. Alice made *great* cookies.

DANA: Well, were you fairly interested in literature as a very young man?

LAUGHLIN: No, I grew up in a house in Pittsburgh with nothing but sets and the Bible, and the sets were never read. Of course, I had children's books to read, wonderful books about pirates.

DANA: When you say sets, you mean sets of books? Like the Harvard Classics?

LAUGHLIN: No, just sets. Sets of Jane Austen, or of Walter Scott, . . .

DANA: Alexander Dumas?

LAUGHLIN: Yes, that sort of thing. My father wasn't much

of a reader, and my mother read awful tripe. Her favorite writer was Lloyd C. Douglas. I don't know if that name means anything to you.

DANA: Oh yes, *The Robe*. I remember the Douglas vogue very well.

LAUGHLIN: So that I really didn't get bitten by literature as a child. I suppose I always *did* write. The whole family lived on one hill in Pittsburgh. Woodland Road, Squirrel Hill. There were seventeen related houses on that road, related by marriage or by blood.

DANA: Amazing.

LAUGHLIN: And at Christmas we always put on a Christmas play. I used to write these plays for the other children to act in. They were written in either rhymed couplets or in blank verse, and they were highly dramatic. They were about princes, and princesses, and villains, and dragons, and all that sort of thing. I really didn't begin to get interested in what I would call good literature until I got to Choate, where I had two really remarkable English teachers.

DANA: Dudley Fitts?

LAUGHLIN: Well, first was Carey Briggs. His method was quite different from Dudley Fitts's. Carey Briggs was a little old man who taught his Honors English class in the library, not in a classroom. His method was to teach boys to *use* books. To find things in books and to use them. Each boy was given a project, and he didn't give us much help, either—I mean he said, "Gentlemen, here is the library, here are the books, there is the card index. You go to work now and find out what you need to know for your project." For some reason, I chose as my project the history of poetic prose. I spent most of that year digging through the library hunting for examples of what could properly be called poetic prose.

DANA: How did you arrive at this project? It seems very avant-garde for the thirties.

LAUGHLIN: Briggs may have dropped a hint that interested me. I dug up people like Lyly and Sir Thomas Browne, all the old boys. Briggs was very inspiring because he really made you love books and taught you how to use them. When I got to Harvard, I had an enormous advantage over most of the other boys in the freshman class, who had never been taught how to use the library or how to look things up. It was a very interesting pedagogic idea.

DANA: Fitts, as I understand it, gave you a letter of introduction to Pound?

LAUGHLIN: Yes. Fitts had been corresponding with Pound for a number of years. Fitts was a friend of Lincoln Kirstin, who ran *Hound and Horn* magazine. Somebody ought to publish Fitts's letters, because they were the funniest letters ever written by anybody. He was a great linguist, and he'd read everything. His letters really entranced Pound, because here was somebody who had read in all the languages Pound read.

DANA: Well, Pound wrote some pretty mean letters himself—funny ones.

LAUGHLIN: Fitts was really the one who got me writing.

I remember one humiliating day with Briggs—not really humiliating, because he was a sweet man—when I had turned out what I thought was a poem. He read it and then lowered his glasses on the rim of his nose and said, "Mr. Laughlin, are you *aware* that what you have written is *not* poetry, but verse?"

Fitts was a very inspiring composition teacher, and he got me writing prose. Through him I became editor of the Choate literary magazine and wrote quite a few pieces for that and helped run it. Fitts later wrote Ezra to say I was coming over and would like to meet him.

DANA: This would have been the summer of '34?

LAUGHLIN: I think so. Gertrude got tired of me because I didn't accept everything she said. I would argue with her, and that was disrespectful, so she cooled on me.

DANA: Well, greatness doesn't like to be disagreed with.

LAUGHLIN: When the summer was over, I went up to Paris for the fall and lived in a tiny rented room in an insurance office. My rent was seven dollars a month, and I ate around in small restaurants in the quarter and walked a great deal.

From that period comes my story "The River," about a young writer trying to adjust to life and decide what he is going to write about.

After some months in Paris, I wrote to Ezra, not really expecting to get any reply, asking if I could see him. To my amazement, he sent me a telegram: "Visibility high." So I took the train to Rapallo in Italy.

Ezra and I immediately hit it off. He loved to have somebody to teach. He was a thwarted professor. And I was ripe to be taught. So he enrolled me in what he called the Ezuversity. No tuition. He found a room for me in the flat of an old German lady. Mornings he would work, mostly at his correspondence, answering letters from all over the world about his historical and economic ideas and about poetry and everything else. He used to say that postage was his highest living expense. Then we'd have lunch together with Mrs. Pound in the dining room of the hotel next to the building where their penthouse was.

The instruction in the Ezuversity simply consisted of Ezra's monologues. He would usually start talking about the mail he had received that morning and then go on to everything under the sun. And it was very exciting talk, because he had an extraordinary mimetic ability.

DANA: Yes, that shows up in his letters, too.

LAUGHLIN: He could remember how Joyce talked and imitate him. He could remember how Yeats talked and imitate him. And he was *full* of funny stories, very *funny* stories, very *nice* stories. Never, in all the years that I knew him, can I remember Ezra's ever telling an off-color story.

DANA: That's interesting.

LAUGHLIN: Then he would give me books to read from his library.

DANA: Like what?

LAUGHLIN: Chiefly what's in *How to Read*. What I call the Pound Canon. The books that he approved of, you know, going back to the Greeks, and up through Catullus and Propertius, then jumping to the Provençal poets and then up through Villon. . . . Oh yes, well, Shakespeare's songs he always approved of. He didn't care much for the plays, but he thought the songs were music.

DANA: So that you'd say he had a consistent curriculum.

LAUGHLIN: Yes. And what was most interesting about reading his books were his marginal comments, what he'd written in the margins of his own books.

DANA: Do you remember any of them?

LAUGHLIN: No, unfortunately I don't.

DANA: How long did you stay with Ezra?

LAUGHLIN: Well, let's see. I think I came in September. Then, in February I went up to Austria to go skiing at St. Anton. I loved skiing. After the skiing season was over, the end of March or April, I came back to Rapallo and stayed on into the summer. Somehow—I can't remember how I acquired it, because I had no money—I got hold of a car and drove up to Salzburg with Ezra, Olga Rudge, and Mary, their daughter. The great thing that I remember about Ezra in Salzburg was when we went to the *Festspielhaus*, where Toscanini was conducting Beethoven's *Fidelio*. As you probably know, Ezra never really liked Beethoven very much. And after about twenty minutes of the opera, Ezra reared up from his seat and said in a very loud voice, which everybody could hear, "No wonder! The man had syphilis!"

DANA: And did he leave?

LAUGHLIN: We *all* left. Toscanini was unfazed. He continued to conduct.

DANA: So, six months with Ezra?

LAUGHLIN: I would say probably that.

DANA: You give Pound a lot of credit for sending you, if you'll forgive the double entendre, in "New Directions."

LAUGHLIN: Well, I didn't finish telling you the curriculum of the Ezuversity. We had lunch together, then he took a snooze, and then we would go swimming or play tennis—he was a whale of a tennis player—or walk in the beautiful hills in back of Rapallo. We'd come back, and Mrs. Pound would make tea, and then there was more discussion. After tea, he would work, and Mrs. Pound would read Henry James aloud to me. Can you imagine that beautiful English voice reading Henry James?

DANA: That's quite an education.

LAUGHLIN: Then we had dinner together. After dinner, he often wanted to go to those dreadful Italian comedies at the movies. In those days, art had not reached the Italian cinema, and the movies were beyond belief awful. But Ezra loved them. He would sit up in the first gallery with his cowboy hat on and his feet up on the rail, eating peanuts and roaring with laughter at these dreadful comedies. The only reason I stuck them out was that I was learning a certain amount of Italian from them.

That was the curriculum. Mornings, I'd try to write stories or poems. Ezra wouldn't read the stories; he wasn't interested much in any fiction since James or Flaubert. But he would look at the poems and tear them to pieces. He would break the points of six pencils crossing out words, saying, "You don't need that word," and, "Here's what you really mean to say." He'd write in the way *he* would say it.

Finally, after I'd been there some months, he said to me, "Jas, let's face it, you're never going to be a writer. Why don't you go back home to the States and do something useful?" I said, "What's useful?" He said, "Waaal, you might 'assassernate' Henry Seidel Canby."

Canby was the editor, you remember, of the *Saturday Review*. He was the famous man who wrote that there was no character development in *Ulysses*.

I said, "Well, how am I going to get away with it?" That puzzled him, and he said, "Well, maybe you're right. Well, go back and be a publisher." So that's how I became a publisher.

DANA: That must have rung some kind of a bell for you.

LAUGHLIN: Well, it was *books*. You know, it was books and authors. Literary. It meant escaping from working in the family steel mill, which I hated. Terrifying place.

DANA: Did you have experience with the steel industry?

LAUGHLIN: Every Thanksgiving my father would take my brother and me down to the mill. He thought this was educational. We'd tour one of the mills, and it was like the *Inferno*. As you know, in those days they hadn't automated the mills, and there was this terrible flame leaping out of the furnaces and hot, molten ingots rolling out of them and then going on to the rollers to be thinned. There were terribly frightening giant cranes moving overhead carrying huge buckets of molten metal.

DANA: Yes, I remember seeing such things in movies. I've never seen them in person.

LAUGHLIN: I think it's all changed now. I haven't been back in the mills since. But I believe now they do things in a very different way. It's all run by computer and the safety . . .

DANA: You must have found it terrifying.

LAUGHLIN: It *was*. It *was* terrifying.

DANA: So you were determined at some fairly early age not to deal in steel, so to speak.

LAUGHLIN: Well, I wanted to avoid it if I could. My brother went into it. But he was lucky. He became a salesman, so he didn't have to work in the mills.

DANA: Now, you actually launched New Directions while you were still a student at Harvard.

LAUGHLIN: Yes. I went back to Harvard and picked up my work where I'd left off.

DANA: What year was that?

LAUGHLIN: I think it was, maybe, the fall of '35, because the earliest date in New Directions books is 1936, which would have been the second term of that year.

What Ezra did to get me started was to write letters to all his writer friends—to Williams, to Kay Boyle, to Cocteau, to, oh, a dozen or so writer friends—saying, "If you have a manuscript, send it to this worthy young man." But the funny thing about my starting was that I didn't know anything about how to become a publisher. I had no instruction, nobody to tell me. All I had done was work on the Choate literary magazine and then the *Harvard Advocate*. That was all I knew. So the first book that we did I printed with the printer in Vermont who'd printed the *Harvard Advocate*. It was a very funny book called *Pianos of Sympathy,* by Wayne Andrews, though he called himself, in those days, Montague O'Reilly. He was an interesting young man. He's now an extremely eminent professor of history or something at Wayne State University. He's just finished writing a book for us at New Directions, a book on Voltaire which is the funniest thing you've ever read. He treats Voltaire with complete irony throughout. Voltaire, though the greatest literary figure of his age, was, as you know, a pompous ass, as well as being a smart aleck. And Wayne has read everything on him, every memoir of the period. Well, anyway, I was in Eliot House and Wayne was in Dunster House at Harvard. He and his family had lived in Paris, and he had grown up very precociously. He had known most of the surrealists—Breton and Eluard and others—very well. So here he was at Harvard, a bit lost and, under the name of Montague O'Reilly, writing delicious stories about old gentlemen who had long hair and piano-string fetishes. That was the first little pamphlet that we published.

DANA: So that was the beginning of New Directions. Are there any extant copies that you know of? Besides those in your own possession?

LAUGHLIN: You don't see it around much, because we printed two hundred copies to start, in red covers, and those were sold off. Then we printed two hundred copies in blue covers, and I think that was all there were.

DANA: And the New Directions annuals followed that?

LAUGHLIN: *The River,* my own pamphlet, may have followed next. Then we did the first New Directions Anthology, the one with the hideous yellow and red cover. The one where we forgot to number the pages.

I started all this business with complete innocence, more or less being taught, as far as manuscript preparation and production went, by the printers I used. As for selling the books, that was the great mystery. What I began to do was—they had a thing at Harvard in those days called the reading period, when you didn't have any classes—I would get in my car and start west to visit bookstores. In some stores I'd sell a copy or two, and sometimes I wouldn't.

DANA: When you say you'd head west, how far west?

LAUGHLIN: The farthest west I ever went was Omaha, Nebraska, where there was a fearsome lady in Matthews Bookstore. Mrs. Matthews made me tremble, she was so irate. Nevertheless, she would usually end up buying one book.

DANA: Well, you must have been quite a sensation at Harvard. An upstart twenty-year-old publisher with . . .

LAUGHLIN: I don't think that Harvard paid any attention to me. I mean, the people . . .

DANA: No circle of friends sprang up around you? Or, . . .

LAUGHLIN: I'm pretty much of a loner. The people on the *Advocate* . . . I was always a member of the *Advocate*, and I would have been president of the *Advocate*, except for the turpitude of another fellow, my best friend, who won the presidency away from me by giving the *Advocate* building a new roof. So that I ended up as Pegasus of the *Advocate*, which meant the poetry editor.

DANA: I see.

LAUGHLIN: In our literary club, the Signet, people knew me as somebody to be avoided, as being slightly off-color and dangerous.

DANA: So, after that, you continued to print Pound. He became one of your staples.

LAUGHLIN: Oh yes, we went right on. He was, at that time, being published by the old firm of Farrar and Rinehart, and he decided that they were crooks. The basis of this harsh and quite unjustified judgment was that one Christmas they sent him a leather-bound copy of his latest book, and he said, "They must be crooks." So he took his work away from them, not much to their sorrow, because in the early days the *Cantos* weren't selling, and started giving it to me. We did *Polite Essays*, which were not polite, and we did his *ABC of Economics*, which is still a text which I recommend to anyone who is puzzled by things like inflation. We did, oh, one after another, there must have been, I suppose, twenty books. I'm very proud of the fact that, with one or two exceptions, we keep all of them in print . . . at some loss. I mean some of his books sell well, his *Selected Poems* sell well, the *ABC of Reading* sells well, the *Cantos* sell well, but with the rest of them it's three or four hundred copies a year.

DANA: Apropos of the *ABC of Economics*, I know that at odd times in your life you have talked about Social Credit as an important factor in understanding what goes on in America. In fact, I went through the annuals and reread your prefaces. You almost always had something pointed to say about American culture, American politics, American economics, . . .

LAUGHLIN: I am still, despite lack of encouragement, a convinced Social Creditor. I picked that all up from Ezra and from reading. Ezra gave me the works of C. H. Douglas to read, which set out the principles of Social Credit. And I am still convinced that some such system is the only solution to the mess we have gotten ourselves into by the pyramiding of debt. You see, our whole economy is based on debt. Borrowing, stocks, whatever you have—debt; private debt, government debt. New York City almost went under last year because of debt.

DANA: Oh yes. You can't save any money on your income taxes unless you're in debt.

LAUGHLIN: Right.

DANA: It's crazy.

LAUGHLIN: I am still convinced, although I don't see any chance that it is ever going to happen, that we have got to get swung over to some kind of a positive economic system, where credit is issued as a social right rather than borrowed from some bank at fifteen percent. There should be a national dividend, which would be paid out in varying amounts from year to year, depending on the economic situation. I mean you would have a little book, and you'd go to the post office, and you'd get your money. Everything would then be switched around from the psychology of borrowing and debt to the psychology of creating credit to represent man's capacity to work and achieve.

DANA: Well, I can see some of your critics saying, "Well, but you yourself are a capitalist."

LAUGHLIN: I am.

DANA: It prompts me to ask you, did those theories of Social Credit affect the way you organized New Directions?

LAUGHLIN: I don't think they affected them at all, because the way I started running New Directions was to ask my father for money, and he'd give it to me.

DANA: So you would say it was a straight capitalistic economics?

LAUGHLIN: He didn't charge me any interest. He *gave* me the money. My father was a very sweet man who worked in the mills. He was in charge of the electrification of the Aliquippa mills. He'd taken an electrical engineering degree at Princeton, and he worked in the company until his father died. And the minute his father died, he quit and devoted the rest of his life to golf, fishing, and shooting birds of various types. But he was a sweet man and very much a gentleman. If I asked him for money, he'd say, "Are you going to publish some more of those books that I can't understand?" And I'd say, "Yes." And he'd give it to me.

DANA: But you organized New Directions on a straight, capitalistic, sound accounting model.

LAUGHLIN: New Directions was never capitalized.

DANA: It was just subsidized.

LAUGHLIN: It was just subsidized. And even after we became incorporated some fifteen years ago, it was never capitalized. I mean, we have stock, but nobody bought it.

DANA: Let's get back to Pound for a moment.

LAUGHLIN: Ezra was a lovable person. You know, people think of him as an anti-Semite monster, but he wasn't.

DANA: Well, his genius has always seemed rather remote and contradictory.

LAUGHLIN: He's a funny case. He neglected his children. He would only see his daughter, Mary, for a few weeks during the summer. And he seldom saw his son, Omar. When Omar got out of boarding school, he'd be shipped off to his grandmother's for the summer. Ezra was remote in that sense. And yet, in the town of Rapallo, he was deeply loved and respected. And nobody ever came to see him in Rapallo and was turned away summarily. If he proved to be a bore, he would be gently eased out. But anybody could come there, and Ezra would talk to them, try to instruct them. He had this wonderfully forbearing quality about people—and he didn't expect people to be as smart as he was.

DANA: Certainly his generosity to other writers is legendary.

LAUGHLIN: You may have read of all the things he did for Joyce . . . and do you know that in the Pound/Joyce letters book there is not one single line where Joyce says something nice about Ezra's writing?

DANA: Is that right?

LAUGHLIN: Not one line. It's always "Me, me, me, me, me."

DANA: He was interested in Hemingway, in Frost, in Joyce, and they were all remarkably different from each other, quite different people. Yet he seemed to have the same intensity of enthusiasm for each of them. You don't see *that* much in the literary scene today.

LAUGHLIN: On the other hand, he was singularly blindered, as a horse is blindered for a race. Would you believe it that he thought that the only important modern French poet was Cocteau?

DANA: That's remarkable.

LAUGHLIN: He didn't pay any attention to Valéry or to Reverdy or the Surrealists. It was a strange sort of an egocentrism that a person had to have somehow entered his orbit in order to qualify for attention.

DANA: You and Pound must have had disagreements. I mean, even as a young man who admired and respected him, there must have been moments when your judgment and his judgment diverged.

LAUGHLIN: I tackled him a little bit about the anti-

Semitism. I would raise a questioning voice about whether it was really the Jews who were back of the financial shenanigans, because, statistically, there are just as many *goys* who were lending out money as anybody else. I did tackle him a little bit about *that*, but he always had one answer. He would say, "Jas, how can somebody whose name is Ezra be anti-Semitic?"

DANA: Did you disagree on literary matters?

LAUGHLIN: No. Well, we may have disagreed a little bit about Shakespeare's plays. All that Ezra could see in them was the music of the songs. You see, his lifelong preoccupation was the idea of suiting the length of the syllables in a poetic line to the notes of the music to which they were to be sung. Now, if you study the scores of his operas—the *Villon* and the *Cavalcanti*—you will see to what lengths he went to approximate the length of the syllables in the French and Italian words to the notes that he provided for them in the score.

DANA: Well, when *you* started publishing French writers, you published people like Breton and Eluard. Was Pound blind to their value?

LAUGHLIN: He didn't read them. I'd send him the books, and he just wouldn't read them.

DANA: How do you explain that?

LAUGHLIN: Because he had this blinkered vision. I mean, if I sent him something of Cocteau, he'd write back and say, "Good work."

DANA: Did Pound connect you to Williams?

LAUGHLIN: Yes. Williams received a letter from Pound, and he then invited me out to Rutherford to see him. I think he wanted to look me over. Because, you see, he had ready at that time the first volume of the Stecher trilogy, *White Mule*. He had that all ready and waiting. He had poems ready and waiting. Williams had had a very checkered publishing history. The only way that he was able to get his first books published (those very interesting experimental books which are totally unlike anything he did later—*Kora in Hell, Spring and all, A Novelette, Descent of Winter, The Great American*

Novel—which are *very* experimental and very interesting in terms of the influence of Gertrude Stein) was by doing them through Ezra's friends in France.

Now this is one of the *big* mysteries. What was the real influence of Gertrude Stein on Williams? Mrs. Williams, when she met Gertrude in Paris, hated her. Despised her. Began talking her down to her husband, so that in his autobiography Williams speaks of Gertrude only in a very cursory fashion. And he doesn't speak of the earlier of Gertrude's books, which I'm sure he must have read. There is a revealing anecdote in Williams's *Autobiography*. The Williamses visited Gertrude and all went well until Gertrude brought out a big stack of unpublished manuscripts. "What would you do with these?" she asked Bill. Nonchalantly he replied, "I'd keep the best one and burn the rest." Gertrude ushered Bill to the door with the remark: "Obviously, writing is not your métier."

Anyway, these early books of Williams could only be published either by privately printing them, as *Kora in Hell* was, in Boston, or done in Paris by McAlmon and George Oppen. So that the only books he had really had done here in this country were *A Voyage to Pagany*—that's the story of his *Wanderjahr* in Europe which was done by McCauley, who then went broke—and the so-called *Collected Poems*, done by George Oppen and Reznikoff at the Objectivist Press. So that Bill was in the odd position of being a hero to *fifty people* in New York. You know, people like Marianne Moore and others of the *Dial* group who had read him and thought he was wonderful, but he hadn't a publisher. Therefore, after he had looked me over and decided that I was well-meaning and solvent, he allowed me to begin publishing him, and the first book we did was *White Mule*. And it had wonderful reviews.

DANA: The story of Williams's very checkered publishing career has given heart to a lot of American poets. Williams held out *all* those years.

LAUGHLIN: He could hold out because he had his doctoring to do, and his doctoring absorbed him. Ezra was always writing to Bill saying, "You're wasting your time in America. Come on over here—here's where the action is."

DANA: And Williams always refused.

LAUGHLIN: Yes, Bill refused. He did make two trips to Europe; one is recorded in *Voyage to Pagany*. And he loved Paris. But Rutherford, New Jersey, was his place. That was his locus.

DANA: I only met Williams once, when I was a graduate student twenty-five years ago. My memory of him is of a very generous, very gentle person.

LAUGHLIN: He was indeed. Can you imagine the amount of poetry that was sent to him? He would read all that stuff. And he would write back to the poets. And he did introductions for any number of C-minus books of poetry.

DANA: That's true.

LAUGHLIN: He was infinitely, infinitely kind. But our relationship is fully documented in the *William Carlos Williams Newsletter*. Dick Ziegler discusses very sensitively our relationship, the rift we had at one time, and then how we made up later.

DANA: Do you want to talk about that briefly?

LAUGHLIN: Well, it's a rift about which you couldn't print anything I said or you'd be in a libel suit. It involves a former employee of New Directions.

DANA: Earlier, we began to talk about the Poet of the Month series. I remember how cheap those books were and how beautifully printed. Fifty cents for Delmore Schwartz's *Shenandoah*, for example. Those were remarkable books, and you farmed them out to small, fine-book printers.

LAUGHLIN: The objective of the series was dual. One, to do good poets and make them inexpensive and to get them out to people, and two, to give patronage and encouragement to hand printers.

DANA: Why did you care?

LAUGHLIN: Oh, I've always been mad about printing and books.

DANA: Where does that interest come from?

LAUGHLIN: I don't know.

DANA: There must have been some point at which you . . .

LAUGHLIN: Well, I used to have—as a matter of fact I still have—a Vandercook handpress.

DANA: You do?

LAUGHLIN: And if I had the time, I'd do some more printing. But it's too laborious, too time-consuming.

DANA: Yes, I know. I'm an ex-printer myself.

LAUGHLIN: I collect fine printing from the past, you know, Bodoni and Baskerville, and printers like that.

DANA: What's the first *beautiful* book you cared about? Did you run into them in Europe?

LAUGHLIN: I think it may have been seeing those two early volumes of the *Cantos* that were done, one by John Rodker in London and one by Bill Bird in Paris.

DANA: Three Mountains Press?

LAUGHLIN: Yes. They are folios, you know. They are gorgeous.

DANA: I didn't know that Bird had done those.

LAUGHLIN: I think it was Bird that did the second . . . and I saw those in Rapallo. Ezra had copies there, and that may have been what set off this fascination with fine printing.

DANA: Well, what made you decide to subsidize fine printers?

LAUGHLIN: I wasn't subsidizing them. Their rates were very modest. We used to get the books in that series out— there'd usually be fifteen hundred in paper and five hundred in paper over boards—we used to get those out for under three hundred dollars apiece. What killed the series was the rise in printing costs. You see, we sold them on a subscription basis. You paid five dollars a year, and you'd get twelve numbers. We never got the subscription list up over about six hundred and thirty-five, and we really needed a thousand to swing it. And the reason we couldn't increase it was that people wanted to pick and choose. They didn't want to take all twelve, because there would be somebody they didn't like.

DANA: Yes, you did many different sorts of poets.

LAUGHLIN: We finally had to give it up after forty-two numbers. But I think it's one of the things I'm proudest of having done.

DANA: It *was* a beautiful series. And, I remember that, as a student with little money in his pockets, to be able to walk into a bookstore and buy a first-rate book for fifty cents was a *joy*. Of course, at that time nobody knew whether these books would turn out to be significant. But one knew, reading Warren or Schwartz or Berryman, that one was reading first-rate work. The question was how much better was it going to turn out to be in the future. It was a remarkable series.

LAUGHLIN: I loved that series. It was a lot of work, because it involved a lot of correspondence with the poets getting them to cut their selection down to thirty-two pages.

DANA: Godine is doing something like that today.

LAUGHLIN: He's done some beautiful chapbooks.

DANA: Right. That series with Scott Momaday and George Starbuck.

LAUGHLIN: He's done some fine books. I have great respect for David; he's really a high-standard man. The quality of design and printing in his books is simply superb.

DANA: Another young press I think is interesting is Ecco.

LAUGHLIN: I'm great friends with Dan Halpern and his patrons, Drue and Jack Heinz.

DANA: It seems to me that's a press that's as committed to a standard of literary taste as you were.

LAUGHLIN: I think Dan's very talented. He's one of the best young editors around. He has uniformly high standards, and he gets a lot of good stuff. You've probably heard the story of Bill Bird's trunk.

DANA: No.

LAUGHLIN: Well, you know who Bill Bird was?

DANA: Yes, one of Hemingway's early publishers.

LAUGHLIN: When Pound moved to Italy, he had a lot of papers that he couldn't take with him in his satchel, so he put them in an old trunk and gave them to Bill Bird and said,

"Keep these for me until I send for them." But he never sent for them. Bill Bird died, and his heirs find the trunk and sell it to the Lilly Library at Indiana University. Among Pound's "stuff" were many translations of the work of Paul Morand, a French writer Ezra admired. I was given copies by Bill Cagel of the Lilly Library and sent them to Dan, asking him if he would look at them and see if they were something he could use in his magazine, *Antaeus*.

I have a high regard for Ecco. I don't care for *all* their books. I'm very limited in the poets I like. I think this is the result of having been under the influence of three truly great poets: Williams, Pound, and Thomas. You know, when you have had to do with poets of the absolutely first-rate, it is very hard to get excited about the ordinary poet.

DANA: I suppose so.

LAUGHLIN: I'd say I'm also very devoted to Rexroth, who had a tremendous influence on New Directions and on me. And also I'm very devoted to Denise Levertov, who I think writes the best free verse around.

DANA: Is there a contradiction in what you've said? You've been influenced by Thomas and Rexroth and Williams and Pound, but you're still very open. To people like Denise, like Gary Snyder, or . . .

LAUGHLIN: Well, I love Gary. I think Gary is one of the most wonderful people God ever made. And I like his poetry.

DANA: He *has* done some remarkable work—*Turtle Island*, for example.

LAUGHLIN: But I don't have the openness to general poetry that I probably ought to have.

DANA: Do you still do all the reading for New Directions?

LAUGHLIN: No, what happens is that manuscripts come into the office, and if they're absolute junk, I mean real crap, the girl at the switchboard desk sends them back with a rejection slip. If they have any merit, they go next to Peter Glasgold, our editor, who is a wonderful guy, tremendously learned, with tremendously good taste. He winnows out what he wants *me* to read. But it just so happens that in the last year he's liked a lot of stuff. So it's come up to me, and I am sweating at it. Coming down in the car, I was reading a novel that—oh, dear—Jack Hawkes, you know, had written to me, saying, "This is my student, C—— H——. You must read her novel." And, as Dudley Fitts once wrote on one of my school compositions, "Beaucoup de bruit pour rien."

DANA: Well, I remember a *Time* article back in the fifties, a one-column piece, which took you to task for being a kind of shotgun critic of literature and having erratic tastes.

LAUGHLIN: That was probably Robert Cantwell, if it was a long time ago.

DANA: It was an unsigned article.

LAUGHLIN: Well, you know, *Time* has always been kind of snotty. I remember Cantwell came up to Norfolk to see me. I was then living with my aunt in her Georgian mansion. And there was Cantwell to lunch with no tie on and two maids and a butler serving lunch, and I think he was a little shattered by it all.

DANA: Well, I can't blame him for that, but pros are supposed to recover from situations like that.

LAUGHLIN: Did you know that *Time*, I think it was *Time*, never reviewed a single Jack Hawkes novel?

DANA: That's extraordinary.

LAUGHLIN: Here's one of the most exciting experimental writers, and they never said a word.

DANA: Somebody once, discussing Hawkes with you, said that there had always been an intimate connection between New Directions and Harvard. You said, "Oh yes, of course," and went on to elaborate.

LAUGHLIN: Well, it's true. I went there, and I keep up. I go back there to committee meetings and to see my friends, particularly Harry Levin, who'll be retiring next year. We'll be publishing this fall his wonderful book *Memories of the Moderns*, essays on everybody that you would want to think about in the modern school. Al Guerard was then at Harvard and not at Stanford, and he put me on to Hawkes. And Delmore Schwartz was teaching at Harvard, and Ted Spencer was one of my dearest friends.

That was a funny Pound story. When Ezra came back in, what was it? '39? Just before the war? Ezra came back, and he was going to try to get to Roosevelt and try to stop the war from happening. When he came to Boston, I got Ted to put him up at his house. Ted was very much intrigued with him and took him out to play tennis. Ezra womped Ted, and Ted really thought he was a good tennis player. Here was this man, ten years older at least, just whupped him.

DANA: It's hard to imagine Pound playing tennis. But it's hygienic.

LAUGHLIN: Well, his theory was very sound. He had the most formidable forehand that I have ever seen, a pivot torque forehand. He would station himself in the middle of the court and wait for anybody to hit anything near him and then zowie, it was gone. It was just gone.

There's always a great fondness for Harvard. All of the New Directions archives will go to Harvard on my death. I've saved every piece of paper that ever came in, and every carbon of every answer I ever wrote. I now have it in a fireproof building on our place, because I have to keep looking up things. But that will all go up to Harvard, and they've got the space for it all set in the Houghton Library with the name New Directions above it.

DANA: You mentioned Rexroth earlier, and I seem to remember reading somewhere that Rexroth and Delmore Schwartz both ran your Norfolk office at one time.

LAUGHLIN: Schwartz's first wife, Gertrude Buckman, ran the office in Cambridge when I had come back from abroad and gotten the thing started. And Delmore helped. At least, Delmore helped the night the Charles River flooded. He carried all the files up from the basement and put them on the third floor.

Gertrude did all the dirty work. She wrapped the packages and put the entries in the ledger and deposited the checks and did all that; but Delmore, I think, used to take the packages to the post office in their car.

DANA: Well, it's hard to imagine Delmore being that organized. Of course, Bellow's *Humboldt's Gift* has cast a certain pall over Delmore's . . .

LAUGHLIN: But you know, *Humboldt's Gift* is very accurate.

DANA: Is it?

LAUGHLIN: Yes. It is *very* accurate. I'm in it, Bob Hutchins is in it. Hutchins is in it as Longseth, the head of the foundation. I'm in it as the playboy publisher.

DANA: Oh, I must go back and reread the book.

LAUGHLIN: No, it's very, very true. And very accurate and very touching.

DANA: How do you see Schwartz at this point in time? As you're well aware, there has been, recently, a great wave of affection for Delmore Schwartz, a reassessment of his career and his works.

LAUGHLIN: I was *so* close to him, until he went mad and turned against me. He was my best literary friend. And he did so much in the way of helping me, advising me about manuscripts and advising me about literary strategy. He was the little Napoleon of literary strategy. You should see the letters in the archive file for the three months prior to the publication of his book *Genesis*. There would be a letter every day, suggesting that I should send something or other, or write to, or call so-and-so, who might possibly review the book. *Every* day.

DANA: It's frightening, because it sounds like what I do to my publisher—only I don't do it every day. I hope that doesn't mean I'll go mad shortly.

LAUGHLIN: No, I feel so, so . . .

DANA: Do you think he was a brilliant writer?

LAUGHLIN: Well, no.

DANA: "The Heavy Bear That Goes With Me," for example?

LAUGHLIN: Oh yes, that's a lovely poem. And so many of the things were so good. What was it? *Dr. Bergman's Belief*, *Coriolanus*—various things like that. They were so heady.

He applied intellect to his work. But I think that *Genesis* did not succeed as a work of art.

DANA: Well, you anticipated my next question.

LAUGHLIN: It just didn't. I don't know whether it was too self-regardant. Maybe that was it. It was too much hipped on his own obsessions about his family and his childhood.

DANA: That suggests that if the writer self-consciously, rather than unself-consciously, begins to mine his own existence . . .

LAUGHLIN: Yes, but, you know, some people can do it successfully. Look at Henry Miller. Every book of Henry Miller is about Henry Miller, and he got away with it brilliantly.

DANA: That's right. Self-consciously obsessive.

LAUGHLIN: And yet in the particular case of *Genesis* it somehow didn't work.

DANA: Does that mean that Schwartz's talent was too fragile, and Miller's was sufficiently supple, and . . . ?

LAUGHLIN: Yes, Miller had such extraordinary exuberance.

DANA: Well, it comes through in even the worst thing he wrote.

LAUGHLIN: So exuberant, so full of pep and stamina. He could carry it off. Although I do think that *Sexus*, *Plexus*, and *Nexus* don't come up to the early *Tropic*s. It seems almost as if he's repeating himself. Did I tell you how I got to know Henry?

DANA: No.

LAUGHLIN: Well, one day I was having lunch with Ezra in Rapallo, and he threw across the table to me *Tropic of Cancer*, and he said, "Well, Jas, here's a dirty book that's worth reading." So I read it, and I loved it. I wrote to Henry and got in correspondence with him, and thus we were able to bring out *The Cosmological Eye*. I never wanted to tackle the *Tropic* books here, because I don't like lawyers and courts and cases. Do you know that poor Barney Rosset, when he brought out *Tropic of Cancer*, had sixty-seven cases going at the same time, in different courts, in different cities, where booksellers had been picked up for selling the book? So that poor Barney, who's to me sort of a culture hero, never made a dime off *Tropic of Cancer*, because it all went in legal fees.

DANA: That's a sad story.

LAUGHLIN: I was just canny enough to know what would happen and to avoid that and to realize that I didn't have the funds to pay lawyers in sixty cases.

DANA: Well, you started to talk about Rexroth, and I know that you used to ski in Utah and used to zing over the other side of the mountains and hide out at Rexroth's.

LAUGHLIN: I stayed with the Rexroths on Potrero Hill in San Francisco in their wonderful old, beautiful, beaten-up house. That was when he was married to Marie. She was Hungarian, a lovely girl. Rexroth partly took over the role of Ezra in my life, in that he advised me what to do and put me on to things.

DANA: Would you say Rexroth plugged you in to the whole West Coast scene?

LAUGHLIN: Well, I don't know. It was just that generally Kenneth could look for three minutes at a manuscript and say yes or no.

DANA: And you *trusted* his judgment?

LAUGHLIN: Oh, absolutely.

DANA: Why?

LAUGHLIN: Well, he was so learned and such a good poet.

DANA: Well, that's two good reasons.

LAUGHLIN: No, he knew everything. He's an autodidact. He's read everything, and he has a photographic memory. He can remember everything that he ever read and can relate it to something else.

DANA: I've always regarded it as a professional disaster that our paths never crossed.

LAUGHLIN: He's a marvelous person. He's a very crotchety kind of person. He calls me up every Sunday, usually right in the middle of a football game, and tells me what I should be doing.

DANA: Don't tell me you're a Pittsburgh Steelers fan?

LAUGHLIN: Oh, absolutely. Did I tell you that I just got an

honorary degree from Duquesne University, and the other person who got one was Chuck Noll, the coach of the Pittsburgh Steelers? We had time to talk while waiting for the festivities to begin, and I asked him about how he trained the draftees that he got. It was most interesting—and so sound. He said, "We don't know whether these guys will be any good or not, but we bought them for ten years ahead. And maybe it will take us that long to teach them how to play pro football, which is entirely different from college football."

DANA: Yes, as professional poetry is entirely different from college poetry. Is professional publishing entirely different from college publishing?

LAUGHLIN: Well, yes, if you talk about this man who's head of Simon and Schuster, who says, "All I care about is the dollar sign."

DANA: You once criticized the whole publishing establishment for "habit, greed, and avarice," I think you said.

LAUGHLIN: That's a slight exaggeration. They're not all like that. I can name a number of publishers who have the highest standards and who are very fine. For example, Norton, and Farrar, Straus and Giroux. And you may quote me as saying that Bob Giroux is the greatest editor in America. Atheneum is good. There are still, I would say, half a dozen commercial publishers that have not sold out to the conglomerates and who are putting out good books. Now, they may not be the kind of books you and I want to read, but they are the kind of books that *somebody* intelligent wants to read. And they are not catering to lower tastes.

DANA: Speaking of not catering to "lower tastes," how did you come to publish Thomas Merton?

LAUGHLIN: I had known Mark Van Doren. He was in the Poets of the Year series. Van Doren had been Merton's professor at Columbia. After he had been down at the monastery in Kentucky for a while, Merton sent a sheaf of his poems to Van Doren to ask him whether he thought they were any good. Van Doren sent them to me, recommending that we publish them. I liked them very much, even though they were religious poems, which don't always interest me. I thought they were spirited in their imagery. So we published his *Thirty Poems* in the Poets of the Year series.

Out of that grew a long relationship. I used to go down to see him at the monastery a couple of times a year, and we had high old times, because he was a very jolly fellow. Full of jokes and japery. I'd go down there and rent a car at the Louisville airport, and the abbot would let me take Tom off. Tom would take off his cassock and put on his blue jeans and his beret, and we would go off for the day around the neighborhood, sightseeing. We'd go to Shaker Town, to Lexington to see the Victor Hammers, who were great friends of Tom's. We'd stop off a great deal at various taverns, and Tom would consume a large quantity of beer and remain as sober as cold stone. He was the last person you would take to be a monk. He was so life-loving and jolly and full of interests.

He was interested in everything—in jazz, in baseball, in almost any subject you could mention, and yet that didn't keep him from his enormous output of work in the monastery. He'd get up at two o'clock in the morning and start writing, and his output was tremendous. Not only the books published, but he wrote over a hundred and fifty of what they call "Conferences," or sermons on tape, which were sent to other Catholic religious institutions for the nuns and monks to listen to.

DANA: What happened to those tapes?

LAUGHLIN: They're all at the Merton Studies Center at Bellarmine College in Louisville.

DANA: Have they ever been published?

LAUGHLIN: Many of them, yes. Of course, they are only interesting to someone who's interested in Catholic theology, because that's what most of them are about.

DANA: They're not literary works in the sense that Donne's sermons were.

LAUGHLIN: No.

DANA: I see. Do you think that Merton was a major poet?

LAUGHLIN: I think that his work got better and better the older he grew, and as he became more secular and less purely

a religious poet. The early religious poems . . . the one on the
death of his brother was a great masterpiece, but most of his
early poems are really not terribly exciting. But as his interests widened and he became deeply involved in all sorts of
nonreligious issues, such as the racial struggle and the anti-
war movement, the poems became increasingly secular, so
that in *Emblems of a Season of Fury*, you get those very fine
poems about the children of Birmingham, and about Adolph
Eichmann and things of that sort. And in his final two works,
Cables to the Ace and *The Geography of Lograire*, you have
him writing a kind of poetry which was totally his own invention. It was poetry based on parody and myth, the combination of the two. *The Geography of Lograire* was planned
to be, you might say, his *Cantos* or his *Paterson*—a poem he
thought he would go on working on for the rest of his life. It's
a poem which has been hardly noticed by the critics. I feel
that it's a major poem. It's based upon his reading in many
diverse fields, ranging all the way from history through
anthropology.

DANA: So it's a work of eclecticism.

LAUGHLIN: Yes.

DANA: You have a taste for that in your publishing efforts:
Duncan, Pound, Williams, . . .

LAUGHLIN: Rothenberg.

DANA: Rothenberg, Merton. How do you account for that
taste?

LAUGHLIN: I don't know. I'm very interested by poetry
which has content and subject matter. I get awfully bored
with poets who just spin poetry out of poetry. I love poems
like the *Cantos* which have all sorts of stuff in them, lots of
history and ideas and people and recollections and places. I
like the concrete kind of poetry where you know just what
they are talking about, where they're doing something with
it. And Merton operates on his material, as I say, by parody.
One of the finest sections of *The Geography of Lograire* is a
pastiche made up of taglines from advertisements in the *New
Yorker* magazine.

He also works with myths, creating myth. He takes, for example, the cargo cults of Micronesia and shapes myths out of his reading. I know the four anthropological works about the cargo cults which he used, but, while their material is interesting, the way he synthesizes it in twenty pages makes it wonderfully mythical and elevated and selective.

DANA: You've touched on two of the key aspects of writing—upon content and subject matter, and shape or form. It's curious that about the same time in a recent conversation with Daniel Halpern the same subject came up. He also expressed a preference for content. He said he wanted poems to be "interesting." I challenged him on that, and I'll challenge you in the same way. Isn't it true that there is a kind of poetry that might be said not to have content in a conventional sense, but whose content is somehow vivified or created by the formal invention of the poet?

LAUGHLIN: A perfect example of that is Robert Duncan. Duncan has created a very real and almost tangible world completely out of his imagination and reading. If you take any given Duncan poem, it is difficult to pin down in any given line what he is writing about. Yet the whole thing has an extraordinary, forceful reality because he has this powerful imagination which is at work and which is creating the Duncan poetic world, just as Pound created the Pound poetic world.

DANA: Is that different from, say, Robert Lowell creating a Lowellian world?

LAUGHLIN: Duncan is ever so much more complex and involved and developed than Lowell. Isn't Lowell a very simple-minded poet, great as he is?

DANA: Do you really think Duncan's more complex than Lowell is in something like *History*?

LAUGHLIN: I think so. Of course, I'm not an expert on Lowell. I'm just saying this from the few poems that I've read.

DANA: Well, if it's possible for Duncan to deliver a sort of negative subject matter via formal excellence, but you have a preference for positive subject matter, how does Duncan fit into the Pound-Merton-Williams preference?

LAUGHLIN: All of these people have created what to me is the test of a first-class poet: they have created worlds—worlds of words, worlds of ideas. Williams did it, Pound did it, Dylan Thomas did it. They have this great imaginative power which creates a world within which they work.

DANA: Would you say the same thing about Thomas's sonnets, which he once called "wild and whirling words"?

LAUGHLIN: I'm speaking of the whole Thomas *oeuvre*. The whole thing put together is a personal, imaginative world.

DANA: The sonnets puzzle the reader even now. "Alterwise by owl-light in the halfway house, . . ." It's somehow the sound and movement of those words, rather than the actual denotations, that provide the "subject matter."

LAUGHLIN: In Thomas, the world is created through a mystique of sounds and symbols.

DANA: Yes, an incantatory quality. I've always felt that Thomas created by incantation.

LAUGHLIN: I agree that he did. I visualize him sitting there reading his own lines to himself and changing them and altering them until he got the effects he wanted. Thomas is highly oral; that is, auditory. Whereas someone like Duncan is more intellectual. There's a tremendous component of learning and reading in Duncan, just as there was in Pound.

DANA: In the sixties, you made a comment on the "literary underground" that I found interesting, if not startling. You said—and I'm not sure to whom you were referring, but it included at least some of the people whom you later published, some of the West Coast poets, the Beat poets—you said, comparing them to poets of your own generation, "They are more difficult to understand than we were."

LAUGHLIN: I think that's true. There was a period there where poetry got awfully difficult, and I'm not sure why. I don't know what forces were operating on young poets. There was a period when the stuff that came into the office was unbearably difficult, where it seemed as if they were just trying not to be understood. I think that's passing. In the manuscripts that have been coming in in recent years, there is more readiness on the poet's part to open himself to his reader on a fairly comprehensible level. Though there still are people . . . I can't understand Ashbery, and there are a number of others. I just don't know what they are talking about.

DANA: Yes. I have trouble with Ashbery. I have the feeling that he may be doing something important, but I don't know what it is. Maybe I'm committed to subject matter somewhat the way you are, because I feel that Ashbery may be brilliant, but there may be no subject matter as such in his work.

LAUGHLIN: I think my interest in subject matter goes back to Dante. To me, the great thing about Dante is that, with all of the allegorical structure and the rest of it, he is always so wonderfully concrete.

DANA: Do you still think that criticism by and large, in America, is in a rather distressed state?

LAUGHLIN: I think it certainly *is* in the popular media, compared to England. If a good novel comes out in England, there are five or six or seven influential papers which will almost certainly review it. Here, on the other hand, where is there that a good book, a serious book, can get reviewed? Chances are, it may or may not be reviewed in the Sunday *New York Times*, because they have so many books to cover that it is impossible for them to cover everything. The other place is the *New York Review of Books*, which tends to give almost all of its space to what I would call "idea books," without devoting much attention to fiction or to poetry. Where else is there for things to be reviewed? The *Atlantic* occasionally had some reviews when Ted Weeks was editor. He had a column which was often very good. There *is* one other place, and that's the *Los Angeles Times*, with Robert Kirsch [now deceased]. You can get reviews there. But otherwise there is almost nothing. New Directions gets most of its reviews either from the underground press or from college newspapers. On poetry reviewing, the best one, of course, is *Parnassus*.

DANA: Do you feel the quality of reviewing in the *New York Times Book Review* is significantly higher than it was ten or fifteen years ago?

LAUGHLIN: It seems to me that it's about the same. If they get a good reviewer, they get a good review. If they get some hack, they get a hack review. But I think the *Times* makes a valiant effort to cope with the flood of books. They go out of their way to try to review at least one poetry book every other issue.

DANA: Well, when you were the young fireball editor, the maverick publisher, you often, in your prefaces to the New Directions anthologies, offered suggestions, directions, as to how things might be improved. You don't do that anymore.

LAUGHLIN: No, I stopped writing introductions to the anthologies a good many years ago, and there were two reasons for that. I thought, first of all, that it was a little bit ostentatious and vain to do it, and secondly, since I seemed to be getting nowhere with my appeal for Social Credit, I got discouraged about it.

DANA: But you also made suggestions about what publishers ought to publish, or what kinds of reviewers ought to review books. Can I tempt you into a comment about a solution to the problem of getting books adequately reviewed to a larger public?

LAUGHLIN: I don't think there is any solution. The newspapers are in business for business. They are only going to have a good literary book page if they get advertising from the New York publishers. Now, there are just too many important newspapers around the country for the publishers to advertise in all of them. I think that some of the publishers advertise in the *Los Angeles Times*, and some occasionally in a Chicago or Washington newspaper, but otherwise they tend not to do much. As long as they don't, there aren't going to be good literary pages.

DANA: But you're not saying that somebody like Harper or Macmillan couldn't buy twelve pages in twelve different newspapers to advertise a book, are you?

LAUGHLIN: Yes, the rates are too high.

DANA: But we're talking about corporations that have millions of dollars in their budgets.

LAUGHLIN: It's pretty thin skating for them on what I would call the "literary" book. In fact, I would venture a guess that the margin of profit on what you and I would call serious literary books is pretty thin. And there just isn't the possibility . . . If you do the arithmetic on what a lot of advertising would cost, as over against the number of copies you'd print and what you're going to make off each copy, it just doesn't work out.

DANA: So, as far as you can see, there is no solution?

LAUGHLIN: I see no real solution to it, unless there were a generation of newspaper publishers who wanted to be patrons of letters by subsidizing a good literary page whether or not they got advertising. Then they might have it.

DANA: Two more questions. First, how do you feel about the National Endowment? When you began, there was nothing like the Endowment. The literary scene was probably as free-wheeling as it could be. Do you think that the entrance of the National Endowment into the literary scene has been a good thing or bad thing?

LAUGHLIN: I think it's been a good thing. I know that they've given grants to a number of very good writers. I know that they have given grants through the CCLM [Coordinating Council of Literary Magazines] to many small, struggling literary magazines. And I can't see how they hurt the literary scene in any way—quite the contrary.

DANA: Well, some people have complained that it has leveled it out, that it propagates a lot of mediocrity.

LAUGHLIN: I will say this regarding the magazines. I think many too many magazines are being published in this country now. When I started, there were about six literary magazines. The result was that the competition to get into them kept standards high. Nowadays there must be between a hundred and two hundred literary magazines. [*The International Directory of Little Magazines and Small Presses* lists approximately twelve hundred titles.] *Anybody* can publish *anything*. And that may not be so good. It may make it too easy for the aspiring writer to get published, and not put him on his mettle to try to write better. That is the only criticism I would make. And it is not the fault of the National Endowment. It's just a fault of the situation that's grown up. First of all, so many colleges have endowed magazines as prestige advertising for the college. Then so many groups—literary people around the country—have decided that it would be fun to have a magazine, so they have a magazine, even if they have to hock their own jobs to pay for it.

DANA: How does the present literary situation, the "poetry scene" so called, strike you? I mean, if somebody asked, "Is American literature in a really healthy state these days?" what would be your reaction?

LAUGHLIN: I think one of the worst things in the country are these courses in creative writing in colleges, because I think that they encourage students who have an emotional desire to write, but who have really no talent, to try to become writers. I see this from the manuscripts that come in to our office. You can tell that this person has learned a certain amount of technical competence and fluency, but he really has nothing to say. I think that these courses in creative writing should be abolished. The real writer, the born writer, the real genius, is going to write whether there are courses in creative writing or not. I think the study of literary history would demonstrate this fact. There were no creative writing courses in the nineteenth century, and yet we had some pretty good writers. I feel that these creative writing courses are a menace.

DANA: When you studied with Pound, though, in a sense you were taking a creative writing course.

LAUGHLIN: No, I was taking a general education course.

DANA: But you were writing.

LAUGHLIN: I was writing.

DANA: And he was reading your work.

LAUGHLIN: Yes, but without much enthusiasm.

DANA: Right. And he did say to you, "Well, I don't think that you should go on with this. I think you should do something else."

LAUGHLIN: How wise he was.

DANA: Well, perhaps you'd advise young writers in creative writing courses to go into publishing instead.

LAUGHLIN: No, I think they should . . .

DANA: Stop writing.

LAUGHLIN: I think that if they are real writers, they are going to write, and they are going to find out how to write from reading good books. And that to devote all this effort to try to shape them and direct them is just a waste of time, because they haven't got the talent.

DANA: Is there a question I should have asked you that I didn't?

LAUGHLIN: Well, I don't know.

DANA: Is there still an avant-garde?

LAUGHLIN: That is a very good question and a difficult one to answer. There is, and there isn't. One thing which differentiated the avant-garde in the old days when I started publishing was that they couldn't get published by the regular publishers, and they were more or less a small group. They had established a small cult audience through being published in literary magazines like *Hound and Horn* or the *Little Review* or the *Dial* or what have you, or in the way that William Carlos Williams did, by publishing his books mostly in Paris and then circulating them largely personally himself. So that there *was* in those days an avant-garde. Now you have a situation where a writer as exotic and as good as Donald Barthelme gets published right from the beginning in the *New Yorker* magazine. And the *New Yorker* is hospitable to people like Borges and the other Latin American writer, Márquez. So that that part of the avant-garde has disappeared.

But the avant-garde still does flourish, in a certain sense, in that there are a large number of very good writers who are doing something which is totally different from what your average, accepted, good writer is doing. Now I would take as examples Walter Abish, three of whose books we have published, who has a kind of construction for fiction which is highly original and totally different from anything that anybody else is doing. And somebody like David Antin out on the

Pacific Coast, who is doing his talk pieces, which are an experiment in trying to make a new kind of poetry out of prose. It isn't prose poetry. I don't know if you've seen his stuff?

DANA: No, but it seems to me that that is the direction really avant-garde literature is moving in. The formerly clear, or what we thought was a clear, distinction between prose and poetry seems to be breaking down.

LAUGHLIN: Right. Now, there has always been prose poetry which was a kind of heightened, imaginative prose, but what Antin is doing is something totally different. It would take a semiotician to explain what he is really up to. And I would urge you to go to the library and read one of those talk pieces and see if you can figure out what he is driving at. I've published them. I don't entirely understand what he is up to, but I find him so damned amusing and such a wonderful raconteur that I enjoy publishing him.

DANA: I met Barthelme in San Antonio in March, and I asked him about his methods of composition—the collage method, and his relationship to various painterly concerns. He said, "I try to write a story the way you write poems." I thought this was a curious sort of crossover, a deliberate move in the direction of a form of literature which may do away with conventional poetry, or at least relegate it to a sort of historical position. Even the novel may be relegated to a position of historical interest. It seems to me the whole thing is evolving into a form that hasn't quite emerged yet.

LAUGHLIN: I think that is true. That it's in the egg still. I get a lot of novels that are written in very bizarre ways, and most of them I don't find at all successful. They could just as well have told the story straight, rather than having gone to all the trouble of mixing up the time planes and the voices of the characters. But there is this drive, this tendency, this persistent discontent with the ordinary way of doing things. The writers are not isolated to the extent that they were before.

DANA: So, in a very real sense, you are still committed to the avant-garde?

LAUGHLIN: Oh, if it's any good, yes.

DANA: Well, you have certainly developed the most startling list of publications of any publishing house in the country.

LAUGHLIN: It's been very much personal selfishness in that I have done the things that I've found curious or interesting or worthwhile.

DANA: You gambled on your tastes. But you had confidence that that taste was intelligent.

LAUGHLIN: Don't ever underestimate the amount of help that I've had in choosing things, from people like Pound, Williams, Rexroth, Denise, Gary. So many of our books come from one of those writers. I trust their judgment. Very often I do something that I'm not too mad about but, say, Gary thinks it's wonderful. Okay, we publish it. New Directions is a publishing house blessed with an amateur, volunteer editorial board which picks out stuff for me to look at.

DANA: Would you say it was a democratic system of publishing?

LAUGHLIN: Well . . .

DANA: Well, ultimately your say is final.

LAUGHLIN: Through all the years, it was very autocratic. I mean, we did what *I* wanted to do. However, we are now in a period of transition at the office, because I've reached a certain age. I've got a wonderful staff, marvelous young people, and I am now insisting that at least two others in the office read and like what we do. One very practical reason, quite apart from my getting old, is that a book that the staff doesn't like is not going to get very far. They're not going to put their shoulder to the wheel and write letters about the book and try to get it reviewed, and to call up reviewers about it if they don't like it. So that, in that sense, I think we are *semi*-democratic. And then we have a kind of "out." If there is something that I want to do, and nobody else wants to do it, then the corporation does not publish it. I publish it personally, and the corporation distributes it. That's what we call "the proprietorship," and there have been two or three things in the last year or so which nobody in the office liked. So I did the book, and they very kindly did their best for it. It's an interesting system which would only work in my particular situation. It still enables me to do a book if I feel very strongly about it.

DANA: Who handles your distribution now?

LAUGHLIN: Norton. We were with Lippincott for many years, and they were very good. They tripled our sales from what we'd been getting ourselves using commission salesmen. Then Lippincott got swallowed up by Harper in a merger, and we decided that the Harper list was just too big. Harper does about three hundred books a year. We felt that our little twenty books a year would be lost. So we're now with Norton, whom we like very much. They are a big firm, but their bigness is really in their educational department. They do about a hundred trade books a year, so we feel we don't get lost in the shuffle. And they're very enthusiastic about New Directions, because they feel it complements their educational books. They have educational salesmen going around showing our books to professors, which is a great advantage. We're very pleased with what they're doing for us.

DANA: So how does it all look to you, from this end?

LAUGHLIN: Well, I think that the whole situation in publishing is very problematic because of inflation. What are we paying now for a novel? Twelve ninety-five. Now how many people can pay that? And what is a paperback? I saw a new paperback advertised the other day for six fifty. And it wasn't a long book. Now, how many students can buy a six-fifty paperback?

DANA: I was talking to a friend the other day who was saying that, one day, bookstores will not stock books anymore. They will all be banked on a computer. If you want a book, you go to the store and ask for it, pay the price of the book, and it will be jet-printed overnight. Bookstores will then reduce all their inventories, and so on.

LAUGHLIN: It's a marvelous idea, I think, because, as it is now, suppose we put out a new book: the stores have it and keep it for about two or three months, and then, if it isn't something that's asked for pretty regularly, they just send back what they have and don't reorder. The worst of the situation is that because of the damned postage rates, which are so horrible now, the stores are no longer eager to special-order. You know what they'll tell you? They'll tell you a book is out of print.

DANA: Is that so?

LAUGHLIN: These economic factors are very worrisome, because they are driving both the publisher and the stores to the best-seller.

DANA: That's very clear.

LAUGHLIN: Something that moves a lot and fast. And this can only work to the disadvantage of serious writing. Roger Straus, bless him, is always sounding off about it. He seems to be a spokesman for the publishing industry. But nobody pays any attention because there's nothing much they can do about it. You see, there *will* be new technological methods which will reduce the cost of books. But what happens is that the minute you get a new technological method, the union demands so much of a raise that the saving on the technological method is wiped out.

DANA: Is there any way out of that?

LAUGHLIN: I don't know.

DANA: But New Directions will carry on anyway?

LAUGHLIN: I hope we can.

Harry Duncan

Harry Duncan founded the Cummington Press in 1939 at the Cummington School of the Arts in Massachusetts. Some of its early authors were Allen Tate, R. P. Blackmur, Wallace Stevens, Richard Eberhart, William Carlos Williams, and Robert Lowell. By the mid-1950s, the Cummington Press was the most important small fine-book press publishing contemporary poetry in the United States. The press later published important first books by Robert Mezey, Stephen Berg, Mona Van Duyn, and Gerald Stern.

Mr. Duncan is now retired from the University of Nebraska at Omaha, where he established Abattoir Editions. His work as a typographer, book designer, and teacher has been a major force in the growth of the present small-press movement.

This interview took place on two separate occasions in Omaha during the hot and stormy Nebraska summer of 1982.

DANA: Harry, your career as a printer spans about forty years. How did you become interested in the printing process?

DUNCAN: The immediate circumstances? Just being exposed to some type and a handpress at the Cummington School of the Arts. The director of the school, Katharine Frazier, for some reason—I don't know why—got interested in this. And she directed—appropriated, really—some funds from the poll tax that all the students had to pay, to buy a handpress in New York. I went with her to look at it, and we found one for about forty dollars. She purchased that and got a little bit of Centaur type. This press sat in the old barn which served as the men's dormitory, and I guess she hoped maybe some art students would turn to block printing and some poets to setting type, and so on. But nobody paid much attention to it, so I fooled around with it.

The first thing I set, I think, was a poem of Robert Frost's, a quatrain. And the thing didn't fit right. The lines were uneven over at the right, so in order to make it fit into a block, I letterspaced the type and *ruined* it that way. I hope all of that has been destroyed.

The second thing was a quotation from Confucius: "Simplicity is the last thing learned. It comes from simple thinking, not from the conscious attempt to be simple." I demonstrated that maxim negatively in my printing of it by again blocking it off, letterspacing the type, and so on. Some copies of that still exist. I saw one the other day. It's very hideous.

DANA: Well, how did you happen to come from Grinnell, Iowa, to the Cummington School of the Arts?

DUNCAN: At Grinnell, my whole practical purpose and training was to become an English teacher. When I graduated from Grinnell in 1938, I had a graduate assistantship at Duke University. Everything was slated for me to continue and climb the ladder in the usual way to learn to become an English teacher. Since I was coming east—I had seen in *Poetry* magazine a notice that scholarships were being awarded for attending the Cummington School, which offered music, painting, poetry, dance, sculpture (I think that was *it* at that time)—

I applied for one of those scholarships and got it. The summer before going to Duke in the fall, I went to Cummington, and that was the beginning of the end of my academic career.

At Duke I had to teach something called Remedial English. The boys would come down from the mountains and other places speaking English in their native way. From the mountains you had a pretty good preservation of Elizabethan English—rumored anyway. "Ain't" used correctly, only in the first person singular. And we had to wash all that color out of their speech and introduce that pale, academically respectable version which we now speak.

DANA: So at some point you did go to Duke?

DUNCAN: I went there for two years and finished my master's thesis on Gerard Manley Hopkins, who interested me at that time. But I overslept for an examination in graduate French, and I never made up that exam. By 1940, I had become interested in printing and completely disillusioned with the prospect of going into what I then thought of as the English department *racket*, which consisted of destroying people's colorful speech and substituting something else. More was going on than that, of course. We were getting into the war, I was a little upset personally, and I had to make an act of rebellion.

DANA: What was it that attracted you about printing? It seems like a very odd choice of career for anybody to make in the 1940s.

DUNCAN: It was. It was especially odd at that time. I wanted to try to find somebody to teach me how to print by hand, and I couldn't. No one was doing it in the whole country. I did get a six-week apprenticeship with Ned Thompson of Hawthorn House in Windham, Connecticut. He was terrific. He set the type for his books by hand, though he printed them on a motor-driven Colt's Armory press. So I at least learned something about hand composition from Ned—and a lot else.

DANA: Well, was he printing literature or . . . ?

DUNCAN: He'd printed a couple of Limited Editions Club books. While I was there he was working on a second volume of his *Maps of Connecticut.* A very nice book. I wasn't much interested in maps of Connecticut, however.

In 1940, when I finally came up to Cummington and tried to make a go of the press through the winter—I was reprinting the Book of Job at that time—I hadn't thought much about the publishing side. But Katharine Frazier originated a program in the school of getting authors to come for a couple of weeks each in the summer—the beginnings of a writer's conference, I guess, except they weren't all there together. And there were some notable writers who came—Marianne Moore, Delmore Schwartz, R. P. Blackmur, Malcolm Cowley, Allen Tate, Jean Garrigue, and others.

DANA: Tell me a little bit about Katharine Frazier's background.

DUNCAN: She was born in New York State near Albany and grew up to be a harpist. She studied with Salzado. When she started the Cummington School, she was teaching harp at Smith College. Where she got the idea for a school of the arts, I don't know.

She was a woman afflicted all of her life by illnesses of various kinds. She cured herself of tuberculosis when she was a young woman, and she was afflicted with chronic insomnia. I envied her, in some ways, because she was one of the best-read persons I've ever known. During her sleepless nights, she read all of Aristotle, all of Plato, all of St. Thomas Aquinas, and also a great deal of contemporary literature. So she was very knowledgeable about it. However, what kept up her enthusiasm and her terrific spirit is a mystery. I don't know. Unlike most merely learned persons, she was always trying new things. She was tremendously interested in what young people were doing. She is, I think, the best teacher I ever had, and I've had some very good ones.

DANA: She was a musician. Was she also a writer?

DUNCAN: She wrote things, *strange* things which probably ought to be looked at again. She had a long fugue, about twenty pages, on another Confucian saying; "When hewing an ax handle, the pattern is near at hand." It was about education.

DANA: A verbal fugue.

DUNCAN: Yes. Her writing, though, lacks the immediacy of common speech, and I think that's why I decided the fugue and the other pieces that I read . . . somehow I didn't want to do them, despite my regard for her, because of this lack of a center of immediate language.

DANA: Samuel French Morse also plays a part there somewhere in the development of the Cummington Press, doesn't he?

DUNCAN: Yes. Sam was a student at the school before I came, and he and Katharine were already friends. It was through Sam that we got Wallace Stevens' *Notes Toward a Supreme Fiction* to print in 1942 or '43. Sam knew Stevens and on behalf of the press asked him if there was anything he had that we could print. Later we did Sam's first book, *Time of the Year*, with an introduction by Stevens. I really don't know how Sam met him. Sam was very young, and Stevens was near retirement from his insurance job. I suspect there was some connection through Trinity College at Hartford. I think Sam went there.

DANA: Well, the first *major* poet you printed was Tate, wasn't it, in '41? *Sonnets for Christmas*?

DUNCAN: *Sonnets for Christmas*, yes.

DANA: How did you happen to connect with Tate? Did Tate come to the school?

DUNCAN: Tate was one of the people who came to the writer's conference in the summer. He told me later that he began with Katharine Frazier in great skepticism and ended up a great admirer of hers. He was extremely supportive after that. He came on the board of the school, helped us to buy a press one time.

DANA: You mean he raised money for the press?

DUNCAN: He didn't raise money for the press. He *gave* us—what? A hundred dollars, something like that, to buy a new handpress. His main support, however, was in his literary connections. He got us the Robert Lowell manuscript to print—*Land of Unlikeness*. To have an intelligence like that working for you was itself a big boost.

DANA: Several publishers I've interviewed—Laughlin at New Directions, Halpern at Ecco, John Martin at Black Sparrow—have cited someone outside the press who had high-powered literary intelligence and literary connections. In Laughlin's case, it was Pound. In Halpern's case, it was Paul Bowles. In your case, it's Allen Tate.

DUNCAN: It *is* Allen Tate, although I mustn't slight the other writers. We didn't call on Blackmur, Marianne Moore, or Delmore, probably just for the reason that they were less cordial. But I also had a very, very high respect for Allen, a respect based on fear. Because I paid my way through Grinnell College in the Depression by winning each year a prize called the Whitcomb Prize for Poetry. In my senior year, Allen Tate had been judge of this contest and had knocked me down to second place. I did *not* win the prize that year. I was just the runner-up. This made me reconsider my own writing. It was a very impressive slap in the face, and I suppose I should be grateful for it. At least I respected and heeded it because of the authority with which it was given.

DANA: Did their Catholicism have anything to do with your publishing of Tate or Lowell?

DUNCAN: No, nothing immediate. Because Allen was not converted to the church until six or seven years later. Not until the late forties. I remember when Paul Williams, my partner, and I first learned . . . I got a letter from Allen . . . no, from Caroline Tate—Caroline Gordon—who *was* a Catholic and had always been hounding Allen to convert, saying that Allen had been baptized, and we could *not* believe it. It was *incredible* to us.

DANA: How old was he at that time?

DUNCAN: He probably was fifty. We had the utmost respect for his mind and his skepticisms. I remember saying to Paul at breakfast that day, "Well, if Allen has done it, there must be something in it. We need to inquire."

DANA: After Tate came Blackmur and Stevens. What made you decide to publish Blackmur?

DUNCAN: Blackmur taught one summer at the writer's

workshop. And his first book that we printed, *The Second World*, Allen Tate got the manuscript for us. The second one we did, called *The Good European*, he sent us himself after we knew him.

DANA: Well, a key question arises at this point. Did the sale of those books—Tate, Blackmur, Stevens, they were all established writers at the time—do a lot to support the press financially in that period?

DUNCAN: Not financially. The only one which sold out in less than two years was Stevens' *Notes Toward a Supreme Fiction*. We then did a second edition of that book. Tate's *The Winter Sea* took many years to sell out, as did both the Blackmur books. It was not a good time for poetry so far as a public went.

DANA: Is there *ever* a good time?

DUNCAN: No, but there were special problems at that time having to do with the war and with a certain retrenchment on the part of literary journals, and so on, connected to the war effort. *The Winter Sea* contains a long poem called "Seasons of the Soul," and Allen had submitted that to either *The Nation* or *The New Republic*, I can't remember which. And it had been turned down with a rejection note that said, "This is very pessimistic, and we don't feel it's the right time for us to publish this." That really teed Allen off. So we got to print that for him. I think that's its first printing. And in my estimation *still*, it is one of the major American poems, although you know Allen's reputation is at a nadir at the moment.

DANA: Well, if the books didn't sell, what was your primary interest in printing at that time? I mean, there must have been . . .

DUNCAN: Well, we certainly were not in it for the bucks.

DANA: There had to be an aesthetic or spiritual commitment to printing and to printing poetry. How did this come about? What was the nature of it? Can you reconstruct it?

DUNCAN: That's sort of to reconstruct my whole soul at the time. I can remember a few specifics. Cummington School is very beautifully situated in the Berkshire Hills, and there was a walk around a hill with wonderful views which Paul Williams and I used to take in the evening. When we first got the manuscript of *The Winter Sea* from Allen, I knew that we had to print it. But I didn't really care for it very much. It seemed to me that it was intellectual, overcalculated poetry. You know it's all in those trimeter lines, tightly rhymed. It has the effect of being very willed poetry.

DANA: Are you saying it was a cold poem?

DUNCAN: Cold? I don't think I used that word to myself, but I think maybe it comes down to that. It didn't move me. However, after setting on the book all day and taking this walk around the hills with Paul, suddenly lines of the poem just came into my head. And I started, and I was able to say four or five of them.

> Brothers in arms, remember
> The hot wind dries and draws
> With circular delay
> The flesh, ash from the ember,
> Into the summer's jaws.

It had stuck so well in my memory, and in this kind of recapitulation, translating from his typescript and my typesetting, to have the lines live in my ear like that, changed my whole attitude and I knew that I had simply in my reading of the manuscript missed its essential passion. That was an experience I got through setting the type for a book. And I don't know any pleasure to equal it. I think it is probably the greatest joy in life to have that happen.

DANA: Does it still happen?

DUNCAN: Oh, of course, it still happens. But not very often, because nowadays I don't think that I get manuscripts anymore which are quite as good as *The Winter Sea*.

DANA: Perhaps it was, as Yeats said, "A poem cold and passionate as the dawn."

DUNCAN: That would have embarrassed Allen, if you had said that about it.

DANA: Well, I'm sorry Tate and I never met, so I could have embarrassed him in that way. It would have been a pleasant task.

In 1943 you published an anthology called *American Decade*.

DUNCAN: Yes.

DANA: Sixty-eight poems, first time in an anthology. I've never seen that collection. Can you talk a little bit about how you happened to publish an anthology and who was in it?

DUNCAN: The anthology was edited by a man named Tom Boggs. I guess he probably tried to peddle it all over, and we were maybe a kind of last resort. Anyway, he was very interested to get this anthology in print. You know, at that time the publication of poetry was very perilous in the United States. It was a bad time for that reason. Tom Boggs was a sort of charming Bohemian from Greenwich Village, and he persuaded Katharine Frazier that she ought to take this one. And I went along, too.

DANA: You're smiling, Harry.

DUNCAN: It's not a bad anthology. It has a lot of Stevens in it, and I think some of the Stevens poems are first appearances, but it's not the sort of book we should have been doing at that time. In the first place, we had to farm out the printing. We sent it to Portland, Maine, for Fred Anthoensen to print. He's a very good printer; he used Baskerville type and did an excellent job, but we shouldn't have been doing that. It was expanding our resources too far. And we shouldn't have accepted a manuscript which was too long for us to produce ourselves.

DANA: It seemed to me, when I looked at your bibliography, a very ambitious leap, very sudden.

DUNCAN: Well, I think Katharine Frazier also hoped the thing would sell very well, and that helped to push it to some degree, but that did not happen. We finally remaindered the rest of the edition to the Gotham Bookmart.

DANA: That raises a question that needs to be asked. How did you market your books at that point?

DUNCAN: Mostly through direct mail. There were a few

bookshops—one in Cambridge (the Grolier Bookshop), Gotham Bookmart in New York, probably one or two on the West Coast—that did take five or six copies of everything we published, which helped a lot. There were certain libraries—the New York Public, Houghton Library at Harvard, the Newberry Library in Chicago, the Amherst College library—they had placed standing orders with us.

DANA: Did you write the libraries, or did they contact you?

DUNCAN: These were simply in response to our direct-mail advertisements. The connection with Amherst College was a little more than that, because Newton McKean, who was then librarian at Amherst, had come to see us. He knew something of the hand-to-mouth way we lived, and he commissioned from us bookplates for certain special collections in the Amherst library. We did three or four for him, and this did help to keep body and soul together.

DANA: So you actually took on sort of classy job printing to pay the bills.

DUNCAN: Well, we also were doing the printing for the Cummington School while it was open in the summer. Doing the music programs. We didn't do the catalogue ever, I'm glad to say. We were too snotty to do that.

DANA: Now, all this time you were obviously teaching yourself about type, about paper, about presses. You didn't get it all from books, certainly. Who were some of the people who helped you to a more sophisticated understanding of the printing process?

DUNCAN: I've already mentioned Ned Thompson.

DANA: Could you formulate his influence on the development of the Cummington Press? What was the biggest thing he did for you?

DUNCAN: I can formulate it in a negative way. Ned simply did not have the intense interest in poetry that I did. I could not, at that time, have *conceived* of doing a book which was a catalogue of the early maps of Connecticut, because to me poetry was the thing that really mattered. Ned taught me not only how to set type properly and efficiently but also how to make the press ready, and the makeready process is pretty much the same whether you have a Colt's Armory or a Washington handpress. It's to get the strike even, so you've got an even impression, which is very important. He taught me how to do that. He had worked with William Edwin Rudge—you probably never heard of him.

DANA: No.

DUNCAN: Well, Rudge's shop in New York City was the place where Peter Beilenson and Ned and a lot of others of the best printers had worked, and the Rudge books were very superior mass-produced books.

DANA: How did you connect with Thompson?

DUNCAN: Katharine Frazier, when she decided to buy a handpress, wrote to all of the famous printers in the country, and she got advice from Goudy, for example, and I think Bruce Rogers.

DANA: Well, how did she know about printers?

DUNCAN: That was just part of the store of information which she provided for herself during her insomniac nights, I think. But, it wasn't only printers; she chose the very best ones.

DANA: When you say Goudy, you mean the Goudy who designed typeface?

DUNCAN: Frederic Goudy. He was still alive then. He, as a matter of fact, went down and looked at the press we were going to buy and told us that it was a good buy. So we had that expert advice. And Ned became a kind of godfather to the printing venture until he got out of printing entirely. His conscience bothered him, and he went to Washington to abet the war effort. He had something to do with cartography in the Library of Congress.

DANA: Has your idea of proper typesetting changed since he taught you, or is it still . . . ?

DUNCAN: No, no, the principles are still the same. We had already printed a book at Cummington called *Incident on the Bark Columbia*. And we had set all of the type for that by hand. We'd also done two anthologies of student work from the summer school.

DANA: One of which you burned.

DUNCAN: The uglier of them. Perfectly dreadful piece of work.

All this time there was a gradual improvement in things. *Incident on the Bark Columbia* was set unleaded in a squarish page. The typesetting was all right. What Ned gave me, though, was a little bit of the confidence of his authority, which got me rid of this squaring off of pages and so on, of that first impulse I had. His dedication to printing was even more instructive in the end, probably. He was living in this little Connecticut town making a kind of marginal living for himself and his family, and doing it . . . you know, he just had the pressroom attached to his house . . . it was probably a great luxury for him to go to New York or Boston . . . and he *liked* it. It was a perfectly satisfactory life to him. I think that that was instructive to me. That you can have a perfectly satisfactory life out of the capital.

DANA: That seems to tie in in some curious way with Confucian ideas about simplicity.

DUNCAN: Yes, I think it does tie in with that.

DANA: At some point you had a German refugee named Gustav Wolf working with you.

DUNCAN: Yes, this was the Book of Job project. One of the writers who came in the summer was a Smith College professor named Alfred Young Fisher. He had just written an essay on the Book of Job as a work of literature, and we liked the essay. At the same time there came to the German refugee camp in Cummington a man named Gustav Wolf, who was from Karlsruhe, Germany, where he had been an illustrator of books, a wood engraver.

DANA: How did you know he was there?

DUNCAN: We knew about him through the Congregational minister in Cummington, Carl Sangree, who was responsible, more or less, for the welfare of the refugees. In getting them jobs and so on. It was Carl Sangree's idea that Gustav Wolf should do a book with us. Since we had this essay by Fisher, we decided to print, over the winter, the Book of Job with woodcuts by Gustav Wolf. Wolf and his wife were to come and live in the Vaughan House, which was the women's dorm. And we turned the kitchen of that place into a pressroom and printed the book there. The book was a handsome *succès d'estime*.

DANA: Yes. Mary Richmond implies in her article about you that it's the first landmark book of the Cummington Press.

DUNCAN: Well, you know, one of the things about publishing is to become known publicly, and *The Book of Job* was chosen by the American Institute of Graphic Arts for their Fifty Books show. In other words, it was honored. So that gave us a kind of moral support. It didn't help to sell the book very much. We couldn't have done it without the patronage of one of the trustees at school, named Margaret Vaughan, who granted us the money. Enough to get us through the winter. Even so, we didn't have enough money for coal in the house. The house was always cold. But we survived the winter, and the next spring. There was no money left after we paid for the binding, and Gustav Wolf had to leave. At that time, the State Department came up to Cummington to make a movie called *The Cummington Story* which was the story—a very much souped-up story—of Gustav Wolf's coming as a refugee to America and getting employed, you know, by a press. The irony of it, of course, was that Wolf was out of a job. *The Cummington Story* became a rather famous propaganda film. Aaron Copland wrote the music for it.

DANA: Well, so far the picture is one of a group of dedicated people living hand-to-mouth in semiprimitive conditions, and funny things often happen during periods like that.

DUNCAN: I remember one day when we were working on the makeready for *The Book of Job* and Gustav was doing a little bit of wood engraving in the bed of the press. I dropped the tympan and frisket on his head, and his head went piercing through all our makeready. That was funny, although at the time he moaned.

DANA: What happened to Wolf after the war?

DUNCAN: His wife got a job at a boarding school in Massachusetts. She was housemother there, and he went there with her. He was not well. He had really been shattered by the Nazi business—although I don't think he was ever in a camp— and the business of displacement. And he'd had a miserable time in New York trying to live, before they came to Cummington. I'm afraid that this somewhat shows in the work he did for *Job*. He died a few years later.

DANA: Mary Richmond says that Paul Wightman Williams was persuaded to undertake book illustrations for the Cummington Press. That makes him sound like a reluctant partner at the beginning.

DUNCAN: That needs qualification. During the winter that the Wolfs and I were living in Vaughan House printing *Job*, one bitter night there was a knock on the door, which was unthinkable as far in the country as we were, on the back roads. It was a soldier, and he said that he'd come because he'd read somewhere about us or heard from somebody about us.

DANA: Was he in uniform?

DUNCAN: He was in uniform, and we invited him in out of the bitter cold night. And put him up for the night and got along with him extremely well. He left the next day and said, "I'll be back." He was discharged from the army some months later. This was Paul Williams.

DANA: What year was this? About '44, '45?

DUNCAN: '44. Anyway, he *did* come back. And after the Wolfs left, he said he would like to stay on and help me print, on the starvation basis we lived on. We *did* have the Lowell manuscript, which had come before the Wolfs left, and Gustav Wolf did the frontispiece.

Well, I was committed to composition of type. The Washington handpress requires two people, really, to run it, and I was very grateful that Paul had come. He had studied in an architect's office in Memphis, Tennessee. He was an architectural designer. And it was natural, since I was setting the type, that he undertook, from then on, the illustrations. At first, these were linecut reproductions of his line drawings. Then he graduated to linoleum cuts, as in the Robert Penn Warren book.

DANA: *Blackberry Winter?*

DUNCAN: Yes. And then to plank woodcuts, which was the method used in the period of incunabula, and that's what he was really splendid at. So far as I know, he is unsurpassed in that. Later, he experimented with metal etched and engraved, printed relief or intaglio. We were able to do intaglios on the Washington press. He really started out to learn the craft himself, and since he was completely self-taught in this, his work is completely original.

DANA: Do you think it would be possible today for anyone to just walk in off the road that way, into a small press operation, not knowing a whole lot about it?

DUNCAN: I'm sure it's possible. It's not so likely anymore, because there is a vigorous movement in the private-press field, as you know. And the field has organs of communication—*Fine Print*, and so on. So people do hear about one another much more readily than they did at that time. Insofar as I know, nobody else was doing handpress work then.

DANA: I guess what I'm asking is, is there time today for somebody who, like Williams, doesn't really perhaps know a whole lot about engraving or etching or block printing to teach themselves to do that?

DUNCAN: The self-teaching is harder when you have many people who are doing it. The natural thing today would be to go to somebody who can give you some instruction. You could go to Barry Moser, for instance—there are workshops all over the country—and learn the fundamentals without the trial and error of teaching yourself.

DANA: Now, you and Williams had a close association for a long time.

DUNCAN: Ten years. He came in '45; he died in '56.

DANA: Did his tastes and his aesthetic concerns influence the production of the press in significant ways?

DUNCAN: Yes. He was a finer craftsman than I. He had a

keener conscience about getting things finished to the nth degree. I'm much more sloppy and careless.

The best printing that I've ever done was with Paul, and under his aegis. In the last two or three years before we left Cummington, we did a series of pamphlets. One by Richard Eberhart. One by Yvor Winters. Allen Tate. J. V. Cunningham. And a pamphlet by Frederick Goddard Tuckerman, *The Cricket*. I think these are the best craftsmanship that I have ever done, and I could not possibly have done it without Paul to act as my gadfly and to carry things to their ultimate, which is, you know, one of the marks of vital craftsmanship.

DANA: What did he do? Can you point to anything specific?

DUNCAN: He had an *eye*, and if I went a little dark with the ink on one sheet, he would immediately say, "Too much. Take some of the ink off." Left to myself, I tend to think, "Well, in a couple of more impressions the ink will be down where it was," and not take the time to stop and take a little bit of ink off.

DANA: Did he cause you, or did his presence cause you, also, to increase your use of cuts, prints, designs?

DUNCAN: Oh yes. And they confirmed me in a conviction that the best work is done by using what you've got. Not by, you know, canvassing the country to find an illustrator, or trying to explore all the latest techniques of reproduction, or anything like that. But with what you have. Making it do. And I think this kind of economy is one of the qualities of craftsmanship which is not very much observed anymore.

DANA: Did you ever disagree on a project?

DUNCAN: Oh, sometimes with great acrimony. For instance, for J. V. Cunningham's pamphlet, *Doctor Drink*, Paul did a kind of abstract, very funny intaglio plate in which, if you puzzled it out, you could see that there was a man with an erection there. And this disturbed me. It riled my hypocritical, puritan conscience, and I attacked him about it. He stuck by his guns. And, thank heaven, we printed it. But I did raise those objections, and we had a quarrel about it.

DANA: It's been said that the two of you innovated certain

aspects of bookmaking. What about Williams's set of original watercolor covers for Tate's *The Winter Sea*? About thirty out of a run of . . .

DUNCAN: There were thirty or thirty-five copies of *The Winter Sea* signed by the author on a special paper. They were bound by John Marchi in white paper over boards. Paul did for each of these thirty copies an original watercolor, and he just put the watercolor down on the front cover, and then we sent them out without any protection whatever, except a dust jacket of thin paper. Madness! Really madness to do that! They were beautiful, and all very different from one another. No repetition. Incredible to be so careless about your work as that.

DANA: Had anybody ever done this before?

DUNCAN: No, no. We just cared enough for the book, and Paul saw in it . . . he got all these images out of the poetry.

DANA: Maybe this is what Kim Merker means when he insists that you are the master innovator of book design among fine-book printers. Whenever I compliment him on the output of the Windhover Press, he says, "Oh, yes. But Harry is the *real* genius. Harry will try things I would *never* try."

DUNCAN: This is only Kim's modesty talking. Actually, the watercolor covers of *The Winter Sea*, I think, are just folly. To send out something . . . just because they were such good watercolors . . . to send them out unprotected that way is irresponsible bookwork.

DANA: But it wasn't folly to do it in terms of the design of the book. You're not saying that.

DUNCAN: No, just that I should have valued Paul's watercolors enough to have protected them at least with a cellophane wrapper or something like that. But the white paper . . . I've seen copies soiled . . .

Books have to have a certain amount of stability, of course, because they are for reading and rereading, and so they have to last to some degree. However, I do not think of books as being a kind of adamantine monument of some sort of indestructible materials. They are perishable. And what you have in Paul's covers, those watercolors, is an immediacy of response to the literature, to what was really there. "The shock of recognition," to use Edmund Wilson's phrase. Something confirmed about that. The virtue consisted in that realization. My irresponsibility was that I just let those out to be worn away. However, I think of books as being, not momentary, . . . but they are a matter of responsiveness. And this does not have to be in terms of marble or gilded monuments or anything like that.

DANA: But their durability has to be protected to a certain extent.

DUNCAN: Yes. Since they're special objects, they should be able to withstand temporal depredations to some degree.

DANA: Somewhere you have written—and I bring this up since we are starting to talk about the *craft* of bookmaking—"Standards of book craftsmanship are based on the hand press. Handprinting must remain the basic direct letterpress technique until traditional book architecture submits to technology."

DUNCAN: Stupid.

DANA: Well, maybe it *was* stupid. You also said, "Design is not applied but *structural*, rising from good materials traditionally worked." Now, that sounds very much like what you've been saying this afternoon.

DUNCAN: These remarks, of course, are not original with me at all. They are simply the mythos of bookmaking that was prevalent until—what? Fifteen years ago, or something? The London *Times* in 1900 said something to the effect that hand printers should establish the criteria for machine work, and I suppose they thought the handprinter had a little more leisure to pay attention to the finer aesthetics of the matter. Nowadays I think that sounds absurd, actually. But we haven't yet found anything better.

DANA: Computer type must give you nightmares.

DUNCAN: Most of the ways in which literature comes to us nowadays look to me anemic. If you bother to look at it, it almost disappears off the page. This is true even if the design is well planned, and so on.

DANA: What do you mean "anemic"?

DUNCAN: It just doesn't have any guts to it.

DANA: When you talk about print having guts to it, or book designing having guts to it, what are you talking about?

DUNCAN: Well, I'm talking about a certain reassuring presence in the quality of ink and the third-dimensional quality of type penetrating paper, because those are things that really did exist as objects. With photo-offset printing, everything is so spiritual.

DANA: Spiritual—you mean . . . ?

DUNCAN: Nothing is embodied, quite. A book is a physical thing. It is the contents of the book which has its soul.

DANA: Meaning the printing of the type is too pale.

DUNCAN: Yes. It doesn't have very much presence in space.

DANA: Is this the quality of the printing process, or the choice of typefaces, or the lack of taste in choosing a typeface?

DUNCAN: Well, the only means that we know of for a natural evolution of alphabetic forms is through handcraft. The alphabet is not an intellectual matter. It is a matter physically realized by the hands of men. Like shoes or fabrics. And maybe someday we'll assign computers the right tasks, the right problems to solve, and get back some graphic presence in books. But most of the stuff we get nowadays doesn't have very much graphic presence. And I care about this because I care about the literature, and I'd like the object which presents the literature to us to have some conviction to it. Not to be a tentative, timid thing.

DANA: While we're on the subject of craft, you said earlier that when Cummington started out it didn't have a "credo," or a set of aesthetic principles. But, clearly, a very strong set of aesthetic guidelines has developed over the years.

DUNCAN: Yes. Those were always in evolution, which is the way aesthetics should be. It's absurd for people to theorize, in my estimation, about aesthetics. Aesthetics are created in the workroom by artists, not by philosophers at desks. Except there's no reason why philosophers should not respond in their own way to whatever is beautiful to them. And some of them were very good at it, of course, like St. Thomas Aquinas with his *claritas*, which is, you know, just excellent for book printing.

I think the whole point of a book is the text—the verbal creation of the author. Type, like handwriting, is simply a system of visible signs which still speech into a special form which waits to be resurrected in the human voice—to be re-created, because no reader will hear a poem exactly the same as another reader or the same as the author wrote it. So it's an interesting business to retrieve what is there. It's the way literature conquers time.

I don't think of typefaces as being illustrative. I think that what should happen is that the reader, in the process of reading, can forget what he's looking at so that he is completely taken up in letting the text be reborn in his ear.

DANA: What you're really looking for is typeface that disappears when the reader . . .

DUNCAN: Obviously, that can only be metaphorical. You know that Beatrice Ward, when she was talking about this, said printing should be invisible. And it never can be invisible. But what the reader needs is the assurance that the typographer, who in his precursory reading sets the terms of the presentation, has done his work well. So that the reader doesn't have to be disturbed by lines which are so long he's doubling, or . . . But it's more than that. He needs to be reassured that there is a certain amount of clarity and integrity to what he is reading, because books are architectural in that sense. The human eye simply, if it's a civilized eye, expects some decent order in what's made for its use. The building is not the important thing, it's the person who lives in the building. It's the work of literature that counts. But we have to house the literature in a way which does it honor, or at least is suitable for it.

DANA: This is a very intense way of printing. How did you arrive at this?

DUNCAN: No great discovery.

DANA: No, but there must have been some moment in the process of becoming a printer when this idea of it presented itself very clearly to you.

DUNCAN: Oh, probably not very clearly until this moment.

DANA: When you set Lowell's book, *Land of Unlikeness* . . .

DUNCAN: That's really not one of our best books at all. Not that the typesetting is so bad, and the choice of Poliphilus for Lowell is good. But it was done on a clamshell treadle press. I printed it by myself without any helper. And the paper isn't very good, and the press wasn't big enough. I think I broke it once. It wasn't big enough to give me the kind of bite into the paper I wanted. Every book I've ever printed has great flaws, and I'm not singling *Land of Unlikeness* out as one of the worst examples.

DANA: Well, let's take a book you think is one of your best. How did you decide what the best presentation of that work would be?

DUNCAN: If by "decide" you mean make an analytical thing of it, I'm not very good at that. I think that probably most typographical designers, who make layouts and preliminary sketches and all of that and consider all these things objectively, are better at that kind of objective approach. But my approach is much more subjective. I read texts, and if it's original it awakens something new in me. And I have a pretty good idea of the limited resources available—the typefaces, the papers, and so on. And more or less intuitively I try to get these things in agreement with one another, realizing my limitations. It's not any very arrogant thing. I don't try to *control* my materials. I just try to get them to fit.

I like to let the material speak. This applies just as much to the typeface as it does to the text. In other words, printers are not fine artists at all. They are the artists of application, and they try to just get things right in that sense. Not to be original.

DANA: Do you remember a work for which you chose the type and the paper and decided at some point that this was not the right type or the right paper? Where you changed your mind *in medias res*?

DUNCAN: Yes, oh yes. I've changed my mind when I realized something was wrong. I should have done it more often, too.

I have set now a long narrative poem about Nebuchadnezzar. We started printing the book. We got two runs done of it when I received a completely revised manuscript from the author. Ordinarily, it would be no problem at all. You'd just say, "Too late. Sorry." But the revisions, which were extensive, were a great improvement, so that raised a question of conscience. I decided to destroy what I'd already printed and go back to square one. My consideration, though, was not entirely on the improvement of the poem. I also saw that the printing I had done wasn't very convincing to me, and so I wanted to do it on another press with a different kind of bite into the paper. So I'm going to do that whole book again. I'm going to use the same paper and the same typeface but get them to marry one another better by using a cylinder press instead of the Washington. It's on a big quarto page, and the Washington just doesn't have enough bite printing four-up to do it properly.

DANA: Have you ever switched types in the middle of a job, or switched papers?

DUNCAN: Not usually. One has a certain limited choice of typefaces. Most of them are good in themselves. I buy designs that I respect, and try to get them so that they are not just narrowly applicable. I don't have any black letter, for instance. Although I once had Victor Hammer's American Uncial, which is a typeface I like. It's surely the most original typeface of the century and very beautiful, to my mind, and very clear and easy to read. But it's too special. It hasn't yet got to the stage where people will just read it without looking at it. And so I don't have it. I did use American Uncial for Blackmur's second book and a couple of pamphlets, including Richard Eberhart.

DANA: *An Herb Basket.* Before we get more deeply into the subject of Victor Hammer, how many of your books have made the fifty best-printed books? Do you have any idea?

DUNCAN: I don't know. I would say more than ten, less than twenty. You know, they no longer have the Fifty Books. Instead they have something . . . The American Institute of Graphic Arts has a show in which I had a book about five or six years ago—the Dean generously permitted me to go to New York for the opening. Well, what a hodgepodge! What a junkpile that whole show was! In the first place, there must have been at least a hundred books, and they were of all kinds—paperbacks, all sorts of stuff—which is fine, I don't object to that. But it was impossible to see it. There was nothing really to see in that massive jumble. I was very disappointed, and so I've never sent a book to that again. This kind of show replaced the Fifty Books twenty years ago, I think.

DANA: How did you come to meet Victor Hammer? You worked with him for a while, didn't you?

DUNCAN: One March day in sugarin' time—an unseasonably mild day—there was a knock on our door in Cummington, and a gentleman entered and introduced himself as the dean or something, a high official of Wells College in Aurora, New York. He had come to tell us about the work of a man named Victor Hammer, who was head of the Art Department at Wells. Victor had set up the Wells College Press and was printing books and had just cut a new typeface. He also wanted to see what we were up to at the Cummington Press. And it was a very pleasant hour we spent with him. You know, it's not hard to figure out who had commissioned him to make this journey. And he must have made a good report when he got back to Aurora, because Victor then sent us this magnificent quarto, a brochure I guess you'd call it, *A Dialogue on the Uncial*, which was in the new type. Magnificent! And a letter from him—"I thank you for the help you gave my cause. I, too, am concerned how to keep body and soul together, but it is not spiritual help we need. It is financial help. Thank you." To be associated in this way with such magnificent work was very flattering. So Paul and I got on the bus, after getting permission from Victor to come see him, and we spent an evening with him, and he very generously told us his methods of damping paper, inking the type, presswork, makeready, et cetera. The whole works. Very generously. Which changed our own way of working.

DANA: Now what year was that? About 1946? '47?

DUNCAN: Yes.

DANA: Where was he from?

DUNCAN: He was from Vienna. He was born in Maria Theresa's Vienna and never really felt any need to get *out* of that, except that, of course, he had got out. He was teaching at the Vienna Academy of Arts when he heard the Nazis were coming and just quietly, without even saying good-bye to anybody, left the school, went home and picked up his wife, and they went down without any luggage to the train station and got on a train for France. This was the night before the *Anschluss*, the Nazi takeover. He went to England for a while and then came to America, where he got the job at Wells College. During the next year we saw Victor three times again. He came once to Cummington, and I think we went twice to Aurora, the last time because he persuaded the trustees or somebody at Wells College to sponsor our printing a book at Wells—with an eye, probably, to our taking over the Wells College Press after he'd gone. He was at mandatory retirement age, sixty-five. We printed the book there, and we looked forward to it so much because we thought we'd be closely associated with him, but he was already taken up with his move to Lexington, Kentucky, where he'd found a job at Transylvania College. So we saw very little of him, but we did William Carlos Williams's *The Clouds, Aigeltinger, Russia, &c.*

DANA: You had already published one book by Williams independently. How did you come to publish Williams?

DUNCAN: Well, when the idea first came to us of going to Wells, we had looked forward to doing a book in American Uncial, which we liked very much. We had just printed a Blackmur book in it. We had a long poem by Robert Lowell called *Dead Briton's Vision*, an invective. We thought that we should find Victor's type in the pressroom at the Wells College Press and could use it. But when we got there, there wasn't

any. There was, instead, Joseph Blumenthal's Spiral type.
Furthermore, when we submitted the Lowell poem, the committee at Wells thought it a little scurrilous to be sponsored
by the college, and so we gave that up. We had the Williams
manuscript on hand and substituted that. It was very well
suited, probably, to that typeface. It was rather long to print
in three months, which was all the time we had. And we didn't
get to include in front a woodcut that Paul had done drawings
for. I'm sorry the book looked so bare.

DANA: Your bibliography says Williams nixed that design.
Why?

DUNCAN: I don't know that he nixed it. I think we just
didn't have time to do it right, so we decided to leave it out.
Tennessee Williams nixed one for *I Rise in Flame, Cried the
Phoenix*.

DANA: How did you connect to William Carlos Williams in
the first place? Had he taught at Cummington?

DUNCAN: Bill Williams came to see us at Cummington once
with his two ladies, Flossie and Flossie's sister, I think. Oh,
what a wonderful visit that was. They stayed overnight. The
other woman, not Flossie, cooked us a marvelous meal. What
a wonderful time. We got along fine.

Then Bill submitted a third book, called *The Desert Music*.
Extraordinary book. We had already designed it, set much of
the type for it, when he told us that it was going to appear in
Botteghe Oscure—entire. And we refused to do it with that
stipulation. We told him how much we liked it and how much
we wanted to do it, but said we were establishing a policy and
sweating blood over it that we would not simply do a reprint.
It's a policy that I never changed and never regretted, except
in that one case, because *The Desert Music* is such a beautiful
poem. And it would have been such a beautiful book, too. A
little, narrow, tall page of Lutetia Italic. Do you know, that's
how we disconnected.

DANA: But he sought you out at the beginning.

DUNCAN: Well, I think so. The first connection, of course,
was our printing *The Wedge*. But we did that without meeting
him, and I think he sent us *The Wedge* through the mail. You

see, at that time poets were having a hell of a time getting published. Especially rather small books. Publishers were doing collected poems and things of that sort.

DANA: Did your relationship with Victor Hammer influence the development of the Cummington Press in any way?

DUNCAN: Abundantly. It changed it in that fundamental way of changing the method of work and improving it. Changed it also in the influence of Victor's character, because he was a really heroic figure, and still is to me. So resourceful, so completely dedicated to printing. His English was not good enough for him to be able to read poetry in English very perceptively. But just after leaving Wells College he finished his quarto printing of the poems of Hölderlin, which is one of the magnificent masterpieces of the century, I'm sure. I know what a marvelous reflection of the text this book is. He did it, you know, towards the end.

Just before leaving Wells he designed, and his son Jacob printed, a book by James Feibleman called *Journey to the Coastal Marsh*, which we published. Feibleman advanced the money to pay for the production of the book. I think maybe this was the first book in American Uncial, as a matter of fact. But during this time Victor had a heart attack. But two months after leaving Wells he had resumed printing on his quarto of Hölderlin. He did it by lopping a quarter of the platen off either end on his press so that he could pull the handle without undue physical strain. He wrote us, "Since I am printing all by myself, thanks to the halved platen, I have also learned how to print alone, undistracted, no conversation." This dashed our hopes. Because I'd always hoped that he would call on me for assistance. I always wanted to work with him. And that dashed that. Later, he sent what he called "a waste copy" of the book. It was magnificent! When I saw it, I wished the book well and lost my selfish interest.

DANA: Did he have any aesthetic impact on the Cummington Press?

DUNCAN: I never agreed with his aesthetic ideas, although I respected them all, certainly. You know, he was out of Vienna.

I was out of Keokuk, Iowa. There was a big difference. He was a much more complete man, more complete printer, than I could ever hope to be. I think for him the whole Judeo-Christian tradition was still active and alive. He was a craftsman who just attacked without the slightest hesitation anything that he felt desirable to do. At one time, one of the reasons I hoped he would call on me for assistance is that he would teach me punch cutting.

And there was a terrific quarrel between Victor and Paul Williams, aesthetically. Victor thought Paul's work was callow and vulgar. Paul thought Victor's work was somewhat pompous, and they never resolved this quarrel, really.

DANA: From 1952 to about 1954 there are no books from the Cummington Press.

DUNCAN: That's not true. There is one book called *Requiescat in Pace: Paul Wightman Williams*. He was killed in an automobile accident in 19 . . . Oh no, now we're at Rowe.

DANA: Yes. There's a hiatus of about two years when the Cummington Press doesn't publish anything. Then it comes back together at Rowe.

DUNCAN: Oh yes, I went to Europe, and when I got back I spent the summer at the McDowell Colony.

DANA: What caused this . . . ?

DUNCAN: The Cummington School—and there was nothing hostile about it—felt that the sort of lever needed had gone since Katharine Frazier's death, and we were sort of an impediment to the school, which was providing our housing.

DANA: You were being tolerated rather than supported.

DUNCAN: Tolerated rather than supported. The trustees very generously said that we should take not only all the back stock, the books we had printed, but also the equipment for the press, which was a very generous settlement on their part. My father had died the year before and left a small legacy, and I decided that I wanted to follow Allen Tate to Rome, so I went to Rome for nine months. Paul went to New York and tried to make a reputation as a painter.

DANA: What did you do for a year in Europe?

DUNCAN: Well, I lived in Rome, and—walked.

DANA: You weren't there studying typefaces or bookmaking or . . .

DUNCAN: No, and I didn't even have the sense to go to Verona to see Mardersteig. Of course, now I could kick myself. But I felt this would be somehow a pompous act. He was one of the very great printers of the century. The founder of, the proprietor of, the Officina Bodoni. He started the press in Germany, then moved to Italy.

DANA: Did you just sit things out?

DUNCAN: No, it was a magnificent year. It was so magnificent that I had sort of a trauma about coming back. By the time I left I had a job translating for an American newspaper syndicate that does releases from the Vatican. I could have stayed. I was making enough money. But either way I decided—whether I came back to America or stayed—I would regret it the rest of my life. A remarkable, red-haired, Jungian witch of a psychiatrist got me over that impasse. I came back, partly because my book of poems was going to be published, and because I'd been invited to the McDowell Colony. I'm not sorry. Not anymore.

DANA: So you went from Rome to Rowe.

DUNCAN: After I got back, at the McDowell Colony, I met a composer named Lee Hoiby, and he and I started to do an opera together, I writing the libretto. We became great friends, and he and Paul and I moved the press equipment to Rowe and bought a Greek Revival house for a song and moved in. The way we were able to keep up the mortgage payments and to keep from starving was to do largely job printing and by moonlighting. I drove a school bus. So we didn't get much publication done. We did a couple of things on commission for the library at Williams College and the Pierpont Morgan Library. And we did the printing for the town of Rowe—Fireman's Ball tickets, the town report, ballots.

DANA: You handset the type?

DUNCAN: Handprinted them all.

DANA: They must have been the most elegant town reports and ballots in the history of the country.

DUNCAN: Well, the town report was so long that we had it set on the Linotype. But Paul did a series of drawings of some of the old buildings in the town of Rowe. Really stunning!

But we did manage to get three things published. We did a book of poems by Bob Price—Robert Price, the late friend of our friend, the painter Stamos, who paid part of the production cost. And we did a pamphlet by Harvey Shapiro and a pamphlet by Don Stanford. That's about all we got published in two *years*. And that gives you pause because, for me at least, the whole point of the thing was the contact with literature and publication, although I loved to print, and I even enjoyed doing the town report. There's a kind of drudgery which you don't experience if you believe in the text that you've got. So when I had a telephone call from Les Moeller at the University of Iowa asking me to come there, I was favorably disposed to try it. And Paul thought it was a good idea, too. Lee Hoiby decided to go back to New York. Then Paul was killed in an automobile wreck.

DANA: You came to Iowa in 1956. Was that Carroll Coleman's idea?

DUNCAN: Yes.

DANA: It's been said that you had a choice between the University of Iowa or commercial publishing, that you had had invitations to join commercial publishing houses. Is that right?

DUNCAN: This was more of a hope, I think, on my part. Because Les Moeller told me that in order to come to Iowa I should understand something of the contemporary printing scene, I did presswork at the Lane Press in Burlington, Vermont. It was a very good experience. I think they would have taken me on. But I didn't even propose myself for that, although Ben Lane was a very nice, sympathetic man. One place that I did perhaps have some in, I think—probably John Wheelock would have given me a job at Scribner's if I'd asked for it. And by then Allen Tate—I don't know whether at this time or shortly before—Allen was working for Scribner's, too.

DANA: Well, your own book had come out in the Scribner's Poets of Today series.

DUNCAN: Right. Through John Wheelock and Allen's recommendation.

DANA: Are you saying you didn't really have a choice in the world of commercial publishing?

DUNCAN: Maybe I had the choice, but it didn't interest me that much. I really was not interested in commercial publishing. That's really true.

DANA: Not even as a book designer?

DUNCAN: No, not really. I felt that it was beyond my abilities. I have never worked at a drafting table planning books. I'd always worked with the type by hand. But I *had* thought of moving to New York as a printer and talked to Joe Blumenthal at Spiral Press about that. He said, "If you come, I would be glad if you'd work for me, but my solemn advice is *get out of New York and stay away from here if you want to get anything done.* This is a rat race. Don't come here." He said, "It's very hard on a printer," and I believed him. I think that was very good advice. So after I'd talked to him I didn't really consider that very seriously.

You know, I was born early enough in the century that I still had the idea that culture centered in capitals, and I tried to get out of Iowa as fast as I could. Instead, I seemed to always be pulled back to the Midwest. And so I accepted that fate. I'm certainly not sorry.

DANA: Well, leaving New England and coming away from a very intimate relationship with other printers and with Williams—what was Iowa City like for you?

DUNCAN: Well, it was dreadful the first year. At least my memories of it are mostly bad. I was desperately lonely. I missed Paul terribly. My mother very generously got me a house, away from downtown Iowa City. A house on Sixth Avenue or somewhere, and I hated the house. I'd come from a very beautiful *old* house and this was a gimcrack, modern, thrown-together . . . One thing that happened that relieved that a little bit was that I met Kim Merker. Kim took my course and helped me with the Paul Williams memorial book. And the Mona Van Duyn. Then Kim started his own press and did the Weldon Kees. Well, that was terrific. I couldn't have hoped for a better student.

DANA: Why did Carroll Coleman want you to come to Iowa City? He had his own press and was employed by the university.

DUNCAN: Well, he had founded the Typographic Laboratory, and he was leaving it in order to be kicked upstairs and take charge of university printing. So he needed a replacement.

When I was . . . this must have been 1939 . . . my father was a traveling man and covered Iowa and had gotten to know Carroll. Once, he took me to Muscatine, where Carroll was in one of these storefronts down near the river. He was working all alone, by himself at that time. My father took me in and introduced me. Immediately, I was completely awestruck by Carroll—working there, so all alone.

DANA: Was this before you went to Cummington?

DUNCAN: No, I had been at Cummington one summer. And, you know, Carroll is a very reticent, uncommunicative man. So when I learned that he'd recommended me for Iowa, it surprised me. I think he probably remembered me from that visit to Muscatine and probably he kept up on some of the books we'd printed. I saw almost nothing of Carroll in Iowa City. I think we had lunch together once or twice.

DANA: I understand the trip from Massachusetts to Iowa was rather spooky. You packed your Washington and your typecases in a U-Haul trailer?

DUNCAN: I had a U-Haul trailer, and it really wasn't big enough to carry all that weight. I remember I had to inflate the tires to one hundred and fifty pounds. And when I went over thirty-five miles an hour in my station wagon with that trailer behind, I began to sway. So it took three full days. I didn't know how to back the damn thing either, but I managed.

DANA: What were some of the other problems of Iowa City?

DUNCAN: I don't blame Iowa City. I blame being isolated in

that house and being so lonely—my own misery. I also found that the J School was very much involved with the timeserving practice of pleasing the communications industries establishment. That was one of the reasons I eventually got less and less printing done. I got so involved in the J School in the last years at Iowa City. I regret very much a university dealing with something so fascinating as the print media and communications being subservient to a doddering industry.

DANA: Do you regret the time that went into teaching?

DUNCAN: No. Teaching, of course, as you know, has its own rewards. Unfortunately . . . , it calls on the same energy. Your writing and my printing.

DANA: And what one finds out is that one has a limited amount of energy.

DUNCAN: Yes. And teaching, of course, is more or less like writing in water.

DANA: Prior to Iowa City, the Cummington book list is largely bolstered by well-known, established poets: Stevens, Tate, Blackmur, Williams. The one notable exception, as a greenhorn, is Lowell. *After* Iowa City, the Cummington Press becomes more involved with first books—with the books of new poets, poets with untried reputations.

DUNCAN: Yes, I think that's so. It's no deliberate thing. It was still a hand-to-mouth operation. That is, one prints what is there to print. The state of publishing in the nation changed by the fifties. The well-known, established figures could get published easily by the New York industry. So I think these people didn't send me manuscripts. Besides, they'd mostly tended to disappear anyway. I don't know of comparable reputations nowadays. John Ashbery is not synonymous to Allen Tate in his position. There is a dispersal of central authority in the literary world.

DANA: Did the Iowa Writers' Workshop have an influence on the Cummington Press?

DUNCAN: It was very powerful when I first went to Iowa City—with Levine, Coulette, Everwine, Mezey, Berg. You know, I went and sat in their halo as an auditor for a whole

year. On the other hand, I think Paul Engle found me somewhat refractory as someone to carry out his purposes. I was
terribly suspicious of Paul at first. I thought he was always
trying to get me to sell out and do what *he* wanted. For instance, he had me print some of his sonnets for a kind of
Christmas pamphlet with Kathy Hefner illustrations. And
I did that. I don't know how he talked me into it. I don't regret it. There was the *Homage to Baudelaire,* which was
more compatible to me because it had good translations of the
poems. But, you know, the pressure from Paul seemed to ease
off after awhile. I did *Golden Child.* It's partly just that one
wants to join the community where one is.

DANA: But at the same time you felt as though he wanted to
use the Cummington Press in some way.

DUNCAN: Yes. This, I realize now, is not to his discredit at
all. It's simply the way that he got things done. He tended
to look around and see what was there and then try to turn it
to his purpose. That's the way he operates. He uses people
around him. I suppose we all do that, but maybe Paul was
better at it than most of us.

DANA: How did you happen to print Robert Mezey's first
book? That was the second in the brief string of Lamont poetry prizes won by Iowa Workshop poets.

DUNCAN: Well, I had accepted the book, of course. The way
the Lamont operated at that time was that submissions were
all by publishers who had accepted the manuscript of first
poems already. Then the publisher submitted it to Lamont
and the award was made, whereupon you had to produce a
thousand copies, or however many, for their membership at a
certain fixed price. That was a worse sellout than probably
any of the work I did for Paul Engle, because I was frantically
confined about time, not only for the publication date that the
Lamont people required but also my job. I had the type set by
Monotype in St. Louis and did the book dry, on dry paper. The
binding's kind of shoddy, too. It's not one of the books I'm
proudest of, because I didn't know how to use those circumstances. I still don't. The way I work is slowly and to let things

kind of grow in my head by themselves. And there's something wilful about the Mezey book. Which is what you have to do if you're going faster than the thing originates itself.

DANA: You had the choice of a lot of poets at that point. Mezey was there. Justice was there. Levine. Jane Cooper. How did you happen to come up with Mezey and then follow that with Steve Berg a couple of years later?

DUNCAN: Bob and I were great friends, and he sent me a manuscript. I never had a manuscript from Phil or the others. They may have talked about it, but Mezey sent me the manuscript of *The Lovemaker*. And Steve sent me his first book.

DANA: Kim Merker is, perhaps, the foremost of your printing protégés of the Iowa City period. What was it about him that caused you to strike up a kind of partnership with him for a while?

DUNCAN: Oh, it was just his interest, that's all. He got the bug early. That's really it. He wouldn't leave me alone. He persisted. And that's not very much like him, as a matter of fact, when you think about it. He's not very insistent. But he did insist.

DANA: That sounds very Confucian. The student goes to the teacher and insists on studying with the teacher, rather than the teacher being handed a batch of students.

DUNCAN: It's in the *I Ching*, you know.

DANA: "Go sit out in the rain for three days, and we may let you in the temple to sweep the floors. Later on, we'll see if you're an able student or not."

DUNCAN: In the *I Ching*, it says, "If a student importunes me once, I will try to give him the answers; twice, I will be silent; thrice, I will turn my back."

DANA: Well, going back to the notion of simplicity and directness, that's part of the mystique you seem to live by. How did you know he was good? Insistence isn't enough to make one a good student of printing. How did you know that he was more than just an insistent young man who thought he wanted to be a printer?

DUNCAN: In a handcraft, the insistence does have a lot more to do with it than you might think. And although he is not the top beginning typographer I've ever had—I think maybe Doyle Moore qualifies as that—it's the persistence that kept Kim with it.

DANA: Would you say that Iowa City had any appreciable effect on your ideas about the Cummington Press? On your aesthetic ideas? On your notions of book printing?

DUNCAN: At Iowa City, I began to see emerge through Kim and others the present renascence of fine printing and private presses, which made me realize slowly that this was not a matter involving my own ideas alone anymore, but it was more or less a community of ideas. This is something that I never could have enjoyed in the thirties or forties. Impossible. And that changes things. One tends to work, therefore, with an eye to what Clare Van Vleet in Vermont might say. In other words, printers support and qualify one another's work. That's new. Early along, in Iowa City, I began to realize that Kim was a critic. That it wasn't only a matter of his showing me *his* efforts, but he was judging mine as well. That, combined with the fact that I never had been able to work alone, as Carroll Coleman has done. I always needed someone to work with me. And this is not only a matter of the right way to run a Washington press; it also has to do with a sharing of work. I'd always worked with somebody, beginning with Katharine Frazier, and this has not changed. Although I never got anybody like Paul Williams again, who was dedicated to undertake the supervision of illustration and who also was very critical and exacting about my own presswork. I never found anybody like that again, but instead there is a dispersed critical atmosphere.

I'm looking forward very much to retiring, because I have the romantic notion that after we fix the attic I can go upstairs and be more perfect than I ever have before and not be interrupted every few minutes by some other concern and really make a book as I think it ought to be made. That's probably a romantic notion, because I can't imagine doing it alone. Anymore, I seem to lose, within a year or two, my best students after I've trained them.

DANA: So you're saying that Iowa City opened up a kind of multisided dialogue among printers. Like poets talking to each other from poem to poem. Did it make your printing more adventurous than it had been? Or more austere?

DUNCAN: Just maybe more companionable. I want to get more austere. That's why I look forward to the garret.

DANA: That sounds really monastic.

DUNCAN: There is something monastic about that. Not hermitic, perhaps, but monastic.

DANA: It sounds a lot like the writer's attitude toward writing. Is it significant that both you and Kim Merker—in Kim's case, he *was* a poet; in your case, you are still a poet—is there some kind of intimate relationship between the way the writer in you thinks about his art and the way the printer in you regards his craft?

DUNCAN: It's just a matter of having an interest in literature which tends to, you know, . . . you want to do something about it, and if you stop writing poetry, that doesn't mean that you care any less about literature. You still want to be part of it, and be in the scene and be active, not just a passive reader. So I think it grows out of the same kind of interest. Although some good printers have never been poets.

DANA: But it's not uncommon for the writer to move from writing to printing?

DUNCAN: No. And I suspect that this is part of the resistance of poets today to the electronic age. A poet always is opposed to his time, and the technical part of printing has become so sophisticated and complex and expensive, the printing industry, the publishing industry, is so monstrous, and poetry still is intimate and personal, I trust, to some degree. So it's natural to turn to a small press which is out of the main industry and using rather simpler means. That seems perfectly natural to me.

DANA: So you think that in the current publishing mess,

since it's mostly a matter of accounting in the big publishing houses now, the small press really has an important function to fulfill.

DUNCAN: Probably more important than ever. In the twenties and thirties, a beginning poet had a certain procedure he followed. First, he began to submit his work to magazines. And, while there are still literary magazines, they again are dispersed in their interests, so there is not a normal course of things. *Poetry* magazine no longer is a kind of stepping-stone to the first "thin book of verse," and so on. Although it can be. I don't think the publishing industry serves poetry well anymore.

DANA: It didn't serve it very well to begin with, but it seems to serve it less now.

DUNCAN: It seems worse than ever. I understand why. I know the reasons, and they mostly seem bad to me. They have to do with conglomerate corporations showing a profit and all that crap. And I don't see any men like John Hall Wheelock anymore, who really care about literature as a whole and want to promote it and that's why they're working in publishing. It's as though everybody in publishing is out for a fast buck. So I think that it is the small presses who've taken over this kind of responsibility, which Alfred Knopf, John Wheelock, and others once had. I don't know if there are any publishers like that anymore.

DANA: Were you aware, Harry, at any time between Cummington, Massachusetts, and Iowa City that you were providing an immense impetus to small-press production in this country?

DUNCAN: No, I had no idea at all, because it wasn't until after I'd been in Iowa City for years that I knew that the small-press movement was growing. I still feel, really—although I know I shouldn't—I still feel almost as isolated as I did at Cummington in the beginning. That's because I want to, somehow. That's a selfish thing. I think that it probably helps my work if I feel like Adam in the Garden.

DANA: Who are some of the other fine-book presses outside

of the Iowa City group—which would include Windhover, Penumbra, the Toothpaste Press—whose work you think is interesting, innovative?

DUNCAN: Probably San Francisco, if anyplace, is more active in this regard than Iowa City. This is through the influence of Andy Hoyem and Adrian Wilson, but there are a great many young people who, I know from being there last year, are not only working very well, but persistently too. And even in New York City, which was a desert to this sort of thing for so long, there are a couple—oh, more than a couple—of good people working there. So it's by no means entirely midwestern. Northampton, Massachusetts, may be the center of fine bookwork in the nation because of the binding that's done there, and because of Barry Moser and his Hampshire Typothetae.

DANA: Are there two or three presses whose work you think is outstanding? At the risk of invidious comparison, of course.

DUNCAN: Walter Hamady at the Perishable Press is probably the most boisterous, obstreperous typographic genius of the age. I wish all of his students had the same spirit Walter has. Walter came to see me at the little shop on Gilbert Street in Iowa City. I remember his standing around watching me print the Agee book, and he said that turned him on. But he's a completely self-made man. He doesn't use the Washington handpress, but he does make his own paper.

DANA: You moved the Cummington Press from Iowa City to, not San Francisco or Northampton, but Omaha, Nebraska. Why?

DUNCAN: That's easy. Because the job with the University of Nebraska at Omaha, as it was offered, said that I would spend half my time teaching and half my time printing and publishing. At Iowa, my job was entirely teaching.

DANA: You called the press you set up here Abattoir Editions.

DUNCAN: Well, I thought the university should have an imprint of its own, so I tried to think of something which was suitable for Omaha, and I knew that Omaha had succeeded Chicago as hog butcher to the world. Abattoir, of course, is a fancy name for slaughterhouse. I didn't really take into account that the meat-packing industry had decentralized and is now scattered all over and that the stockyards are two-thirds deserted. I also thought that we might be able to use that quotation from Wordsworth, "We slaughter to instruct," as a motto. And many a time I've thought I ought to print it and post it conspicuously for my students' sake.

DANA: Has anybody at the university ever said, "Gee, why would you want to call your press the Slaughterhouse Press?"

DUNCAN: I think several people have asked me about that.

DANA: Were they upset?

DUNCAN: Oh no. People don't get upset about words anymore.

DANA: I see. Is there any difference in philosophy of Abattoir Editions and the Cummington Press? Do they serve different functions? Do you work from a different set of ideas?

DUNCAN: Philosophical differences—that's too highfalutin. But I did use the Cummington imprint a couple of years ago when I printed some dirty poems by the Earl of Rochester and I thought maybe that they were a little too *much* for the university imprint to appear on. I put the Cummington Press on that.

DANA: How much does the university support Abattoir?

DUNCAN: It is a kind of unofficial support. That is, they have given me a nice place to work and they pay my salary, but I don't think anybody likes to think of the publishing program as an *official* university activity. Maybe they do, I don't know. But I have seen little evidence of that. The support that they do give in the way of . . . oh, if there's money left over in the college budget at the end of the semester, I am in competition for it, and I have been able to get pieces of equipment and some paper and other things that way. The university has been extremely generous to me. There has been no rejection or anything.

I think I told you about the committee that was formed

when I first came? Of campus worthies—good men and true, all of them. I ran into a little trouble about the John Logan manuscript, which was one of the first books I printed here. I can't remember what the trouble was. The book is called *The House That Jack Built*. It's a kind of long, meditative autobiography, and there was something in it which I thought might be questioned by the official powers. So I tried to get members of my committee to read this, to help take some of the onus off me, I guess. Well, they were all too busy. They didn't have time to read a manuscript, an unpublished manuscript, and make a criticism of it. So I made the decision myself on that occasion and went ahead with the book, and I have never been reprimanded for any of my editorial choices since. I don't know whether this is a source of gratification or not. One would like to feel that somebody cares enough.

DANA: Does this gloss what you meant by, "Well, the university doesn't like to think of its relationship to the publishing"?

DUNCAN: That's right. Unlike the University of Nebraska Press in Lincoln, Abattoir Editions has been a kind of under-the-rug game, which is fine with me. It prevents that bureaucratic thing. It keeps the amateur standing, which is important for a small press. I think it's fine.

DANA: Which of the books you've published under the Abattoir imprint do you think rank among your best-designed, best-printed books?

DUNCAN: I never venture to make that kind of criticism of myself. I always think the next book that I'm going to do is going to be my masterpiece and that finally I will do something without blemishes and the awful mistakes that I usually make, and it doesn't usually turn out to be that, and so I have an incentive to print yet another book.

When I work on a book, I try to make it as good as I can, given the amount of help I get from the muse. Because these things cannot just be willed. You have to have some kind of mysterious participation of the imagination, you know. And this is something you have to wait for. You can't command it automatically. This kind of inspiration, or whatever you want to call it, comes from a connection made subconsciously, half-consciously, between typeface, paper, page size, and text. And if these do not fall together in some kind of thing worth pursuing, then I'm very helpless. I just wait. I have to wait. They *have* fallen together with Kees. And the Charles Gullans book which I'm going to set this fall I've put on a little formal page, twelve mo [duodecimo, twenty-four pages] or smaller. The type is not small; the type is good sized. The lines are not long, you know. Wintersian.

DANA: What's a normal pressrun for an Abattoir book?

DUNCAN: I suspect that the average is about two hundred, maybe a little more. This is not a matter of calculation. It depends on the amount of paper that we can get for a reasonable price. I did five hundred copies of Dick Duggan's novel because I had the peculiar feeling that that was the only way we could come out paying for the rather expensive photoengraving, the plates, and all the cost of composition, and still sell the individual copy at a reasonable price.

DANA: Which of the Abattoir books has sold the best for you? And how do you sell these books? Do you have advance subscription?

DUNCAN: Well, we did have a distributor here in Omaha whose name was Richard Flamer. That was convenient because he handled all the shipping and the bookkeeping and so on. But he petered out about a year ago. So we now have a new distributor, Jim Sitter; he runs the Bookslinger in St. Paul, Minnesota.

DANA: So you don't have a lot of people who just take standing orders for . . . ?

DUNCAN: Yes, we do have seventy—something like that—standing-order customers.

DANA: Probably among those seventy customers are those people who collect books because they are, first of all, the artistic product of your particular presses, Abattoir and Cummington, and secondly because they're limited editions and increase in value, usually at a pretty rapid rate. How do you feel about book collectors?

DUNCAN: I don't really print books for collectors. So far as I have a conscious sense of audience, I print books for some-body who is going to discover the text of the book—poems, stories, and so on—with the same delight that *I* discover it as I am working on the book. So I don't tend to think of books as being a series of products, of a printer as an artist. I think of books as being an unexpected confluence of text, type, paper, and so on. I tend to think of them individually. I do see that there are certain habits that I have and certain ways of think-ing which haven't changed very much from the old days in Cummington. I still persist in that. I think that's idiosyncratic, probably, but I don't think what a printer is going to do is express himself. A lot of printing which is self-expressive I think is a pain in the ass.

DANA: What are these idiosyncratic ideas—two or three of them—which you see as having carried on down from the earliest days of the Cummington to the present situation in Omaha?

DUNCAN: Now you're asking me to examine my own preju-dices, and I do have some that I can identify. I don't know that they'd be important ones or the large flaws in my work.

I believe that a book should graphically be an integrated thing. I've always had trouble with title pages because, from the beginning, the title page has been a kind of display ad-vertisement. I think maybe all display advertisements grew out of title pages of books. Be that as it may, I do not like the title page to look different in proportion or typographic style from a page of text. Therefore I save the title page for last, and the reason is that it's difficult for me to make a display page which does not violate the conventions of a text page. This is solved for me just by tending to use the same size type, although I don't always. But to me, this matter of inte-grating the typographic design of the whole book rather than shooting off fireworks at the beginning is important and is a prejudice.

Another thing is that I am very definitely old-fashioned and sort of sixteenth-century Venetian. I usually start out with what's called a golden section, which is based on a proportion of two to three, and determine the margins in that way. This is the only thing that I do on a drawing board. When I get a page size and a probable length of line, and so on, I sit down and draw out a golden section. I'd never abide by it strictly, but it gives me a place to start. This gives a kind of Renaissance look to much of my work, and although I sometimes try deliberately to avoid it and work asymmetrically or another way, I find myself returning to that conservatism.

From the earliest days, I have objected, perhaps for the same reason that I object to title pages, to the size of capital letters. It seems to me that from the beginning of printing these were drawn to overpower the lowercase. It's true in some of the handsomest type designs. Nicholas Jensen—his capital letters are, in my opinion, too heavy and large for his handsome lowercase. So I have tended to try to find capital letters which are smaller. Lately I've been combining fonts. I did a book a couple of years ago which has for its lowercase a handsome Bembo Narrow Italic which Alfred Fairbank designed. But to me the type is ruined because he made the capital letters to go with the capitals of Bembo Roman. And the capitals seem to me to overpower the lowercase. So I used, with a sixteen-point Bembo Narrow Italic, the fourteen point Joanna Italic capitals. I like it. It makes an even texture. Your eye doesn't go bump every time a capital letter appears on the page. I think that this evenness of texture is one thing that I always want if I can get it. And in the type that I've been buying lately, I usually have the capitals cast to align with the lowercase from a size smaller of the type. I've done it with Walbaum, the Poliphilus . . . It's not necessary with Joanna, where the capitals seem to be the right size. And it was not necessary for that very handsome Romanée that we got from Holland early along in Cummington.

DANA: That evenness of texture you talk about. That's what every artist would like to have.

DUNCAN: Well, it can be a monotonous thing. But I do not think the variety to the eye which is provided by going bump on top of a letter is the right kind of variation.

DANA: In your opinion, what would constitute a good relationship between the writer and the printer?

DUNCAN: Well, in Clifford Burke's book, which I reviewed for *Fine Print*, I objected to one thing he had to say. He said, "Occasionally one may find a poet accommodating enough to make changes in the text which will help solve typographical problems." To me, this has everything ass-backwards. The pleasure of a printer is in solving the problems which the text presents to him. And if he thinks that things are up for grabs and that by writing the author he can persuade the author to make this or that change for the sake of the typography, I think he's spoiling part of the fun for himself, which is that you are strictly regulated by your text and keep it inviolable to any typographic consideration. The whole fun for a printer is in finding a typographic form which will accommodate and solve these problems because, of course, the pleasure is in the difficulties you encounter, and in keeping them out of sight.

Lawrence
Ferlinghetti

Lawrence Ferlinghetti, in a brief partnership with Peter Martin, founded City Lights bookstore and publishing company in San Francisco in 1953. The publication of Allen Ginsberg's Howl, *and the trial of City Lights on obscenity charges, resulted in a landmark judicial ruling against censorship, and in national prominence for the publisher and the writers of the so-called Beat Generation.*

In addition to Ginsberg, Gregory Corso, and Jack Kerouac, City Lights authors include Kenneth Patchen, Malcolm Lowry, Edward Dahlberg, Julian Beck, and Antonin Artaud.

Mr. Ferlinghetti was educated at the University of North Carolina and holds an M.A. in art from Columbia and a Doctorat de l'Université in art from the Sorbonne. In July 1981, the loft offices of City Lights Bookstore, where this conversation took place, were hung with more than a dozen of the publisher's canvases, some of them very recent. A well-known poet, Ferlinghetti is also the author of more than a dozen books, including Pictures of the Gone World, A Coney Island of the Mind, *and* The Populist Manifestos.

DANA: You said, when I talked to you earlier on the phone, that you're "on leave." What's that mean?

FERLINGHETTI: Well, I'm painting. See, these are all my paintings.

DANA: I noticed them on my way in. Does that mean you're giving yourself more to painting these days than to publishing? Or writing?

FERLINGHETTI: Oh yeah.

DANA: Why is that?

FERLINGHETTI: I have a co-editor here, Nancy Peters. The one that did the *Literary San Francisco* book. She's the main editor here. She's the brains of the outfit.

DANA: Is there some reason that you're moving away from publishing?

FERLINGHETTI: Well, there are just a lot of other things I want to do. The business doesn't leave time enough to do them all, so . . .

DANA: When did you get interested in painting? Didn't you do an M.A. at . . . ?

FERLINGHETTI: The paintings on this wall are from the fifties. I've been painting a long time.

DANA: You did an M.A. at Columbia on Ruskin and Turner, didn't you?

FERLINGHETTI: Yeah.

DANA: How did that all start? The interest in painting.

FERLINGHETTI: Well, I was on the GI Bill in Paris at the Sorbonne, and I was going to an art school at night, and two, three days a week. That little black and white one there, I did in those days.

DANA: Does your move toward painting reflect the discontent with American poetry expressed in your manifestos recently?

FERLINGHETTI: Well, no, I think it's the other way around.

The manifestos really enunciate what I wanted to happen with the Pocket Poets series.

DANA: What you *wanted* to happen with the Pocket Poets series?

FERLINGHETTI: Yeah. Well, it's what we're still *trying* to make happen. There can't be a revolution when there isn't one. For instance, in the fifties, when we published the Beat writers first, there was this whole group of writers that no one was publishing. Now, if J hadn't been in India . . .

DANA: James Laughlin?

FERLINGHETTI: Yeah. If he hadn't been in India in the fifties, he probably would have picked up on all these properties. Like Ginsberg had sent Laughlin poems before *Howl*.

DANA: Oh, he had?

FERLINGHETTI: And when I published *Howl*, JL wrote me and said, "Ginsberg suddenly got good." Well, I mean this is strictly *my* point of view. I don't know if J will agree with me or not, but he was in India editing *Perspective USA*. He left New Directions in the hands of other people. I mean he was still the owner, but he had other editors there while he was away. I think they sort of had different tastes than he did. I've never discussed this with him, and I don't know whether this is true or not.

All I know is that in the fifties there was this hiatus when no one was publishing this hot group of writers. Grove Press didn't exist yet. This was, say, 1953. So that's when we rushed into the gap. And New Directions was always my model and ideal as a publisher. JL is the greatest of the contemporary publishers. Of the publishers of the avant-garde, or of belle-lettres, or the modern classics. There's no one else that can compare with him.

DANA: Well, you're going to come pretty close.

FERLINGHETTI: The quality of his list, you know. And I never dreamt that I would ever get published by New Directions.

DANA: How *did* you happen to get published by New Directions?

FERLINGHETTI: Well, *A Coney Island of the Mind* was a

book that I wrote sort of all at once. I didn't even have time to submit any of them to magazines. I never had submitted any poems to magazines, and that's unusual. Usually an unknown poet gets his first book published by getting poems in separate magazines, and then he goes to some book editor and says, "Look here, this poem has been published in *Harper's*, and this one's been published in the *Podunk Review*, and . . ."

DANA: That's right, ". . . and I've got a lot of boilerplate."

FERLINGHETTI: And so that makes it something you can list on your title page and blah, blah, blah. *Coney Island* I just . . . New Directions had always been my ideal when I was a kid in New York, so there was no question in my mind where to send it.

DANA: Did you know Laughlin at all at the time? You'd never met him?

FERLINGHETTI: I was just an unknown. One of the thousand unknown poets, ten thousand . . . and he'd just gotten back from India not long before. This was 1958, '57 sometime.

DANA: That's not long after you started the bookstore.

FERLINGHETTI: We started the bookstore in June of '53. And we published our first books in '54. I published my own first book as number one in the Pocket Poets series, *Pictures of the Gone World*. And then we did Kenneth Rexroth, Kenneth Patchen, and *Howl* was number four. Then there was *True Minds*, by Marie Ponsot, who is now being published by Knopf.

DANA: When you published your own first book, did you think you were launching a publishing company or your career as a poet, or both?

FERLINGHETTI: Well, yeah. When I started the bookstore with Peter Martin—Peter Martin is a book dealer in New York. He has the New Yorker bookstore. It was really his idea to have the first all-paperbound bookstore in the country. There weren't any trade paperbacks then. There was no place to get quality pocket books. They were merchandised like toothpaste in the drugstore, and the people didn't know what they had.

DANA: Right.

FERLINGHETTI: You could get Avon books and Penguins and Signet, and that's about all there was. European publishers have always had a paperback. You could read books in paperback for modest prices. But in this country paperback publishing didn't start until the mid-fifties. There was Penguin, but Doubleday Anchor was the first quality paperback, in about '54, '53, somewhere in there. And New Directions didn't go into paperbacks until late in the fifties.

DANA: Well, New Directions did have that Poet-of-the-Month series they farmed out to small presses in the late fifties.

FERLINGHETTI: But mainly all New Directions books were hardcover 'til about '57? '56?

DANA: Yes, even the New Classics series were hardback.

FERLINGHETTI: I was very surprised when I heard right back from them in '58. He said, "I was just writing to you, and then I found your manuscript on my desk." And I sent it in cold without any introduction by anybody, no letter of recommendation. I didn't know anybody.

DANA: Well, that's the way it's supposed to happen, right?

FERLINGHETTI: I have a suspicion that Kenneth Rexroth was advising Laughlin at that time. Because I know that when Laughlin was out of the country Rexroth was hollering and screaming about what was happening here.

DANA: In San Francisco?

FERLINGHETTI: Yeah. And trying to get New York interested, get the East Coast establishment interested. We were doing poetry and jazz at The Cellar, and Kenneth was sounding off about, "Hey, there's a lot happening here and no one's paying any attention," and he must have written Laughlin about it.

DANA: When you started the bookstore, did you think you were going into the book business or the publishing business, or both?

FERLINGHETTI: Both.

DANA: So you really *knew* you were going into publishing?

FERLINGHETTI: Right from the beginning. My partner had no idea of that. In fact, he sold out and went to New York after the first year. He had published a little magazine, sort of an early pop-culture magazine focused on films. It was called *City Lights* magazine. It was . . . they didn't call it Xerox in those days, it was something-o-graph.

DANA: Multigraph.

FERLINGHETTI: There were about four or five issues of just a small pamphlet stapled together. But he wasn't interested. He was very surprised when, after he'd left, he found out we were publishing books. That's what I had in mind, because I'd come from Europe, where the bookstores and the publishers are often the same company. The big publishers in France— I'm not sure whether they're bookstores or publishers first, like Gallimard. And in Italy it's the same way.

DANA: So did you have that in mind when you came back from Europe?

FERLINGHETTI: Yeah.

DANA: Why did you want to go into publishing?

FERLINGHETTI: Well, it's hard to say.

DANA: I know while you were in high school you did some work in a printshop in Bronxville.

FERLINGHETTI: Oh yeah, I did. I got involved with printing at a very early age, and I always liked printing.

DANA: Was that because your foster-father had a big library?

FERLINGHETTI: Oh yeah, he had a classical library. Half of it was in Latin, some in Greek. He was a self-educated classical scholar in the old Southern tradition. Old families in the South would send their children to France to be educated, and so forth. By the time he came along, the family was fairly impoverished, but the classical tradition still existed in his family. All the books were in his house. This was in Natchez, Mississippi. Well, it's all in that biography of mine by Neeli Cherkovski.

DANA: But did he do anything or say anything that led you to . . . ?

FERLINGHETTI: Oh, yeah, he was a big influence on me to general literacy.

DANA: General literacy?

FERLINGHETTI: It was like *The Autocrat of the Breakfast-Table*. Oliver Wendell Holmes. When you came to the dinner table or the breakfast table, you were supposed to be able to converse intelligently and even wittily.

DANA: Then one had to have some source material.

FERLINGHETTI: He was liable to say, "Young man, you've been to school, . . ." Later, "Young man, you've been to college. Who was Demosthenes?" Or something like that. Or, "What did Horatius say when he was crossing the bridge?" Oh, and he used to give me silver dollars for memorizing poems, which I would have to recite at the dinner table.

DANA: Well, some people would say that should have turned you off of poetry and off of literature.

FERLINGHETTI: No. I would meekly pipe up with some line—say, I was about nine years old—and he would say, "No, no, young man." Then he would launch forth in his histrionic recitations like Mark Twain. In fact, Mark Twain was his hero. He dressed like Mark Twain. He was not from Missouri, but he was sort of like Mark Twain, same style of man, very handsome. It's hard to impart this tradition to a generation today. Kids are not interested.

DANA: But he never said to you what Pound said to Laughlin: "Go home and start a publishing house." Or "Go out and be a poet."

FERLINGHETTI: Oh no. But he always wanted to be a writer himself. He never made it because he had to . . . I don't know. He got involved in making money, I guess.

DANA: That's a big diversion.

FERLINGHETTI: You can't do both. Our publishing company really doesn't make money and never set out to make money. It's survived, and broken even all these years, but it's always . . .

DANA: How much money did you put into the publishing end of it when you started?

FERLINGHETTI: Five hundred dollars.

DANA: Five hundred dollars?

FERLINGHETTI: I had five hundred dollars, and Peter

Martin had five hundred dollars. That's what we started the store on.

DANA: So did you buy mostly books or . . . ?

FERLINGHETTI: Yeah.

DANA: Well, how did you finance a first book out of that?

FERLINGHETTI: We couldn't get the door closed. As soon as we got the place open, it was open 'til midnight seven days a week right from the beginning. It still is. There was no place to buy paperback books then. Now, of course, there are thousands of paperback bookstores.

Another thing about the publishing end . . . I read that a successful publisher, like some of the big publishers, not necessarily big ones, but usually in their history they had a big hit in one of their very first books. And that was the case with *Howl*, which was the fourth book we published. Luckily, we were busted by the police, who gave us all this free national publicity.

DANA: You sent that book out of the country to be printed, didn't you?

FERLINGHETTI: It was printed in England, yeah. In those days, the exchange was such that it was much cheaper to get books printed in England.

DANA: Did you start out printing them in England?

FERLINGHETTI: Yeah.

DANA: Your own book was printed in England? The first one?

FERLINGHETTI: No. My very first one was set here locally by a printer named David Ruff, and it was printed here. Set and printed by hand. But after the first one, they were all printed at Villiers Publications in London.

DANA: So *Howl* was not the first one to be printed abroad?

FERLINGHETTI: No. I think it was the third one. No one bothered the Patchen and the Rexroth and the Marie Ponsot. Then Customs first seized *Howl* as an obscene book, and then the local police raided the bookstore.

DANA: Cherkovski says in his biography that you sent a manuscript of *Howl* to the ACLU before you printed it, is that correct?

FERLINGHETTI: Yeah.

DANA: You did?

FERLINGHETTI: Yeah. We knew exactly what we were doing. We figured we might very well get busted for it, but in those days it was important to take a stand on the question of censorship. This was the McCarthy Era.

DANA: So, in a sense, you deliberately started out to challenge the law.

FERLINGHETTI: Sure. Well, it wasn't so much that. We wanted to publish what we wanted to publish, and if they wanted to make something of it we were willing to . . .

DANA: You were *willing* to challenge the law.

FERLINGHETTI: Yes. But we took the precaution of making sure the ACLU would defend us—ahead of time. That's why we submitted it to them.

DANA: Well, this is an academic question . . .

FERLINGHETTI: See, we wanted to make sure that they would defend us, because if you didn't have the ACLU to defend you, a little business like ours couldn't have made it.

DANA: Would you *not* have published . . . ?

FERLINGHETTI: That was one of McCarthy's main tactics, and the tactics of the government in persecuting the underground press in the sixties, the counterculture press in the sixties—one of the main tactics was to involve them in legal proceedings and make them go broke from the cost of the legal defense.

DANA: What would you have done if the ACLU had said, "No, we won't"?

FERLINGHETTI: Well, I don't know. Hard to say. Obviously, we didn't have any money at all to hire a lawyer. As it turned out, we not only had the ACLU, but we had Jake Erlich, who was a famous criminal lawyer who smelled the amount of publicity he could get out of the case and rushed to the defense.

DANA: How long did the case run?

FERLINGHETTI: Oh, it ran about three weeks one summer. The summer of '55, I guess it was. There's a whole book on the subject called *Horn on Howl*. Horn was the name of the judge.

DANA: How did you feel about it by the time it was over?

FERLINGHETTI: That opened up the whole set of questions which Grove Press was later able to use for publishing D. H. Lawrence and Henry Miller. It established the legal precedent that a work had to have redeeming social significance, and if it did have redeeming social significance, then the question of obscenity could not even be raised, according to the judge.

DANA: Do you think that principle's in danger at present?

FERLINGHETTI: Yeah, it's quite possible. It's a continuing battle. It's a continuing battle in every age, whether it's . . . It's a battle against the police mentality, which is a continuing thing the world over. It's a little bit like what they say about ecology: "Every victory is temporary. Every defeat is permanent." Well, it's not necessarily permanent. There can always be another court case. But, yeah, today, it seems to me . . . Well, the newest book we just published, *UnAmerican Activities*, it's a history of government subversion of the underground press in the sixties and seventies, and it brings it up to date with the Reagan administration's latest attempts to water down the restrictions on wiretapping and search-and-seizure regulations, making it easier to do those things without telling anybody. All those things can be done very quietly without anyone realizing you've done it. Just change a little administrative rule here and there, and you can have another McCarthy pretty easy.

DANA: Yes. The rules the game is played by can make a lot of difference.

FERLINGHETTI: They sure do.

DANA: Can we go back to France for a moment?

FERLINGHETTI: Yeah.

DANA: Is it true you found a Prevert poem on a paper tablecloth?

FERLINGHETTI: Oh, sure. I was in the Normandy invasion in the navy. And then I was in Brittany, along the coast, after the invasion. I was in a few towns along the coast, like St. Brieuc and St. Malo. I was in Cherbourg. And I remember finding part of a Prevert poem on one of those paper tablecloths, the kind they always had in the cheap cafes?

DANA: How did you know it was his? Or did you *not* know it was his?

FERLINGHETTI: Oh, I didn't know it was his at the time.

DANA: It was just a poem in French that interested you.

FERLINGHETTI: Yeah. See, he had been an underground poet, really, during the German occupation, and people passed his poems around. The French passed them around. Before they were ever printed in a book. And then I got ahold of one of his books during that same month. But I remember I lost that one, and it wasn't 'til I got back to France several years later on the GI Bill that I got the book again. By then there were something like 300,000 in print.

DANA: Did you then meet Prevert?

FERLINGHETTI: No, I never met him. I wrote him a lot of letters, and he never answered.

DANA: How old was he then?

FERLINGHETTI: Oh, he died about ten years ago now. I think he was . . . He couldn't have been more than forty-five at the end of the Second World War, in the late forties. Maybe he was forty years old. He did write me a postcard from the Riviera many years later.

DANA: Was this after you had published *Paroles*?

FERLINGHETTI: Yeah. He sent me a two-line postcard.

DANA: What did it say?

FERLINGHETTI: I remember he had an American friend who had taken care of one of his children, and she had translated a lot of his poems, and he was always insisting that she be his translator, except they were absolutely atrocious translations.

DANA: Well, I won't ask who she was, then.

FERLINGHETTI: I don't know what her name was. I don't know whether she was an ex-mistress of his or what. Probably a typical literary situation, if she was.

And when Penguin wanted to publish the same book—in fact they did, they took our City Lights edition and made it a Penguin. The chief editor of Penguin was Tony Godwin in those days, and he was very enthusiastic about it, and when . . .

DANA: Now, *you* did those translations, right?

FERLINGHETTI: Yeah. And when Prevert insisted that they use his friend's translations, Penguin said, "Well, we'll just drop the whole project. We're not going to *deal* with *those* translations." So then Prevert said, okay, use mine.

DANA: What attracted you in that poem you found on the tablecloth, that stuck by you all those years?

FERLINGHETTI: Generally, Prevert's poetry is very visual, which is really maybe the most obvious characteristic in my own poetry. It's super-visual poetry. Later, I think he got a little bit too superficial; he really didn't develop. He became more and more musical. A lot of his poems were made into songs, and he became very popular, but he didn't grow as a poet. He became lighter instead of more profound.

DANA: Instead of denser?

FERLINGHETTI: His later books really didn't interest me very much. It was just the one book called *Paroles*.

DANA: Later, on your second trip to France, you seemed to have picked up on a group of writers, including Artaud.

FERLINGHETTI: I started reading Artaud in '63. The translator is here in North Beach still. Jack Hirschman. He was the translator of our volume. Just saw him up the street.

DANA: Out of all the people you could've picked from that group of French writers, why did you choose to publish Artaud?

FERLINGHETTI: Well, he was not my type of writer, but he's a very important revolutionary writer. I don't think New Directions would have published Artaud. He was too . . .

DANA: Probably not.

FERLINGHETTI: For one thing, he's a junkie, or he was. Heavy on drugs, and quite a madman. Of course, when you've spent many, many years in an insane . . . in a mental institution . . . obviously . . . This book was the first Artaud in this country, the first Artaud published in America.

DANA: Then you must have thought his revolution was . . .

FERLINGHETTI: It was very important to the French theatre and to French poetry in general. It happens the translator . . . even looks like Artaud. He sits up in the Puccini Cafe all day long.

DANA: What did you think that Artaud might introduce into . . . ?

FERLINGHETTI: Have you read Artaud?

DANA: Very little.

FERLINGHETTI: Well, I mean you can't ask me a question like that if you haven't read any Artaud. I mean it's like trying to . . . Am I supposed to give a three-hour lecture on Artaud to tell you what he's all about?

DANA: No, about a five-minute . . .

FERLINGHETTI: That's impossible.

DANA: . . . statement about what you saw there back in 1963.

FERLINGHETTI: Why do you pick on this Artaud book? Why not any of the other seventy-five books?

DANA: I don't know. The Artaud is a special thing.

FERLINGHETTI: Well, all books are special. What about Julian Beck? Do you know Living Theatre?

DANA: No, I don't.

FERLINGHETTI: Living Theatre was in New York City for many years before it was run out of the country by the Internal Revenue Service. They padlocked the Living Theatre in lower New York. Living Theatre went to live in Europe, consequently. And between these two books you have the most important things that were happening in American theatre or in international theatre in the fifties and sixties, I'd say. They both had an enormous influence on American avant-garde theatre.

DANA: Are you referring to breaking down the walls between audiences and players?

FERLINGHETTI: Artaud was one of the direct and most powerful influences on the Living Theatre. It's a madman's vision, but it's not. I'm calling him a madman, but that's just from a straight point of view. What he's saying is what some of the psychiatrists in the sixties were saying; it's not the poets that are mad but the society that's mad. And this would be one of Artaud's main messages. So he may seem to you to be a raving madman, but he's actually . . . because he doesn't conform, he's much saner than the person working in the bank or on the railroad.

DANA: You're talking about the . . .

FERLINGHETTI: I mean, this is the tradition of the outsider which Colin Wilson outlined in his book. Going back to François Villon, Baudelaire, and Edgar Allan Poe. Whitman considered himself an outsider. Ginsberg, the outsider. The poet as the alienated bearer of Eros. I have that in one of the *Populist Manifestos*.

DANA: When you started City Lights, did you have that clear a perspective on . . . ?

FERLINGHETTI: You see, another aspect is Artaud as an anarchist, politically. And the poet as anarchist is an old and honorable tradition. As the bearer of Eros, he represents the free individual, the free spirit, so the State is his natural enemy. Any repression by the State or by anyone is the enemy of the poet. This naturally puts the poet in the alienated position.

DANA: When you started City Lights, did you think of yourself as an anarchist press?

FERLINGHETTI: Of course. It still is. Did you read this *Literary San Francisco* book? You ought to get a copy, because a lot of these questions you're asking are in there.

DANA: Well, it's one thing to read things, it's another to hear you say them.

FERLINGHETTI: Well, it's written better than I can say it off the top of my head. The whole history of our publishing and bookstore is in that book, so you can get a lot of facts out of it.

DANA: Who's had the greatest influence on City Lights besides yourself, directly or indirectly?

FERLINGHETTI: J Laughlin. And Rexroth, indirectly. J's never advised us to publish such and such a book or suggested we publish such and such a book. Generally, I saw his press as a model.

DANA: But Laughlin says, "Well, yes, I listened to Kenneth

Rexroth. I listened to Gary Snyder when he said publish so and so." Did Ginsberg, for example, ever suggest people to you?

FERLINGHETTI: Oh yeah, definitely. Allen tends to proselytize his whole gang. "Publish me, publish all my friends."

DANA: Is it true you turned down Kerouac's *On the Road* once?

FERLINGHETTI: No, I never had a chance at *On the Road*, unfortunately. Jack was way ahead of me. We were much too small for his possibilities, even at that time. No, I never had a chance at *On the Road*. He offered me *other* books. We did *Book of Dreams*. Later we did *Poems*, and I have an unpublished Kerouac manuscript, over a hundred pages, called "Poems All Sizes." The original manuscript.

DANA: Are you going to publish it soon?

FERLINGHETTI: His widow won't allow us to publish it.

DANA: Oh.

FERLINGHETTI: But I won't send it to her, either. I've got the only copy.

DANA: Well, it's a standoff.

FERLINGHETTI: Yes.

DANA: Who else besides Ginsberg had any direct influence on what you published?

FERLINGHETTI: Well, Ginsberg didn't *have* very much influence on what we published, because I've never published across the board. We've never wanted to be known as exclusively the publisher of the Beat poets. I didn't publish the Beat poets across the board. I turned down the manuscript of *The Naked Lunch*. That's the one that I did have a chance at. Burroughs' *Naked Lunch*.

DANA: Why did you turn it down?

FERLINGHETTI: *Naked Lunch* is about this junkie. And the heroin addict is a particularly Burroughs consciousness, which sees no love in the world, no joy. And it's really a very fierce consciousness which, at the time, I wasn't much interested in. As you see Burroughs' later works, you see how this first book fits in in his great worldview, which is something else. But, at the time, having just the first book to go by, and even then it was only scattered pages which Ginsberg had assembled, there was just this junkie's story, this junkie consciousness, and it's a matter if you like to eat shit or not. That's what . . . I mean that's what they call junk, and if you like to, if you have a taste for that, fine, but at the time I wasn't interested.

DANA: If the book came to you now would you publish it?

FERLINGHETTI: Well, by hindsight, when you see the body of work around it now, that's different.

DANA: Suppose it came in, just as an isolated item, would you still turn it down?

FERLINGHETTI: It's possible. I don't know.

DANA: You once wanted to do a sampler of Marianne Moore's work.

FERLINGHETTI: She was willing to go along with it, but her publisher, Viking, wouldn't let her.

DANA: Oh, that's what happened.

FERLINGHETTI: Yeah. I had the selection all made and everything and spent a lot of time corresponding with her publisher, I think it was Viking, but they wouldn't let her do it.

DANA: Marianne Moore seems like an odd choice for City Lights.

FERLINGHETTI: Well, no. She's a very important poet. Her language is a great influence on a lot of modern poets.

DANA: But, philosophically she would be at an extreme from somebody like, say, Ginsberg.

FERLINGHETTI: She likes baseball. That's what I mean. I wasn't publishing in the Pocket Poets series just one type of poetry.

DANA: You were looking for a range of interesting writers.

FERLINGHETTI: I mean, *True Minds*. Did you ever see *True Minds*, by Marie Ponsot?

DANA: No.

FERLINGHETTI: Well, this is Catholic poetry. She's a Catholic with a capital "C." Her new book is just coming out from

Knopf. It's her first book since *True Minds*. It's around here somewhere. It's called *Admit Impediment*, which comes from the same Shakespearean line as the title of the first book: "Let me not to the marriage of true minds admit impediment."

"Let me not to the marriage of true minds admit impediment." This is as far as you can get from Ginsberg. I mean, . . . In fact, that was sort of the principle of . . . I wanted to do that, have a very wide-ranging, catholic list. Small "c" catholic.

DANA: Right.

FERLINGHETTI: For instance, in the bookstore there, right below you, we'll have the *National Review* sitting right next to the publications of the Communist Revolutionary party. Or we'll have *Time* magazine right next to a Marxist journal, or something like that.

DANA: I see.

FERLINGHETTI: So what else in the Pocket Poets series? I mean Ginsberg was not very interested in a poet like Prevert. For one thing, so much of the Ginsberg school is homosexual. He's not much interested in heterosexual poets.

Among his close friends that he always pushed, I never published a book of poetry by Gary Snyder with Philip Whalen. I didn't publish any books of poetry by either of them, even though we had some separate poems by Whalen in the *City Lights* journal. I never felt like publishing a book of their poems. I did publish Gary's prose. And that's the way it went. *I* never published whatever *he* proposed.

DANA: It sounds as though you were "cautiously resistant" to that influence.

FERLINGHETTI: The trouble is, with most small presses, they publish one clique, like "Our Gang." You could say that's what Don Allen does. It's all one school of poetry.

DANA: Or, as we used to say, "a stable," with poets as horses.

FERLINGHETTI: That's usually what lowers the political position of the press. Because it lowers its credibility, it seems to me.

DANA: But it also has the effect of insuring, for a certain period, the flow of a particular group's work, right?

FERLINGHETTI: Oh, sure. Well, another thing, J Laughlin has a principle that when he takes an author, he'll publish *everything* that author produces. Since he published my *Coney Island*, he's published ten or eleven books of mine. Whatever I offered, . . . he has done the judicious editing, . . . he went ahead with it. He really backs up the authors that he picks. He backed them up, right for their whole career. I've never done that. Ginsberg's the only one where I've published every book. I've turned down books by a lot of other authors who wanted us to publish a second book of theirs.

DANA: Do you think that . . . ?

FERLINGHETTI: Well, for one thing, New Directions is a much bigger operation than ours. I realized in the sixties that there was room for a West Coast–type New Directions, or a West Coast Grove Press. There's a big vacuum that still exists out here for such a press.

But it would have been a matter of becoming a full-time businessman, a full-time editor, and not doing anything else. I could have had a big press or a big, long list like Grove Press by now. I didn't feel like spending that much time on it and . . .

DANA: Richard Kostelanetz in a recent article criticized you for not being experimental enough.

FERLINGHETTI: Me personally?

DANA: The press, City Lights.

FERLINGHETTI: Well, Richard Kostelanetz will criticize anyone that will make a sensation. If he can make a sensation by criticizing the pope for wearing his beanie backwards, he'll do it.

DANA: Are you saying he's wrong?

FERLINGHETTI: Well, no, not necessarily. Why doesn't he send me these great experimental works he wants me to publish. I just haven't run across them. It's hard to publish a book without having the manuscript.

DANA: Are you saying that poetry seems to you now generally less experimental?

FERLINGHETTI: No. It isn't less experimental. But whether it's great or not, that's something else. I mean, for instance, there's plenty of experimental poetry being written in the techniques of Ginsberg's style. I don't know, have you read any of his books on poetics?

DANA: I try not to read too much about what he says about poetics.

FERLINGHETTI: Oh, it's very important. A very important body of beautiful theory on poetry.

DANA: Well, I have my own ideas about critical theory.

FERLINGHETTI: In other words, you don't know what I'm talking about.

DANA: I think I know what you're talking about.

FERLINGHETTI: What?

DANA: I just read what you had to say about his . . . what is it? The Disembodied School of Poetics and their interiority and the relationship between one's interior self and breath and what did you call it in French? Not laissez-faire, but . . . ?

FERLINGHETTI: Well, there's a very important book down there called *Improvised Poetics*, and it's worth reading. The trouble with Ginsberg's followers, . . . mainly you could say it's the Graphic Consciousness School of Poetry, where the form is defined as a graphic consciousness. So you have a lot of practitioners in the Ginsberg school that define the poem in that manner. Like Philip Whalen and Gary Snyder, for instance. Philip Whalen will have a poem which will be titled "Take 7-21-81," and it will be what ran through his mind at a certain moment on that date. And you may have "Take 2" for the same date. And maybe he spoke it into a tape recorder. Or maybe he wrote it down. Anyway, that's the take, and that's a poem set on the page as a poem. Usually with slant lines, and with *cd* as an abbreviation for *could* or *wd* for *would*. Just the mannerisms that Robert Creeley developed, for instance. The poem as a graphic consciousness. It's a very valid concept. It assumes that consciousness is basically poetic, which is not necessarily so.

But, besides that point, if you have a genius mind and a really interesting consciousness setting down what's going through his mind, transcribing as directly as he can what comes from his consciousness that moment, then you get a very interesting piece of writing. Because when mind is comely, what mind says is going to be comely or interesting.

And so with Ginsberg. Ginsberg has this omnivorously pack-rat intelligence. It consumes information omnivorously, and whatever comes out of his mind is very interesting because he's got a very unusual consciousness. Whereas when younger followers of Ginsberg use the same technique, not having interesting minds in the first place, what comes out isn't very interesting. So you get enormous, dreary amounts of modern poetry following this technique.

DANA: Well, you're almost talking about the law of the computer: Garbage in, garbage out.

FERLINGHETTI: No. It's not necessarily garbage, but I wish Kostelanetz would send me some of these great experimental works that I refuse to publish. If you see him, tell him to send them.

Another thing I would never answer . . . I get a lot of attacks not only in the press but on my own poetry. I think the best rule is never to answer a critic unless he's right.

DANA: Can we talk about the National Endowment? What do you think its influence has been on the small-press scene?

FERLINGHETTI: I think it's compromised practically every small press in the country. It's a matter of what Albert Camus called "guilt by complicity." Including you're going to get this story published in the *American Poetry Review* . . . ?

DANA: Not necessarily.

FERLINGHETTI: . . . which, I believe, in the past has been supported by grants from the National Endowment for the Arts.

DANA: Yes, it has.

FERLINGHETTI: And this is compromising to any publisher,

James Laughlin with Pepe, Gertrude Stein with Basket, southern France, 1934.
Photo: Alice B. Toklas.

James Laughlin. Photo: Virginia Schendler. Courtesy of the New Directions Publishing Corp.

Harry Duncan. Photo: Nancy Kimmel Duncan.

Harry Duncan (right), Theodoros Stamos (center), and Paul Williams during the early days of the Cummington Press. Photo: Prescott Barrows.

Lawrence Ferlinghetti. Photo: Ann Resor Laughlin. Courtesy
of the New Directions Publishing Corp.

Lawrence Ferlinghetti (center foreground) with Shig Murao, in the courtroom in
San Francisco during the Howl *obscenity trial, 1957.*
Courtesy of City Lights Books.

David Godine. Photo: BBJ/Garfield.

John Martin (left) and Charles Bukowski, 1985. Photo: Michael Montfort.

Daniel Halpern. Photo: Mark Hillringhouse.

Daniel Halpern (left) and Paul Bowles, 1975.

Sam Hamill. Photo: Paul Boyer.

Tree Swenson. Photo: Connie Wieneke.

Jonathan Williams at Middle Creek Falls, Scaly Mountain, North Carolina, 1951. Photo: Francine du Plessix Gray.

Jonathan Williams in the Erik Satie sweater by Astrid Furnival, 1984. Photo: John Menapace.

to let itself be subsidized by *any* source, particularly government. When Albert Camus talked about "guilt by complicity," he was talking about under the German occupation. Who collaborated with the Germans, or who didn't collaborate but didn't say anything. Let's say like the good German who didn't say anything under Hitler.

DANA: Collaboration by omission.

FERLINGHETTI: I mean, you went along with it. Like, if you go along with Ronald Reagan's new rationalization for supporting countries who have no human rights, then you're guilty by complicity. So if the small press takes money from the U.S. government, say, under Reagan, by complicity you're guilty of supporting this policy which ignores human rights around the world. To go back to the Vietnam days, so many little presses I knew, supposedly dissident presses and writers, took money from the National Endowment for the Arts, a branch of the U.S. government, which with its other hand was killing millions of people overseas in the middle of the war.

DANA: So you're not talking about the quality of a press's production, but its moral and political quality.

FERLINGHETTI: Yeah! I don't care what they publish with that money, it's . . . George Hitchcock was a good case in point. George Hitchcock had a press, what was it called now . . . ?

DANA: You're talking about Kayak Press?

FERLINGHETTI: Kayak. He received several grants from the National Endowment for the Arts, and George was a communist in the thirties. He was an anarchist. I don't know about the communist part. That was before I got here, but he was very radical. He was an anarchist who made his living as a gardener. And when the House Un-American Activities Committee came to San Francisco in its last visit, in the late fifties—no, in the sixties—he was called up in front of the committee and they asked him what he did and he said he worked underground. Then later he said, "with roots." He was a gardener, and he told 'em to fuck off, and he wouldn't answer a single question. In fact, it was at the San Francisco

City Hall, and that's what all the witnesses told the committee more or less, and the committee never came back. They were really sort of laughed out of town.

But now George, ten years later, took these grants from the NEA. And he justified one grant by offering a five-hundred-dollar prize for the best poem on Fidel Castro. He was publishing radical literature financed by the government, which is one argument for taking the money and running. Take the money and run. Or you could take the money and build bombs to blow up the johns at the University of California, which another grantee did. That's the revolutionary argument for taking the money. That's an opportunist, pragmatic rationalization, whereas from the strictly moral point of view or the point of view of Albert Camus, you're compromising your press.

In fact, I'm always very conscious of my connections with particularly French and some Italian intellectuals who might read in some American publication that City Lights Press just received a grant from the NEA. They wouldn't see all the rationalizations and the fact that we were allowed to publish anything we wanted with that money. All they would see is that City Lights Press took government money, which is the same government that is carrying on an imperialist foreign policy around the world, et cetera.

DANA: So, as far as you're concerned, it doesn't matter how many small presses come into existence as a result of government grants or how many go out of existence as a result of the loss of government grants. You don't think that money has, by and large, had any positive effect.

FERLINGHETTI: Well, I know editors who did very well on it. I know some local editors who put out some of the most soporific issues you could imagine who lived very well for a number of years on these grants.

DANA: In your view, it's been largely a kind of gravy train?

FERLINGHETTI: Sure. No doubt about it.

DANA: With negative moral and political implications.

FERLINGHETTI: And people have gotten fat. Maybe that's

why there isn't any poetry with any real heart to it being published these days. I mean it's the same in the other arts. It's the same in painting. It's the same in sculpture.

DANA: What about a press like Blue Wind over in Berkeley?

FERLINGHETTI: I don't know Blue Wind.

DANA: They've been publishing people like Anselm Hollo, for example, who did *Red Cats* for you years ago.

FERLINGHETTI: What's revolutionary about that?

DANA: I didn't say it was revolutionary. I just said, "What about that?"

FERLINGHETTI: He's a real competent translator and poet, but he's been in the university world all these years. I wouldn't say that was publishing someone new and . . . He's a real nice man, but he was very much originally influenced by the American Beat poets and is continuing in that line. I don't see it as anything new, even though he's a very fine poet. If you're citing him as an example of the new and exciting works that Blue Wind Press is publishing, I don't know whether that's any argument for anything.

DANA: Well, they're publishing other poets too, members of the so-called Actualist group.

FERLINGHETTI: Well, I've read some of what you might call Actualist poetry, but I really didn't see very much exciting going on in it. It's a term that really doesn't mean anything. It's a very dumb term, actually.

DANA: What are your future plans for City Lights as a publishing house?

FERLINGHETTI: We have too many books lined up. We have a new version of Neil Cassady's *The First Third*. The authentic manuscript has finally turned up. Fawn Cassady, Neil Cassady's widow, recently sent me the version that should have been published in the first place, but which was lost for many years. So we have to reset Cassady's *First Third* completely. It'll be a completely new book. We have a lot of books on the back burner.

DANA: How many books, on the average, would you say you're publishing a year now?

FERLINGHETTI: Six to eight.

DANA: Six to eight a year?

FERLINGHETTI: Yeah.

DANA: Is that down from what you published in the past?

FERLINGHETTI: No, it's about what it always was. We're putting out a new journal starting this winter, called *Free Spirits*. Basically, it's a surrealist publication. It's going to be edited by American surrealists. Nancy Peters and Phil Lamantia are the West Coast editors. The editor in Chicago is Franklin Rosemont. He publishes a surrealist magazine called *Arsenal*. And then there's an East Coast editor named Paul Buell. And this *Free Spirits* will be an amalgam of surrealism, anarchism, and socialism. The subtitle of the magazine is going to be *Annals of the Insurgent Imagination*. It's a very politically committed magazine, but politics isn't the main thing.

DANA: Well, do you think there's something *new* in surrealism today that wasn't there twenty years ago?

FERLINGHETTI: Well, what American surrealists have you read?

DANA: Almost every poet you read employs surreal effects.

FERLINGHETTI: Oh, well, we're not talking about that.

DANA: So you're looking for a pure American surrealist?

FERLINGHETTI: Well, I'm not a member of the surrealist group myself. I was when I was in Paris when I wrote *Her*. *Her* was a surrealist novel. That was years ago.

DANA: Who *are* the chief American surrealist writers?

FERLINGHETTI: Philip Lamantia is the best known.

DANA: Then, in your view, you're still looking for the new and the revolutionary to publish.

FERLINGHETTI: Well, I mean, you don't want to publish the old. I'm not gonna publish Theocritus and Virgil at this point. If they had a new translation that was better than the old translation, I'd publish it.

DANA: Isn't it true that all revolutions finally grind down and become currency?

FERLINGHETTI: Well, I don't really use this word "revolutionary." You won't find it in any of our jacket blurbs or in this sheet here. I mean you really have to stay away from throwing a word like that around, because "revolutionary" can mean so many things to so many people.

DANA: What would *you* mean if you used it?

FERLINGHETTI: Well, I'm not using it.

DANA: Okay, how about "new"?

FERLINGHETTI: "Make it new." That's what Ezra Pound said.

DANA: How would you know the new if you saw it? Or where do you think the new will come from, if there is another round of newness?

FERLINGHETTI: That's an absurd question. It's like saying, "What's going to happen tomorrow?"

DANA: But there are contexts in which that would not be an absurd question, right?

FERLINGHETTI: Well, there are a lot of people who can answer it. Say "What's new?" and they'll give you a definition of new, but what's wrong with the dictionary definition?

DANA: I don't know.

FERLINGHETTI: I mean this is absurd. I mean what's going to happen tomorrow? First off, let's get rid of Reagan. You need a form of world socialism, with a central planned economy which has nothing to do with national boundaries. Ecologically planned economy, because capitalism is the most wasteful system that's ever been devised. Wasteful ecologically. It's wasted the face of the earth. It has to be nontotalitarian, supernationalistic central planning for the world's restructuring of the economy in general. Everyone laughs at Mitterand and thinks that Mitterand isn't going to have a chance, that the French economy can't possibly survive the transition to socialism under Mitterand. But I think they may be wrong. I certainly hope they're wrong, because I think Mitterand is right and Reagan's wrong.

DANA: So you're talking about a sort of world federalism.

FERLINGHETTI: Well, federalism is still a pretty mellow term, except it's based on national states. I mean nationalisms themselves have to go. Nationalism is certainly a barbaric hangover from earlier times. It's like states' rights had to go. It was part of the Civil War in this country to abolish states' rights. So that now it's the national rights that have to go. We're going to have world civil war unless the national rights go.

DANA: Boy, we're a hell of a long way from that, aren't we?

FERLINGHETTI: I mean, I don't have to pledge allegiance to the American flag. I feel just as much allegiance to the French flag or to the ecology flag or to the Buddha flag . . .

DANA: Well, a lot of countries don't share that view.

FERLINGHETTI: . . . or to the Marilyn Monroe flag.

DANA: So you think that literature and art can't change until some of these other changes occur? Or is it a two-way street?

FERLINGHETTI: That's what people publish for. They hope they're going to be able to change the consciousness enough to make things in the world better.

John Martin

*Black Sparrow Press began in 1966, when
John Martin, an office supply executive in Los Angeles, sold
his collection of modern first editions to finance the enterprise and began publishing works by Charles Bukowski.*

*Operating presently from his Santa Barbara house,
garage, and what was formerly the pool house, Martin continues, stubbornly independent of commercial literary
trends. Black Sparrow's list includes not only Bukowski, but
Paul Bowles, Robert Creeley, Clayton Eshleman, John
Fante, Paul Goodman, Robert Kelly, and Diane Wakoski.
And the press has recently acquired rights to all of the work
of British iconoclast Wyndham Lewis.*

*It was a brilliant California summer day in 1981 when I
met the publisher for the first time at his house in the Santa
Barbara foothills. Red-haired, energetic, voluble, he was
generous in clearing his calendar for our conversation. I left*

two and a half hours later, under the shadow of his hundred-year-old dragon's blood tree, carrying an armload of Black Sparrow books.

MARTIN: I want to get one idea across. If endeavors like Black Sparrow are going to go on from year to year, there's got to be more than just the energy of the publisher behind it. You need people like Barbara Martin, who designs all our books, and my assistant, Julie Curtiss, and my printer, Graham Mackintosh, to supply their creative expertise. You need kindred spirits. Graham has done the typesetting on all but half a dozen of the four hundred Black Sparrow books. And when you're dealing with somebody like that, there is a kind of give and take that keeps *you* going and alive as much as it keeps him going and alive.

DANA: Are you saying that he chooses the types? Faces? Sizes?

MARTIN: He designs the pages. But that's the least part of it. You're taking the manuscript to somebody who knows what he's looking at.

DANA: As a piece of literature.

MARTIN: Yes. And even if he's not interested in the author, he respects him. You never fear any kind of snide or hostile reaction. I mean he'll print anything that you respect and bring in. You don't run into any kind of moral censorship. I'm not talking about censorable material or anything like that. But there is a resistance to new *ideas* that you can run into in another ambience—a very conservative printer, for example—that you don't run into when you're with somebody like Graham. I'm talking now about format and the use of color as well as content.

While Graham does design the text pages, the covers and title pages of Black Sparrow books are designed by my wife, Barbara. She had a modest art education before she moved to the West Coast. And because of her art skills, working for the May Company, she got into their graphics department and then into laying out newspaper ads. That's what she was doing at the time I met her and long before I considered publishing, or even knew what publishing *was* exactly.

When I began to publish, she felt she could do a better job of designing the books than a printer. And she could, and has kept doing it. She has turned out over four hundred designs. Each one is unique, beautiful. She is the famous one. It's like owning a ball club and getting a right fielder out of the family.

DANA: Well, her taste must be close to yours.

MARTIN: We're interested in the same kinds of art. If you go through the Black Sparrow covers, you see everything from vorticism to the Bauhaus to pop art to art deco. I think every major twentieth-century art movement is reflected somewhere in the designs of the books, but in a subtle way.

DANA: And that's her doing?

MARTIN: Yes. But her style, on the other hand, is her own.

DANA: My questions today really fall into two categories. The press itself and how you started it, and your book collecting and its relationship to the press.

MARTIN: Well, the book collecting came first and started before I was even a teenager. I was born in San Francisco. I moved to Los Angeles in 1942 and went to school and lived in Los Angeles until 1975, when I moved to Santa Barbara. My father was an attorney in San Francisco; he was killed in an auto accident in 1939. Then my mother raised the family from that point forward.

With my father vanishing out of my life when I was eight, the library which he left took on extra meaning for me. I liked being surrounded by his books. Later, I found out that I was not interested in very many, if any, of his books, because he liked popular literature. But as I got into my teens, they were tradeable.

DANA: What sort of books were they?

MARTIN: Well, he did read some interesting things. He had a set of Maupassant. Some Thomas Mann. But I found I could trade those books in used-book shops for those I wanted at a time when I had no money at all. So that's what I did. I transformed his library into my library over a period of time. When

I was about eighteen, I began to read what we call the moderns, and by chance one of the first books I picked up was *The Journal of Albion Moonlight*, by Kenneth Patchen. That was a wild beginning.

DANA: Were you a student at UCLA or some other school?

MARTIN: I never went to college. There was no money for me to go to college. I went to work when I was eighteen, as soon as I got out of high school. But by the time another ten years had gone by, I had an education in the field of twentieth-century English and American literature to a degree that I doubt any college would have educated me.

DANA: Then, you must have had a circle of literary friends.

MARTIN: Yes, I did. One by one, I would meet people with similar interests. There were two in particular who were very influential. One was an older man now dead, William Hillman, who first introduced me to the works of D. H. Lawrence and Henry Miller. He had the only completely infallible taste in the arts I've ever encountered in my life. When someone like Jackson Pollock began to paint his abstract paintings, within six months Will Hillman would know all about Jackson Pollock. And he would be enthusiastic about it. Many years before I met him, when he was an undergraduate up at Berkeley and Wallace Stevens' *Harmonium* was published, he championed that book on campus, much to the amusement of his professors. He was the most avant-garde person I've ever known. He would pick up right away on something new that was happening and go to the source, so to speak. The writers he got interested in about 1952 were the Black Mountain poets: Charles Olson, Robert Creeley, and Robert Duncan. And he got me reading them. He had already introduced me to Pound, Stevens, Williams, and . . .

DANA: Was he a professor?

MARTIN: No, he was an attorney, and a pianist. And with modest means he had assembled what would now be a marvelous book collection. All first editions, because he read them as they came out.

Initially, about 1948, I had become interested in Wyndham

Lewis, D. H. Lawrence, Henry Miller, and Virginia Woolf. It was later that I began reading the post–World War II poets, the Black Mountain figures, Denise Levertov, the Beat writers. This was long before most of these new writers had major publishers. I mean, Denise has been with New Directions for so long you think she has always been published by New Directions. But that's not the case at all. She was published by White Rabbit. That's where I first read her. And she was published by City Lights.

A lot of people I know have now become totally postmodern and have lost interest in pre-1940s literature. But I've always maintained my interest in and tried to develop my understanding of the people I read originally and who turned me on to reading. Everybody from Paul Bowles to Wyndham Lewis to D. H. Lawrence, Henry Miller, Wallace Stevens, Pound, William Carlos Williams. I was encouraged by the two or three friends I had then who were also interested in contemporary literature. There was very little interest of this kind in 1950, and we gave each other support and encouragement.

I ended up with a collection of two or three thousand books without a single book that I would want to take out and say, "No, this isn't good," or "No, this book doesn't count."

DANA: You said there were *two* men who influenced you.

MARTIN: The other was a friend of mine named Bill Piper, who became a well-known rare-book dealer. He was about six years older than I was. He also became a close friend of Will Hillman. And he built up, during the course of the twenty-five years that we more or less collected books together, extraordinary collections of D. H. Lawrence and James Joyce, who were his two favorite authors.

Then he was able to leave the workaday world because of his knowledge, which began with the love of reading, to become a very successful, self-employed, well-paid, rare-book dealer. It's one thing to go into something because of the commercial aspect; it's another thing to work into it through a love of the thing itself. A good example would be somebody who knows a lot of modern painters and loves their work and finally realizes he has the expertise and the business sense to become a dealer in their work. That's the way Bill got into dealing in rare books.

DANA: It's the perfect way to find a career.

MARTIN: Right. And that, of course, is the way I found publishing.

Our primary debt would be to Will Hillman, who, as I say, had an interest in almost every field of the arts. His own field of greatest expertise was music. I can remember, as early as 1950, when I was still in my teens, he loaned me a record by Charles Ives. The only record in print at that time by Ives. I took it out to UCLA, where I had a friend who was a graduate student in the music department, because I was very excited about the record. To play it for him. And we were playing it in the student lounge when the head of the music department came in and made us take it off because, he said, it wasn't music. But that was not untypical of the reaction to postmodern painting, music, and literature of that caliber in the forties and fifties.

DANA: What were you doing for work at that time?

MARTIN: I was working my ass off. I had hard, low-paying jobs with lots of responsibility. I always seemed to be able to find that kind of thing.

DANA: For example?

MARTIN: I went to work for a company—at the time I was only one of three employees—and in ten years, along with the two owners, we built that company into a million-dollar-a-year business that employed about forty people.

DANA: What kind of business was it?

MARTIN: It was a large office printing and supply and furniture company.

DANA: So did you also, then, pick up a lot of know-how about . . . ?

MARTIN: Yes, how to take something that hardly existed and add people, add the right people, and get accounts, and learn how to keep them. So, yes, that was all a perfect preamble to what I ended up doing for myself.

And, without realizing it, this whole time I was buying books as they came out, books that had never been reprinted. If you wanted to read, in 1950, *The Unvanquished*, by Faulkner, the only edition was the first edition. The paperback revolution had not yet started. If you wanted to read *The Sound and the Fury*, you had to go out on Saturdays, which Bill Piper and I did religiously, and scour used-book shops looking for the books you wanted to read.

Then we would trade books back and forth, so we could each read everything in the total library. We were reading all the time. It was a fine time. There was no sort of—excuse the expression—academic bullshit being laid on us. You could really look at the thing as it existed and make up your own mind as to whether it fitted in with your concept of what literature was there for, what it could and should accomplish.

DANA: Without a critical haze?

MARTIN: Right. Without being told we either should or we shouldn't like this. As a result, I got to like some books that were very unfashionable at the time and which are great books. Like *Sister Carrie*, by Dreiser. I named my only child Carrie, after that book. That, to me, is the first great American modernist book. It was published in 1900, in the dawn of the new century. In many ways it opened the door for everything that followed. Hundreds of serious books. There are lots of writers that I came to like that perhaps I would have been told I shouldn't like.

DANA: Who besides Dreiser?

MARTIN: Sherwood Anderson—very unpopular at the time. Marvelous writer! *Winesburg, Ohio* has hardly been equaled yet.

DANA: And it's still neglected.

MARTIN: Of course, and always will be. As far as I am concerned, I am a total elitist, and while this has nothing to do with intelligence or IQ, it does have to do with your grasp of art. I think at any given time in our culture there are only a few thousand people capable of being receptive to the best art, and the rest are just not tuned in. They're another kind of radio station; they won't pick up those greatest broadcasts. They pick up something else—something less, if you will. Popular culture.

Another writer I never would have been allowed to approach through academic channels at that time is Henry Miller, who I think is a great American writer. There will come a time when *Tropic of Cancer* and *Tropic of Capricorn* are spoken about in the same breath as *Moby Dick*. They are as great in their century as *Moby Dick* was in its century. Just as *Moby Dick* can be read as a boy's adventure story, you can, I guess, read the *Tropics* the wrong way—as pornography. It's up to the individual. But, on the other hand, if you want to read *Moby Dick* as a great transcendental or metaphysical statement about life, you can read the *Tropics* in the same way.

There have always been two parallel streams in American literature: the people you might call "insiders," the ones who conform to accepted standards, which sometimes are also our academic standards. Now, some of these people are very good writers, like Robert Lowell, but they conform in a way that limits their vision. Their work is of interest only up to a point. But then, most people are interested in life only up to a point. So these kinds of writers—like Lowell, for example, or Updike—completely satisfy this kind of expectation of what literature should be.

DANA: Well, Lowell's heritage was very prescriptive: Calvinist, Catholic, Harvard.

MARTIN: Yes, all kinds of social and moral conditioning with which he cooperated and which kept him from emerging fully as an artist. On the other hand, there has been this other parallel stream of "outsiders." Mavericks, beginning with Walt Whitman. To my way of thinking, *Leaves of Grass* is the first great *modern* literary statement made in the world. And to this day, perhaps, the greatest and most astounding.

Anyway, I had the advantage of approaching literature through the work of these outsiders—like Lawrence, for example, who I think is the greatest twentieth-century figure of them all—men who were really, in their day, shunned, considered immoral, censored.

DANA: So when did you actually make the transition from reader to publisher? Were you ever a writer?

MARTIN: No, I never wrote poetry or fiction or anything like that. I *was* under contract for three years, in my twenties, to the Frank Music Company and wrote a musical for them called *Spectre of the Rose,* a property Ben Hecht made a movie out of. I knew the songwriter, the lyricist, who was doing the lyrics for the piece, and he pulled me in as a writer on the book, as kind of a favor.

DANA: Was this when you were working for the office supply company?

MARTIN: This was between office supply companies. I lived off that for three years. Then I went to work for the office supply company I mentioned earlier, after I got married and needed the steady work, a "future."

DANA: So you really made the transition from reading to publishing.

MARTIN: What happened was, I got married and had a child and experienced the usual economic chaos that people experience when they first get married and have children. And worked very hard, helped build up this company that I was working for into a very successful company. I had also accumulated this library of two or three thousand books that, it gradually dawned on me, had a lot of value. So I applied a little expertise to gathering, filling out author collections, things like that. And about 1965 I sold that first collection for enough money to go into publishing—fifty thousand dollars. At the time I sold it, I had a real sense of doing it for a purpose, but I really didn't know what that purpose was. I hated letting go of those books. I'd had them around me for fifteen years. It was a wrench, but it was just something I felt I had to do, that it was imperative. So I put the money in the bank and . . .

DANA: Did you feel that the books had gotten too valuable just to have around?

MARTIN: No, I had no such feelings. Believe it or not— without knowing why I was doing it, I felt that there was a very good reason. And that once I did it, that reason would be clear. So I just went ahead on that basis. After the books were sold and the money was in the bank, it suddenly dawned on me that all the new poets I'd met or corresponded with or whom I liked—not a single one of them had a publisher. Not a regular publisher.

DANA: How did you happen to be corresponding with poets?

MARTIN: Well, you'd read a book you liked, and you'd find that the person lived in Buffalo or New York City or Los Angeles or Berkeley and . . . I guess my first reason for writing them would be, "I see you have published some other books, that I can't find in bookstores. Do you have copies for sale?"

DANA: So you wrote them as a collector?

MARTIN: No, as a reader.

DANA: As a reader, first, but as a collector next?

MARTIN: Yes. If I liked one book by someone, I wanted to read everything they had written. I had this "completist" mentality. If I liked somebody's fifth novel, I was dying to read his first four novels. Then, if the book was out of print and I couldn't find it anyplace . . . In the case of contemporary poets, you couldn't find them—they had never been distributed to begin with. The only way you could get this type of book was to write the author. So I would write some writer I already knew and say, "Do you know where Michael McClure lives?" "Do you know where Robert Duncan lives?" "Do you know where Robert Creeley lives?" I'd finally get an address or the address of some small publisher, like Golden Goose Press or whatever, one of Creeley's early publishers, and find out there were still a few copies left, or there weren't. And sometimes this is how I would get back to the author. The publisher would say, "I don't have any, but Creeley has some." Or Snyder has some. Or Robert Duncan has some. And they always did.

DANA: Is this how you first made contact with Bukowski?

MARTIN: Yes. I'd read his stuff first in a couple of magazines. I had found out that certain contemporary "little" magazines printed a wide variety of new writing, and you could see who was being published, who you liked. You didn't have to buy twenty different books. You could read a hundred different people by reading a half-dozen magazines and then get the books of the ones whose work you felt you would like.

DANA: Let's go back to the sale of your collection for fifty thousand dollars.

MARTIN: A friend said to me about this library, "You realize this is valuable. These are all first editions. And you're meticulous, so every one of them has the dust jacket. And they're all in as nearly new condition as is possible to find them." Visually, it was a gorgeous thing. I had everybody from Henry James to Allen Ginsberg. And I had become friendly with people like Ed Sanders, who was sending me *Fuck You*. It was impossible to buy, you couldn't get it. You had to be on the mailing list of a hundred or whatever. So, anyway, people kept telling me, "This library is valuable."

Looking at it, I'd think, "I have an opportunity that most people don't have, unless they inherit money or are given money or something like that." I had something I could sell and get a lot of money for. Should I do it? That was the first question. And if I do it, what should I do with the money? I don't want to take it and just live well for a couple of years. I'd rather keep the books. But I had the feeling that if I sold the books it would be clear to me at that point what to do with the money. It sounds a little mystical, but that's the way I felt about it.

Here's the whole story. I was standing by the books—I remember it was a Sunday afternoon. I was holding Ezra Pound's *Personae*, 1909. You know, reading it. I was very relaxed, very comfortable. To this day I believe a voice said, "Sell the books." As simple as that. And I walked over to the phone, right at that point, and called somebody I knew who was a book dealer who supplied libraries, helped them build collections.

DANA: Who was that?

MARTIN: His name was Dick Mohr. He has a successful business called International Book Finders. You send him a list of the books you want, and he searches for them. I had found that he was a quick way to find any rare book I wanted to read. He was one of the people who had told me, "This is a valuable library." So I called him. I said, "Do you really think you could sell my books?" He said, "Do you have a catalog?" I said, "Yes." He said, "Well, can I pick it up?" and I said, "Yes." He picked up the catalog that afternoon, said, "I'll read through it and I'll get back to you. What do you want for them?" I said, "Well, I don't know."

He called me back that night and said, "I think that collection is worth fifty thousand dollars," which kind of bowled me over. He said, "I'll work on it." He happened to be going to Santa Barbara the next day to meet with people in the library and with Hugh Kenner, who was at UCSB at the time. Dick took this catalog, and they bought the collection the next day, on Monday. Good-bye, books.

I accepted the fact that they were sold, but there was some horrible interim anxiety. A week later, they came and packed them up in boxes. They cleaned out the living room in about twenty-five minutes. Four burly college kids. I kept telling them to be careful. Then the books were gone, and there were all these empty shelves and Dick Mohr standing there, saying, "Don't worry. When that check comes, you're going to feel a whole lot better."

But I still didn't know what I was going to do with the money, not precisely. I knew that most of the people I was reading who were young, or relatively young, were having a difficult time getting their work published. That, even if they had a book ready, it might have to wait for three or four years until a publisher came along. And then, in those days, it was always a one-shot deal. Each new book would be from a different small publisher. At that time, in California, Auerhahn was doing books, Oyez was doing books. And Graham Mackintosh had his White Rabbit. But there were many more authors than publishers.

DANA: Did you know Mackintosh at that time?

MARTIN: Just by letter, because I was buying his books, and Oyez's books, and I was buying Auerhahn's books. I didn't care what they published. I knew that here were publishers who, no matter what they did, I was going to be interested. So I wrote them all, saying, "Send me everything you do as you do it."

DANA: In other words, a standing order.

MARTIN: Then they wouldn't follow up. Most were totally inefficient, as far as taking care of business, which was a drain on them—they were creative spirits, often poets themselves. On the other hand, I had just taken a small business with only three people at the beginning and helped build it up into a successful company. Its name was Office Supplies Unlimited. We did everything—the rugs, the drapes, the desks, the printing, all the supplies. In a period of ten years, we wiped out the competition in West Los Angeles. Every order that was placed was delivered the next day, without exception. That was our guarantee. If we couldn't deliver the next day, we would deliver it the next day free. We never had to.

So I knew how to begin small and build up a business. I was used to working under pressure, getting things done, dealing with people. This was the 1960s and money was easy. I was used to quick success. So, I felt on the side I might do some literary publishing. I had seen that the average small literary publisher was determinedly noncommercial. He had no sense of urgency, his only focus was the book, the actual printing process, format, the pleasure of the author and his friends, the publication party. All of which are important, but you can't stop there. After that, you've got to take your wares into what Robert Kelly calls "the neutral terror of the marketplace." You've got to develop an audience for your authors, persuade bookstores and distributors to carry your books, solicit reviews, collect accounts, and so forth.

DANA: Distribution *is* important.

MARTIN: Yes. So I started out. I had no idea how difficult it would be. I decided the first person I wanted to publish was Bukowski.

DANA: How did you decide that?

MARTIN: I wanted to publish somebody who was completely unknown, who I thought would become recognized.

DANA: How did you become familiar with his work?

MARTIN: Through reading his work in magazines. He was very prolific in magazines in the late fifties and early sixties. And there were, at that time, a lot of magazines being published. Again, one-shot things, or two issues and that was it. Bukowski had had a couple of books published—chapbooks. There had also been two interesting books that LouJon Press did: *It Catches My Heart in Its Hands*, which is a line from Jeffers, and a book called *Crucifix in a Deathhand*. Then I found out he lived in Los Angeles. It was the first time I'd ever run across an author whom I thought was important who was living in my city.

I wrote him a letter. I don't remember how I got his address. I told him what I had read of his, what books, that I liked them and would he mind if I came by sometime. He wrote back and said, well, it was Christmas, and he was in the process of finding a new place for his wife and his infant daughter to live—that he needed his privacy, and they were moving out. But as soon as the dust had settled in January, he would get in touch, and, sure, come on over. So, in January, I got another postcard saying come on over Friday night. I went over, we talked and had a good time.

DANA: Where did he live?

MARTIN: He lived in a dilapidated neighborhood in East Hollywood, in literally the most dilapidated house on the street. It was a little court with bungalows. That's the kind of place he liked and had always lived in. He worked at the post office, which kind of blew my mind, and hated it. He felt that if he could write full-time he could make it, but that working in the post office he could never finish enough work to get the ball rolling. Well, that was ridiculous because he was so prolific. He'd written a thousand poems. More than most poets write in a lifetime. So there was really no reason, if poetry had been marketable, why he couldn't be living off his work. It wasn't because he couldn't write enough. It was because there was no money in it. It was because no serious publisher was interested in Bukowski.

So we talked about that for awhile. I was the only person he knew at that time who had an income of any substance. I was making two hundred dollars a week at a time when the average wage was a hundred or a hundred and a quarter. So I wasn't *that* much ahead. Maybe I had seventy-five dollars more a week than some other working stiffs earned.

So the first five things I published, simply because they were easy to print, were broadsides. They were all by Bukowski. This was not going to be a big thing. I wasn't thinking in terms of making a living off it. Then I did a little chapbook of his, about four pages. And then I published Ron Loewinsohn's *L'Autre*, the first full-length book that I attempted.

DANA: That was in '67?

MARTIN: Yeah. I think that was '67.

DANA: When you were printing the Bukowski broadsides, were you calling yourself Black Sparrow?

MARTIN: Yes, right from the beginning.

DANA: How did you come up with that name?

MARTIN: Well, I had admired the Black Sun Press because it was an elegant expatriate press in Paris between the wars, and it was run by a couple, a man and a wife. Unfortunately, the similarity ended there, because Harry and Caresse Crosby were wealthy. He was a nephew of J. P. Morgan. So I didn't have those advantages. I was living from week to week with a wife and a small child. But I admired the Black Sun Press, and somehow I wanted the word "black" in it. Then I remember getting a very pretentious ad from some publisher at that time like the Purple Parrot Press or the Pink Swan, or whatever.

DANA: Oh, yes. The large, elegant bird.

MARTIN: I thought, why do they always pick some exotic animal? What I'll do is go out and find the most common city-dwelling animal there is. And after having gone through Black Rat and things like that, I came up with Black Sparrow. It was after I'd read a poem by Williams. It's either in *Journey to Love* or *The Desert Music*, a poem about a sparrow. He's walking and he sees a sparrow in the street. A car had run over it, and all that's left of the sparrow is a dried wafer, but somehow the sparrow hasn't been annihilated. It still *exists*. Man has first built the city there, and then laid down asphalt, and then run a car over the poor little sparrow, and the sparrow still somehow has its integrity. The markings on its wings . . . are still clear. You can see that it was a sparrow. I liked that. And I thought I'd combine the elite black with the ubiquitous sparrow.

DANA: With the image of the survivor.

MARTIN: Yes. So that's where that came from. Then I asked Bukowski, "Design me a logo—a sparrow—I don't want something that looks like a fancy swan." Bukowski is a good visual artist, and I still have the drawings, two or three drawings. They look like very mangy crows. Well, I didn't want it to be fancy, but I didn't want it to be funky, either. So Barbara, somewhere along the line, the fifth or tenth book, or broadside, or whatever . . . the little logo appears in the back for the first time, looking very different than he looks now. He was fat and stubby. She's redesigned him twice, and each time he got a little more sleek and hungry, and now he's practically streamlined.

DANA: And then?

MARTIN: Of course, the minute we started putting out books—this was in the mid-sixties—and from the outside it looked like there was going to be some kind of continuity, you didn't have to worry about manuscripts. I published Robert Kelly. That would be our second full-length book, a book called *Finding the Measure*. And Kelly was pals with Diane Wakoski. And Wakoski was pals with Clayton Eshleman. And Eshleman was pals with Jerome Rothenberg. And Rothenberg was pals with David Antin. And you find yourself weeding out the people in the circle who are not quite right for you and publishing the people in the circle, as Ezra Pound used to do, who you think are really writers. I'm still publishing Diane Wakoski, and I'm still publishing Eshleman and Kelly and Bukowski.

About three years after I did the first broadside, Bukowski *really* started to complain. He called me up almost every day—"I can't go on in the post office. I just can't do it. It's driving me crazy." Well, I had published some books by this time, including a full-length book by Bukowski, and I was already taking in more money than I was spending. Not enough for me to live on, but some. Maybe two hundred dollars a month, or something like that. So I told Bukowski, I said, "Okay, I'll pay you a guaranteed hundred dollars a month for life if you'll quit the post office." So he sat down and made an agonizing list of what it would cost him to live and found out that he could live on his savings and a hundred a month. And he quit the post office.

DANA: How old was he by this time?

MARTIN: At that point he would have been about fifty.

DANA: Was he divorced from his wife at that time?

MARTIN: They were never actually married. She had lived with him awhile, bore him this child and then . . . there are some hilarious poems about it in his book *Mockingbird, Wish Me Luck*. He just couldn't go on. It drove him crazy. It wasn't that she was so terrible to live with, but her idiosyncrasies— he just couldn't handle them. And he'd always lived alone anyway. He didn't want to be a family man, although he's always been very close and devoted to his daughter and supported her faithfully. He just didn't want them under the same roof with him. So he moved them out just before I met him.

DANA: How old was he when he met her?

MARTIN: Well, I would say that would have been 1965. He would have been forty-five. So about the time he was fifty he quit the post office. It was the last day of the year. He took it easy on January 1. "It's a holiday," he said, "I'm going to start writing January 2." And he started *Post Office*, which has been his most popular book. He called me about the twentieth of January and said, "Well, you can pick it up." I said, "What?" He said, "My novel." I said, "What do you mean?" He said, "It's done." I said, "You're crazy." He said, "No, it really is." I said, "You mean you have written a novel in three weeks?" He said, "Yes." I said, "Well, how long is it?" He said, "Oh, I don't know, a hundred and fifty pages. That's enough to say everything I want to say about it." So I went over there, he handed me the manuscript, I took it home and read it, and it was great! I said, "What are you going to do now? You going to do a novel every month? I can't publish twelve novels a year by Bukowski, you know." But he slowed down after that. But, just on pent-up energy and the fear of not pulling this thing off, he literally burned the novel out in three weeks. I think it's almost unparalleled. He did rewrite it once carefully, and it came out about a year after he finished it.

I just ordered the sixteenth printing of *Post Office*. It has probably sold now around fifty thousand copies in my editions. It has been translated into a dozen languages and really done much better in foreign translation. Right at this moment, Bukowski has nearly a million copies of books in print worldwide.

DANA: Well, his reputation abroad seems . . .

MARTIN: It's just like Henry Miller.

DANA: Yes, much bigger than it is here.

MARTIN: I don't know why, but writers like Miller and Bukowski become much more popular in Germany and Italy and France. *Not* in England. He is really still relatively small potatoes in England. At one point, in Germany, year before last, he was the best-selling American author. Outselling Capote, outselling Norman Mailer.

DANA: That's surprising.

MARTIN: Outselling everybody. He had a sort of omnibus volume that contains *Post Office* and *Factotum* and some stories. This book—I think it includes those two novels, and it's a ten-dollar hard cover—sold two hundred thousand. That's big bucks. You're talking about a two-million-dollar gross for the publisher, less discount, and Bukowski gets a dollar a volume royalty.

DANA: I take it he doesn't live in the most dilapidated house on the block anymore.

MARTIN: No. Bukowski lives very well now. Although he's careful with his money. He realizes that he could live to be eighty, and so he doesn't throw it around. He goes to the racetrack, and now that he doesn't need to win at the track, he wins almost constantly. When he did need to win, when he was working at the post office, he couldn't win for losing.

DANA: Have you ever gone to the track with him?

MARTIN: No. That would either be an incredible high, you know, or an incredible low. Most of the time in those days it would have been an incredible low. So I just didn't want to be part of it. But he would call me up in the beginning of our relationship. He knew I worked and that fifteen or twenty dollars was not going to break me. He would call me up, from the pits, choked with despair because he'd lost twenty dollars at the track. But I learned. I'd say, "I'm putting a check for twenty dollars in the mail tonight. You're covered." Boy, he'd brighten up; he'd feel good, chipper. You know, a publisher, for such a small sum, that he could keep a writer together—it's a great feeling.

My first full-length book of Bukowski's was *At Terror Street and Agony Way*. In the beginning, I was leaning heavily on signed limited editions, because you didn't have to print too many copies, and you could sell them for a premium. But then either you go along with that and develop it even further, or you suddenly realize that these writers could have a following of twenty-five thousand, and you should shoot for that. You can't do that by selling expensive books. So if you look at a list of everything I've published, you'll see at a certain point the paperbacks become primary. And the editions get larger and larger to where now, with a Bukowski book, my first printing would be ten or fifteen thousand, which is still small by industry standards. But for a small press it's large.

DANA: That *is* a large run for a small press. What sort of a person is Bukowski?

MARTIN: A wonderful person. I mean, I know that he can be violent, and there have been some tough times at parties and things like that. I've read the accounts and talked to the people who were there. I've never seen that side of him. So when we're together or when we're talking, there's never been any problem. I consider him a great friend. If I needed to know something, and I wanted to go to the one person in the world who would give me an absolutely straight answer, I'd go to him. I mean he is the only person I know who is at all times capable of being one hundred percent absolutely straight. I could go to him and say: "What do you think about this?" And that comes through in his writing.

DANA: Did you ever consult him on a really influential decision affecting Black Sparrow?

MARTIN: No. I've never consulted anybody on influential decisions, because I feel that the worst thing you can do is run anything by committee. When a manuscript is passed by a board, it's almost sure to be mediocre.

DANA: Right.

MARTIN: Because you compromise. The very best thing is going to offend half the people on the board, so it doesn't get published. And the very worst thing isn't going to appeal to most of the people on the board, so you're going to stay away from that, too. What you end up with is a very bland compromise. Everybody says, "Well it's not terrible, at least. You know, I wish he'd do this other thing." I would rather see the idiosyncratic, unique choice of an individual than committee publishing, which I don't see any value in at all. Then you might get the grand failure, but you'll also get the great success.

DANA: Did Bukowski ever turn you on to other writers?

MARTIN: No. He's so out of the literary scene that . . . I take that back—there is one writer whom I've become very interested in and have started to publish regularly. In Bukowski's novel *Women*, there's a scene where he's giving a reading in Hollywood and some English teacher comes to see him and says, "Who influenced you?" And he says, "John Fante." The woman says, "Who's John Fante?" He says, "Well, he wrote *Ask the Dust*; *Wait Until Spring, Bandini*; *Dago Red*." He rattles off this list of Fante's titles as dialogue. I remember correcting the proof on it, and I thought, does he mean *Wait Until Spring*—comma—*Bandini*, the way it's typed, or is he rattling off one title after another, and is one called *Wait Until*

Spring—period—and the next one called *Bandini*—period? I should have called and asked him, because I changed the comma to a period on the proof and it was—actually the first printing is published that way—an error. The title is *Wait Until Spring, Bandini.*

The reason I thought that the whole thing was a joke was that the Bandini Company is a leading manufacturer of fertilizer in California. So I thought the whole thing was a put-on, that there was no John Fante and that these books didn't exist, and I mentioned it to him. I said, "That was pretty funny. I mean it looks straight and then you throw in 'Bandini.'" He says, "What are you talking about? That's John Fante, my hero." But he'd never mentioned Fante to me, and I'd known him at that point for nearly fifteen years. So I didn't take him seriously. I said, "I'll have to see what that is all about," with no intention of doing so. But Bukowski mentioned it to a friend of his in Los Angeles, who went to the LA Public Library and Xeroxed *Ask the Dust* and sent it to me. I read it and thought it was a great book, a marvelous novel about Los Angeles, so I published it with a foreword by Bukowski, and now this season I'm doing a novel just finished by Fante called *Dreams from Bunker Hill.*

DANA: Yes, I saw that on your list.

MARTIN: So that's the one writer Bukowski has turned me on to.

DANA: You're reviving a reputation.

MARTIN: Yes, I love to do that. One of the things that I like doing as a publisher is going back and publishing the people that I enjoyed reading as a teenager or as a young man in my twenties. Paul Bowles, for instance. I did his *Collected Stories*. Forty years of short stories. How often do you find that much work by one author, all available, who's good? That book was nominated for the American Book Award and was on *Time* magazine's recommended list for six weeks.

DANA: Is that why you're interested in Wyndham Lewis's work?

MARTIN: Yes, because I realized that you can get too far

away from the beginning of something. There's too much distance now between postmodern writing and the modernist writing that made postmodernism possible. It's not that I'm looking for structure or form. What I'm looking for is content and meaning, and I'm not convinced that writing always has to go through a series of progressive steps until it finally becomes either surreal or Dada or just sounds, you know, like Richard Kostelanetz. He would say, "Yes. That's where the strength, the clarity of writing does go. It's a natural development of the genre." I say, "I don't think so." Form has become more important than content and, in my opinion, form must be determined by content. Fifty years later people have already forgotten their literary antecedents, particularly the ones that have not been reprinted to death. So it's useful to republish a modernist writer like Wyndham Lewis, whose work hasn't been available and hasn't been chewed and swallowed and digested a thousand times by academics. He's a wonderful writer whose work is as fresh as when it was first published. He is as good a writer, at his best, as anybody who wrote between 1920 and 1940—that incredible twenty years between the two wars.

DANA: How much Lewis are you going to reissue?

MARTIN: I'm going to reissue a lot. I'm going to reissue it until I go broke, I guess.

DANA: *Tarr*?

MARTIN: The first Lewis fiction we'll publish will probably be *Self-Condemned*, which, perhaps, is his greatest novel, but written towards the end of his life. The text is not quite ready yet. It's being worked on. The parts that the original English publisher took out, we're putting back.

DANA: How have you gotten hold of the original, uncut manuscript?

MARTIN: These things are all conserved in libraries, but scholars have to go and do the work of comparing the published text with the manuscripts and then restoring what was cut out.

DANA: So are you paying an editor to do that?

MARTIN: They get an honorarium, but they don't get what they're worth. The main benefit to them is academic. I see to it that they get a few hundred dollars and as many copies of the book as they want.

DANA: Is an English scholar editing Lewis?

MARTIN: The man who is working on *Self-Condemned* is Canadian.

Another Lewis book that will soon be available is *Filibusters in Barbary*, which Lewis wrote when he traveled in Morocco in the late twenties. It's a very interesting book and gives you a very clear look at the Arab world at the time, especially the colonial Arab world. That one will appear in the spring. Meanwhile, we have published Lewis' *Blast 1* and *Blast 2*, which many people consider landmark examples of modernist thinking and typography. Marvelous content that shaped a style that was utterly fresh and new, which is the way it should be. I've also just brought *The Apes of God* back into print. So those are the things that are current. In a few years we'll have a whole Lewis series in print, and I'll continue publishing one or two titles a year.

DANA: What are the legal problems associated with bringing out-of-print work back into print?

MARTIN: There's an estate you deal with.

DANA: Do you have to deal with his English publisher?

MARTIN: Not unless they own rights. But no publisher has the rights to these things anymore.

DANA: So he's in the public domain.

MARTIN: No, he's not in the public domain; the rights belong to the Lewis estate. Whenever I express interest in a title, the estate allows me to reprint it.

DANA: Great way to pick up a great writer.

MARTIN: Yes, it is. Next year we're going to edit our own *Blast 3*, which will be a journal in the same oversize format as Lewis's *Blast 1* and *Blast 2*. It will include Lewis studies and reproductions of his paintings, because he was as great a painter as he was a writer, one of the great British painters of the twentieth century. He's the only British painter of the twentieth century to actually launch and sustain a new movement, an original movement in painting, which was vorticism.

Only now are people getting past Lewis's "image" as portrayed by his contemporaries. He was a feared man in his day, because of the savage satire he could unleash when provoked. He had little patience or pity for imposters. If he felt some artist or writer was a fake, he didn't, in a nice, gentle article, suggest the man might be a fake. He would write a ripping attack from which that man might never recover as an artist or a writer. So he was, except by his friends, deeply feared and hated in London. Then, in the thirties, there was the inevitable flirtation with fascism, which Pound and others suffered from. Lewis never went as far as Pound and later lost interest in right-wing politics. But fascism was a big number in some intellectual circles in England and America in the thirties.

DANA: Well, the tendency is still there.

MARTIN: You have to remember that Pound and Lewis were, in their own way, two of the most talented and capable men in the English-speaking world and were trying to live on the equivalent of what now would be twenty-five dollars a week. Neither enjoyed any real support or recognition. So, they developed over a period of time a very deep hatred toward the situation of society that placed them in that ignoble position.

DANA: So the *Blast* that you're going to publish, number three, is really a Lewis issue.

MARTIN: We're trying to show Lewis's unique sensibility, which was penetrating and honest and totally unforgiving in terms of the way it applied itself to art. If you called yourself a painter or a writer, you'd better produce, or you'd better step out of the way. What he called the Lewis gun would be turned on you. And, of course, this attitude is as unacceptable today as it was then. Today, it's "You're okay, I'm okay." Everybody's an artist. Every book is as good as every other book. Every poem is as good as every other poem. Every picture . . .

DANA: You and I know that's a lot of bunk, though.

MARTIN: We tell kids in grade school, "You can be an artist. You want to paint? Here's a brush. Just keep at it, and you'll be an artist." Well, artists are born. There's a small handful given to each generation. You can't take a population and turn them into artists. What I'd love to do is turn Lewis's savage, withering, uncompromising kind of sensibility loose again. As both critic and artist.

DANA: That would be wonderful.

MARTIN: As far as *Blast 3* is concerned, we're publishing contemporary poetry, we're publishing stories. We're publishing previously unpublished Lewis. We've got some unpublished Pound. We've got reproductions of Lewis's artwork. We've got articles on Lewis. We've got a long book by Roy Campbell that was suppressed by the publisher in 1930 and never published, about Lewis. So it will have both a scholarly and a current interest. It's being edited by Seamus Cooney, who also helps me in many ways. I couldn't function without Seamus Cooney. I send him proofs of all our books, and sometimes in the margins he writes, "Asinine! Why can't this idiot *learn* French before he uses it." Any false pretense . . .

DANA: Phoniness.

MARTIN: . . . he tears it apart.

DANA: How much does Black Sparrow make a year?

MARTIN: I'm ashamed to say how little I make, a lot less than people think, because we publish a book every three weeks and reprint ten books a year. That takes all the money I can lay my hands on.

DANA: A book every three weeks?

MARTIN: And they're elegant, if I may say so. They look like there's a lot of money there, but that's where the money is—it's there. It's not here, in our bank account. So it's getting harder and harder to pay taxes and live on what's left. I know millions of other people are struggling these days, and I'm not complaining, but at the same time, when a publisher has been as active as Black Sparrow has been, there's usually a lot more money.

DANA: Is that because you pay your authors well?

MARTIN: They get what they earn. Sure, I pay full royalties. Bukowski gets by far the most.

DANA: You pay ten percent? Fifteen percent?

MARTIN: We pay ten percent at most. If you're a commercial publisher and you're printing twenty thousand copies, there's fifteen percent there for the author. But my editions are still three or four thousand copies on the average.

DANA: Are you hurt by the tax inventory legislation?

MARTIN: Oh, I don't know. I guess I'm hurt by it. I'm hurt by inflation, I'm hurt by recession, I'm hurt by having to pay decent wages. There's no margin anywhere, really, to pick up the slack for anything unexpected.

DANA: Yes. What do you do when your postage rates go up? How do you try to cope with that? Do you print more copies?

MARTIN: I just close my eyes and pretend it never happened. I don't do anything.

DANA: You don't print more copies?

MARTIN: No, because there's no quicker way to go broke than to tie up your money in unsold copies. In fact, if I were to do a book like Bukowski's new book, which will be out in August, after ten thousand paper, let's say, I would be much better off doing twenty-four thousand in paper, because I'll sell them, in a year; but I can't afford to tie up that money for a year, so I'll print ten and reprint. They'll go fast, at first. I'll have to reprint in a hundred and twenty days because I can't afford to pay for more than ten thousand.

DANA: Are you printing letterpress?

MARTIN: No, not in that quantity. We do do letterpress books, but only when the page count is under a hundred. We do the letterpress covers and title pages, and the rest we print offset.

DANA: How do you manage your distribution?

MARTIN: Well, distribution only seems like a mysterious thing.

DANA: You're a very distribution-oriented publisher.

MARTIN: Other small publishers think that I have a secret.

That if I would reveal it, they would be able to enjoy wide distribution. The only secret of good distribution is to have something that people want to buy. Then there's absolutely no problem in distribution. The mail is filled every day with people placing orders for books. It's when you're publishing your friends and yourself, and the work is not very good, and it's not very attractively done, and it's amateur . . . you hardly care. It's flogging a dead horse. You could take those books, if you had some magical means, and you could put one on every cigar counter and market check-out stand and airport in the country, and you'd sell a hundred and seventy-five copies.

DANA: It would sit there.

MARTIN: It would sit there. Because it's no good. I won't say it's *no* good. Because there's a lot of commercial publishing that has no more to distinguish it than this form of veiled vanity publishing. But it's not good enough to carry its own weight in the marketplace.

You can say, "Okay, the American consumer doesn't know anything. If it's flashy, he'll buy it." Up to a point, that's true, but if you put out a product—I don't care whether it's packaged food, whether it's clothing, or whether it's a form of publishing—and it's really first-class, it gets distributed and sold because that is what distributors and bookstores are looking for. Something that will sell. These are aggressive, sharp people. And they are always pressed. They never have the luxury of sitting back and watching the money roll in. They survive because they have this instinct for what they can sell. And if your books are something they can sell, they carry them. That's the secret of distribution.

DANA: Did you go around to LA bookstores to sell, at the beginning?

MARTIN: No.

DANA: Never?

MARTIN: No.

DANA: How did they know you existed?

MARTIN: Well, I would send out mailers. In the beginning I depended almost entirely on first-class mailers, which I made as attractive as possible. There would be a folded broadside with a poem from the book, with a statement about the book, and the price. Even though I haven't done that for ten years, I still get letters saying, "I haven't been getting your flyers recently. Could you send all the ones I've missed?" Because people actually kept them. A friend of mine went to Northwestern about 1970 or '71 to lecture, and he went to the men's dorm and walked in and the lobby was covered with Black Sparrow announcements that had been tacked up by students. That's how I did it. I did it by producing a product that was originally attractive and then following up with a book that, when they got it, they weren't disappointed in.

DANA: Attractive direct-mail advertising that reflects the quality of the press itself.

MARTIN: Yes. I used to send out an individual mailer for every book I published. You said a book every three weeks was a surprise. That's only eighteen books a year. In '69 I did twenty-five books, while I was working full-time and had no help.

DANA: Hard work.

MARTIN: That's another thing that's missing from some independent publishing efforts: the willingness to stand there hour after hour on Saturday and Sunday and pack books, answer mail, type invoices, deal with the printer. I used to work from seven thirty in the morning until about six at night on my regular job. I was the first one to arrive and the last one to go home. I'd get home about quarter to seven. I'd have dinner. I'd go to my Black Sparrow office and work until about two in the morning. I did that for a year or more. And then I'd work all day Saturday and all day Sunday. I did that for over a year until I finally quit my job.

DANA: And then Barbara said, "You need help."

MARTIN: Well, it wasn't until about '74 that I hired my first employee, and I had been at it since '66. Before that I did everything—the bookkeeping, the shipping, the editing, the proofreading.

DANA: Everything except the design and the printing?

MARTIN: Everything except the design and the printing itself.

DANA: Well, that brings us back to Graham Mackintosh. You picked him as your printer?

MARTIN: No, he was there. I asked Bob Hawley, "Who are you having your books printed by? I would like to do a full-length book." He said, "Graham Mackintosh. Graham would love the work. He's trying to establish his own shop." So I went to San Francisco, met him, gave him a book. He printed it. The first one was *L'Autre*, by Ron Loewinsohn. The next was Robert Kelly's *Finding the Measure*. Then he printed Bukowski's *At Terror Street and Agony Way*. Graham was working without capital and without help. It was a very touch and go process. The books took longer to produce than either one of us would have liked. And he didn't charge enough. He'd sit down and give you a price, and I'd say, "Graham, I want to get it as cheap as I can, but how can you do a whole book for six hundred dollars?" And he'd go through the figures and say, "No, everything's fine." I don't know what he was figuring in for himself, for his time. So his shop finally collapsed financially. At that point I didn't know whether I should turn to fine printing and produce just a few books a year in small editions, or whether I should try to be a trade publisher and print paperbacks in quantity. I hated to give up that beautiful look, but I also wanted large paperback editions that were as cheap as possible. Well, I didn't have to give up either. Barbara began to design the books, and they couldn't be better, in my opinion.

DANA: Very handsome.

MARTIN: Well, to get back to Graham, there was a famous printer in Los Angeles; his name was Saul Marks. He had the Plantin Press. Saul was interested in Graham, even though he'd never met him, because Graham, like my wife, is a natural as a designer and as a printer. So when Graham's shop folded, I called Saul, and Graham went to work for him in Los Angeles for about a year, maybe a little less.

Now, Graham marches to the beat of a very individual drum.

The ambience of his own shop was "casual" to say the least. Saul's shop was like an operating theater. There wasn't a spot of grease on the floor. There wasn't a scrap of paper. Everything was done in an almost ritualistic way. When Saul had a form ready to be locked up in the press, a page of type, he would walk over and very carefully wrap a string around it very tightly, slide the type onto a spotless metal tray, and then he'd carry it over to the press and lock it up. The process was a loving ritual—all it lacked was music. On the other hand, Graham would walk over and squeeze the type together, pick it up, and run across the shop as fast as possible before the type collapsed and fell onto the floor. Saul used monotype, which he worked over for hours, adjusting by hand, so if it did fall it would have to be completely reset. To risk dropping it was a crime in his eyes.

So their attitudes toward printing procedures were very different. Graham was as interested in the text as he was in the printing process. Saul, while he had an appreciation for the text, was interested mainly in his work as a printer. In fact, Saul once told me, "It's so much easier to print dead authors. You know, you don't have to listen to their foolishness. I wish most writers would stay out of here and let me do my work." It's really like a great musician, say Horowitz, playing a Bach cantata. Bach would say, "Listen, you tunesmith, play it the way I wrote it." And Horowitz is saying, "Listen, you scribbler, stay out of my way and I'll interpret this for you and make something out of it."

DANA: "It's mine now. It's not yours."

MARTIN: Yes. Well, all I could use Saul for was small books. I couldn't afford him for a full-length book. A friend was using a printer up here in Santa Barbara, Noel Young. He was a job printer, and doing everything. Letterheads, invoices. But he really wanted to print books. And Graham ended up working for Noel. Later, Noel left and the business became Mackintosh, Inc. Later the pressman—Richard Jimenez—who has done all of my presswork here; Graham; the shop manager,

Lynne Stark; and myself took it over as partners. So, finally, Graham and I are actually partners.

DANA: The end result of a long association.

MARTIN: Yes. Tortured growth in some ways, because, you know, there's nothing more susceptible to tension and error, or disaster, than printing.

DANA: Have you ever had any real difficulties with your writers?

MARTIN: No, not really. Once in a while there might be a misprint that escapes everybody, and the author involved might be upset. But that's about as far as it goes. One reason I've always published in Santa Barbara or Los Angeles . . . I think it's much easier if I keep my life separate from the social life of my writers. If I was seeing them as friends regularly, on a day-to-day basis, it would be much harder to deal with their work. For one thing, you tend to overlook shortcomings in a manuscript by one of your friends. So, while I have very good relationships with my authors—Diane Wakoski and Robert Kelly and Bukowski—there are many of my writers I don't know personally.

DANA: For example?

MARTIN: I've never met Joyce Carol Oates, who's given me seven books to publish and who's been very important financially. We have a very friendly relationship via the U.S. mail. I never met Gilbert Sorrentino. I've met Paul Bowles, but I haven't seen him for ten years. I've never met Mohammed Mrabet, the Moroccan that Bowles translates, and I sell a lot of his books.

I think it's an ideal way to do it, frankly. I mean, Creeley has a highly charged, highly emotional life. A lot is expected of him. I may not correspond with him for two or three years, and then along will come a perfectly friendly letter and a manuscript. And I can just pick up right where we left off. No problem. Where, if I was going through all of the ups and downs with him, I couldn't have that kind of relationship.

DANA: It would cloud the situation for you.

MARTIN: Right. So he can turn to me, and if there's any baggage in his life—emotional baggage that's unpleasant—I'm not part of it. I've never disappointed him. I've never failed to pay him. He's always been pleased with the appearance of his book. We've sold out every edition we've ever done. So there's nothing that's ever gone wrong.

DANA: And you'd like to keep it that way.

MARTIN: And I'd like to keep it that way.

DANA: Where are you on the question of National Endowment grants to small presses?

MARTIN: I don't get them.

DANA: Are you interested in them? Have you thought about applying for them? I'm really asking you two questions. Do you think that's a useful and good way to . . . ?

MARTIN: That's a hard question to answer. I mean, you can always use more money. It's like saying to somebody, "Do you think so-and-so should get an inheritance from their parents, or not?" You could make a case either way. You can say, "No, they shouldn't get it, because they're never going to grow up as long as they get that money every month. There are areas where they are going to be irresponsible. They're never going to develop a career. They will never get serious about their lives. You're going to find a forty-five-year-old surfer, eventually, because he's got that thousand a month from home."

On the other hand, you can say, "Well, yes, they should have it, because that money enables them to do a lot of things that they couldn't do otherwise. Why not have your life, within limits, as pleasant as possible?" I mean, how much can you do on a thousand a month anyway? All you can do is a thousand dollars worth of things. You can't stop everything else, and that thousand dollars can't be central.

So you can make a case either way for grants. I mean, if somebody walked in here and wrote a check for twenty-five thousand dollars and said, "Here. Do some advertising. Produce the next few books a little bit better than you would be able to ordinarily," I'd be delighted. On the other hand, if it doesn't happen, I'll get out and I'll get that twenty-five thousand by selling more copies of books I've already published. I'll hustle harder. So I can't answer that question.

DANA: But you, yourself, have never applied for such a grant.

MARTIN: Not yet.

DANA: Is that because you don't need it?

MARTIN: No, I always need it. I need it right now. You need it all the time. That's the one thing with small-press publishing. There never comes a time when you don't need more money. Not in order to take time off, take a vacation, but to pay bills that are waiting to be paid. Maybe they're not due, but they're waiting to be paid. And you would like to pay them to get rid of them. So it's a hard question to answer.

I was talking to one of my distributors today who depends on grants, a company named Bookslinger. They do a very good job for me and for a lot of the small presses. And I was told there's a bill coming up in the U.S. Senate this week to eliminate NEA funding to individuals of all kinds—artists, entrepreneurs, whatever. In other words, the grants will go only to established entities, as opposed to individuals. For example, the NEA currently gives grants every year to individual poets. Five thousand dollars, ten thousand, whatever, depending on how much the application's for and who the person is. That will all be cut out.

Now, you might say, "Well, that will weed out the people who don't belong there in the first place. It will mean that a lot of bad poetry won't get written." Granted. It also means that some good poetry won't get written, too. And you can say, "Well, a lot of publishers will go under without grants." And, of course, given the way we think about things in America, with our so-called capitalistic system, a thing doesn't really have its own integrity unless it supports itself. You could say about those publishers who go under, "That's okay. They should go under. That's nature's way, you know." But then you have to realize that there's a lot of suffering involved. Just because somebody can't make a financial success of their press doesn't mean they don't feel deeply about it, and doesn't mean they aren't making a contribution.

DANA: David Godine has an interesting idea on this subject. He said money should be given to libraries with the stipulation that they buy the books of small presses.

MARTIN: Well, that would be interesting, to rely solely on the expertise of librarians.

DANA: He thinks this would be better than giving it to small presses who allow their books just to sit.

MARTIN: Right. But, you know, David Godine, whom I admire very much for his energy and for the kind of publishing he does and for his standards of production, is a man with a private trust fund. So he goes to sleep every night. He knows he's going to have money tomorrow to live. He has said himself, in interviews, that he's gone into that fund occasionally to keep his company going. And I know what he's talking about. I've sold off a lot of stuff over the years to capitalize various things I wanted to do. To produce a very expensive book, and so forth. So, David Godine is not thinking from the standpoint of a very small publisher with no cash on hand. He's speaking from a sheltered position.

DANA: Well, he wants to get small-press people to put the emphasis on distribution.

MARTIN: On selling their books. Yes, I agree with that. Has Godine ever gotten any grants?

DANA: I don't know.

MARTIN: I would be in a kind of an awkward position if I were to take a grant now, in 1981, because my image as a publisher—Black Sparrow's image—is one of a very successful enterprise.

DANA: Tremendously successful.

MARTIN: People would say, "Well, what the hell? This is like giving a grant to Alfred A. Knopf," if you want to go to an extreme.

DANA: No, it wouldn't be. It's a very successful enterprise, but it's a small enterprise. You could say the quality of Black Sparrow's enterprise ought to be sustained by grant money.

MARTIN: I just don't want to do it unless I have to.

DANA: You think of yourself as an independent publisher. Could you define what you mean by independent?

MARTIN: Well, independent of everybody but my authors. In other words, I'm not publishing books for any market or to make anybody happy or to make money. I'm publishing books to satisfy my own aesthetic requirements and the publishing needs of my authors. And not necessarily in that order.

DANA: Okay. When you began to put Black Sparrow together as a press, did you have any models in mind for yourself? Presses you wanted to be like?

MARTIN: Not presses. I had the model of the office supply business I had built up. I saw that it was possible to start with only a little money, no customers, and rented space, and go from there. In a business sense. The second month you're doing a little bit better, and the third month you're doing a little bit better. Maybe you fall back the fourth month, but the fifth month you'll make it back, plus some. So that was my model, in terms of surviving as a press.

DANA: How much money did you actually have in the press at the time you began?

MARTIN: Well, I sold the books for fifty thousand dollars. After I paid taxes and the agent who sold them, I had about thirty thousand.

DANA: Did you put that all into the press?

MARTIN: Not at first. I put about five thousand dollars in, and I thought "That'll do it." Then about three months later, I put in another five thousand dollars. I said, "That'll certainly do it." In another six months, I put in another five or ten thousand dollars. I thought, "Well, now that's it. I'm not going to put any more in. I've only got ten thousand left. I'm not going to put in that last ten thousand." Well, I put in that last ten thousand, and then I put in, like, five hundred dollars out of my salary. Finally, it turned around to where, on a regular basis, more money was coming in than was going out. The actual process of capitalizing your own business became clear to me. It was like filling a bucket until it overflowed. You had to keep filling the bucket, and then finally you got the overflow.

DANA: So by the time you published, say, Kelly's book you had . . . ?

MARTIN: Not that early. It would be about 1970, really, before I had put everything I had into it, and it started to come back.

DANA: But you didn't think of yourself as the New Directions of the West, or the City Lights of southern California?

MARTIN: If the press has any unique quality, that is because I simply was unaware of New Directions as a publisher or City Lights as a publisher—what their internal picture might be. I was aware of individual books which I liked very much and which got me interested in publishing books of my own, and of their editorial policies, but I had never really gone over to their side of the fence—in my imagination—and thought about what it might be like to be a publisher. I just went ahead and did my thing. So all I really know is what it means to me to be a publisher. I have no idea what it has meant to Ferlinghetti. I can't imagine what it's meant to James Laughlin. His has been a much more formalized sense of publishing, because he had the means to capitalize, to print, publish, and distribute on demand. I always had to do it out of receipts of sales, where at any time he could bring in whatever he needed from the outside to do something big. He's never had to take a book away from anybody or fight for an author. I mean if he lost them, he lost them. You know, it just wasn't going to be the making of him. If I lost Bukowski, I would have problems. If Bukowski got restless, I would fight for him. I would have to. I would have to stop publishing for a while and devote my energies and my time and my thought to keeping him in the fold.

DANA: How *do* you see the future of Black Sparrow at this time?

MARTIN: I don't know, because it has always been such a day-to-day situation. I don't mean that from day to day I'm threatened with going out of business, but I never structure what I'm doing in such a way that I will know exactly what I'm going to be doing a year from now. That just closes the doors on all kinds of ideas and opportunities you'll overlook if you're single-mindedly working toward some kind of a limited goal.

I want the thing just to keep going and expanding and strengthening itself. The moment it becomes static it will fall of its own weight. And that's the way it should be, in my opinion. That's why I'm a little leery of grants. They keep things going that should be allowed to fall of their own weight. We have this idea, because we're human, that everything we have that we love should go on forever. Whether it is a love affair or a relationship with a child or liking a certain kind of art. We don't want our feelings to change. We don't want the situation to change. But it's normal for things to start, to grow, to come to fruition, and then to end. There is some statistic that eighty percent of all new businesses fail within ten years. Mine hasn't. At some point, it will probably come to an end, but I have no idea when that will be.

DANA: Is your new Arabesque imprint another branch of the tree? The art books and portfolios you want to do?

MARTIN: Well, I don't know. It may be that Black Sparrow and Arabesque will continue for the rest of my life. But then how long is that going to be?

DANA: Are there any other titles besides Harvey Mudd's *The Plain of Smokes* in the Arabesque series?

MARTIN: No, that's the only published portfolio. The poems by Mudd and the prints by Ken Price are first-rate. It's sold out. Next year we'll publish the text and images inexpensively as a Black Sparrow book. Now we've started another project, a catalogue resume of the American photographer Paul Outerbridge. He's very interesting and, in my opinion, one of the few photographers whose work can be thought of as fine art. I consider photography a craft. I'm not very interested in it. But I think Outerbridge is one of the exceptions. He was as much an artist as any painter of his time.

DANA: I don't know his work at all.

MARTIN: That's what I like to hear. You know, just as with Wyndham Lewis, sometimes the very greatest people are edged off stage, kicked off the stage. You just love to pull that trump card out and say "Charles Bukowski" or "Wyndham Lewis" or "Paul Outerbridge." You throw the card down and suddenly he's a big thing, because he always should have been a big thing. That's what really excites me about publishing—to be able to change the direction of thought or change opinion. Make something visible that was invisible before. That's where it's at.

Daniel Halpern

   The Ecco Press has quickly distinguished itself as one of America's premier small publishing houses,
and its Neglected Books of the Twentieth Century series has
kept in print important literary works which would otherwise be lost to interested readers.
   Ecco's list also includes the work of Nobel Prize winners
Czeslaw Milosz and Eugenio Montale, and also John Ashbery, Paul Bowles, Louise Bogan, Italo Calvino, Elizabeth
Bishop, Mark Strand, and Robert Hass.
   Daniel Halpern founded the Ecco Press in 1972 while
teaching at the New School of Social Research in New York
City. In 1969, with the encouragement of Paul Bowles, he
started Antaeus magazine, which he still edits. In the fall of
1979, in his apartment on West Thirtieth in New York City,
we discussed the press, its emergence, its outlook, and
James Michener's endowment of the National Poetry Series.

DANA: Were you literary as a student?

HALPERN: No, I was involved with gymnastics. It started in junior high school. I got interested in the "all-around" events, through a coach there who was an ex-Olympic star, Jack Beckner. I actually participated in an AAU meet when I was twelve, in seventh grade.

DANA: How did you get from AAU to literature?

HALPERN: I'm not certain. My father was very sports oriented. He played professional basketball for a while, but got drafted by the military before he actually played with the Syracuse team. He was a friend of Bob Cousy's, in fact, who also played for Syracuse. So, growing up, as long as I played basketball or baseball, we were close. He didn't really understand gymnastics. Then I switched to my mother's side. She was interested in music and literature. Although when I graduated from college, I graduated in psychology, not English.

I went to San Francisco State and California State at Northridge as an undergraduate. At San Francisco State I had to take dumbbell English, and after the third or fourth week, Mr. Freund, the instructor, said, "Don't bother coming back. You can't pass it. You can't write." But I neglected to drop the class officially, so he called me in at the end of the semester. "You're going to have to take the test," he said, "because you're registered for the class." So I took it. You were required to write a story or essay; that was the final test. It was read by various people in the English department. It turned out I had passed. A few days later, Mr. Freund called me in . . .

DANA: Were you surprised?

HALPERN: I didn't care. It didn't mean anything to me. It was required, and I had to take it sooner or later. I figured I'd take it at a junior college if I had to take it again. Anyway, Freund said, "You passed. I don't know how, but I don't want to see you in another English course in this school." I said, "Don't worry, I'll never take another English class." And I never did.

DANA: Later you went to Columbia, right?

HALPERN: After San Francisco, I went to Europe for a year and just traveled around—the Middle East, North Africa, and Europe. During that year I started writing a little poetry. But, you know, I hadn't read poetry.

DANA: How old were you by this time?

HALPERN: Eighteen. The people I traveled with—we were all hitchhikers—would pass books around, and I was introduced to what Mr. Freund would have called serious literature. That was 1964, the beginning of my literary education.

DANA: You weren't traveling in literary circles?

HALPERN: Oh no. People would say "You've got to read this, or this," so I started reading—*The Stranger*, by Camus, *The Immoralist*, by Gide. I didn't know anything about it. But I was getting there, if slowly and late . . . through the back door. But I never considered taking English classes when I got back to America. I started by writing bad love poetry and wistful, nostalgic poems about Egypt and North Africa. I finally finished the three years at Northridge and received my degree in psychology.

Before returning to America I had been drafted. I was in Iraq at the time, Baghdad, on my way to India. So I made a decision not to continue east but to come back to Israel, where I spent a few months in a kibbutz outside of Haifa before returning home.

DANA: How was life in the kibbutz?

HALPERN: Only interesting. I worked in the fields and with the cows. I recuperated in Israel from the Middle East, where I'd been for nearly three months. Once back in the U.S., I became a conscientious objector, which meant I worked at Cedars of Lebanon, a hospital in Los Angeles, for the next two years. After I graduated, I met Paul Bowles, who was teaching at Northridge.

DANA: Your Morocco connection.

HALPERN: He told me a lot about Morocco, and he said, "You've finished school? Why don't you come to Tangier?"

DANA: Well, how did you meet Bowles?

HALPERN: I met him through a professor named David

Posner. He introduced me to Bowles. I had just read *The Sheltering Sky*, and it was trying to change my life. It was a revelation to me, an unbelievable book. I had planned on going to East Africa. My idea was to live and teach in the jungle, but I fell in love with Morocco.

DANA: Where did you get such an idea?

HALPERN: Well, it was easy for me to imagine then. I wanted to get as far away from this country as possible.

DANA: Did you have a lot of family money to enable you to travel freely?

HALPERN: No, I didn't have any. I traveled cheap! I'd spend about fifty dollars a month, wherever I went.

When I got to Morocco, I took a job at the American school there, and lived in Jane Bowles' apartment. She had gone to Spain, where she was hospitalized. Her flat was in the same building as Paul's. It was simply and beautifully furnished and cost me thirty dollars a month—for two bedrooms, a kitchen, a large living room and terrace, and a fireplace. You could buy wood for about ten dollars a ton in those days. I'd keep a fire going all day during the cold, damp winters. I spent a great deal of time with Paul. He would give me books to read, and then we'd talk about them.

DANA: So you had a kind of mentor-student relationship.

HALPERN: A great education. Paul was endlessly patient. And he'd met everybody. I had never met anybody who knew Tennessee Williams, Gertrude Stein, Sartre, Copland, et al. By this time I had become fascinated, like everybody else, by the Paris of the twenties. He knew Djuna Barnes, for example—I had read *Nightwood*. I had an education one could have only in that way. Firsthand information. We used to take long walks, and he'd talk about all sorts of things, such as how he went about composing music. He was initially a composer and did some of the incidental music for Tennessee Williams' plays. They were close friends. And in time I met, through Paul, Tennessee Williams and various other people.

DANA: What writers did he point you in the direction of? Were they all twenties writers or . . . ?

HALPERN: No. He gave me books I wouldn't have dreamed of reading then—books by James Purdy, for example. And James Merrill, Thom Gunn, Alfred Chester, William Burroughs, and Camus, who is one of Paul's favorite writers. What else did I read? Of course I read Jane Bowles' amazing novel, *Two Serious Ladies*.

DANA: And you stayed in North Africa for three years?

HALPERN: Two years. *Antaeus* began in Tangier. It was Paul's idea.

DANA: I didn't know that. That was 1969?

HALPERN: Yes. I'd applied to Columbia and been accepted. A few days before leaving Tangier—I was going first to Denmark—he said, "It's too bad you're not staying around for another year, because . . . have you ever thought of editing a literary magazine?" I didn't even know what a literary magazine was. I mean, I saw the quarterlies that came to Paul, and I knew what the *Paris Review* and *Poetry* were, but I was not involved at all with that world. He said he'd back the first issue if I did the rest. Before I left, I thought about it. I didn't want to go to New York. It terrified me, first of all. I'd never been there—here—and I had no money. At that point I had a plane ticket and, well, a couple hundred dollars. When I got to Copenhagen, I thought, well, you know, this seems to be one of those things that happens once in your life, and you should do something about it. So, after Scandinavia, I returned to Tangier for another year and began the magazine. I was able to get work by well-known writers primarily because of Paul's involvement with the magazine. "Paul Bowles and I are starting a literary magazine. Can we hear from you?" I must say that most of the writers—Tennessee Williams, John Fowles, W. S. Merwin, Jerzy Kosinski, Lawrence Durrell—were extremely generous. I wrote a letter and they wrote back.

DANA: Who gave the magazine its name? And why *Antaeus*, rather than the *Tangier Review* or . . . ?

HALPERN: When I came back from Copenhagen, Paul said, "Let's figure out a name. Well, we could call it *Atlas*." After the Atlas Mountains in Morocco. I said that it might give us the wrong image. People will think it's a bodybuilding magazine. Then Paul suggested *Antaeus*. I didn't know what that was.

DANA: What is it?

HALPERN: Antaeus, in mythology, was the North African wrestler Hercules had to wrestle with. You know, the man who had his feet on the ground? He derives strength from the earth, his mother. Hercules figured this out and lifted him off the ground. Strangled him. However, in the first issue Paul writes a story in which he reverses the myth. Hercules is made out to be a liar. He has actually been beaten by Antaeus. Antaeus is relating this story to a traveler as they're walking into the mountains. He's telling him how Hercules had come and been beaten and returned home and told people that he'd won. They get all the way into the mountains and finally Antaeus robs this guy he's telling the story to, takes his money and leaves him. A typical Bowles story.

DANA: Is that related to the philosophy of the magazine?

HALPERN: Both feet firmly planted on the ground? I suppose. We publish a surrealist poem now and then.

DANA: Did you think of it in those terms at the time?

HALPERN: No, it just seemed like an odd and interesting name relevant to that area, where the magazine began. It's a name that proved to be quite difficult at first. People would say, "Antaeus? What's Antaeus?" But I'm glad we used *Antaeus* instead of the *Something Review*.

DANA: What did your first issue cost you?

HALPERN: The first issue cost Paul about nine hundred dollars. Printed by an Englishman named John Sankey, who taught me printing basics. He also printed City Lights books. His shop was called Villiers Publications. He was extremely patient; he had to teach me everything about printing. All the printer's marks and vocabulary. I knew nothing. And, very patiently, by mail, we put a magazine together. It was surprising to me that there was so much to learn! I imagined I would be sitting at a desk reading manuscripts, saying yes, no.

DANA: What happened after Bowles' nine hundred dollars?

HALPERN: Well, then I came to New York and went into the MFA program at Columbia. There wasn't any money for the second issue. Then I met somebody who was interested in Tangier. Michael Palmer was his name. He was a banker. He said, "Well, how much do you think you'll need for the next issue?" I said, "Eighteen hundred dollars is what it will cost to print it." He sat down and wrote out a check for eighteen hundred dollars.

Well, after the second issue was printed, I got a subscription from a Drue Heinz. I wrote back as I did to all subscribers, saying, "I'd love to fill your subscription, but at this point we don't have the backing for future issues." I got a letter back saying, "I will be in New York on such and such a day. I'll be having a little party. Why don't you come over and we can talk. Stop by around nine." Well, I walked into a black-tie party for about three hundred people. I'd only been in New York a few months, and I almost always wore a pair of blue jeans and a tee shirt. And there were Rockefeller and Lindsay talking to each other. Lillian Hellman and Truman Capote. Warren Beatty with Renata Adler. I didn't stay long.

So I didn't meet Drue that night, but the next day she called. She said we ought to have lunch and discuss the magazine. She had been interested in publishing a literary magazine and had heard that *Antaeus* was just starting, so after much discussion with her about writers and literature and the first two issues of the magazine, she said she would like to become the publisher. That began a relationship that is now in its fifteenth year.

DANA: It's curious. Why would anybody get into the business of publishing a literary magazine? There are so many of them. Very few of them are self-sufficient. Probably none of them.

HALPERN: I'd say none of them.

DANA: You just simply walked into this whole thing. Well, it's not naive on your part.

HALPERN: Sure it was. I didn't know anything that was

likely to happen. I didn't know any of the people in that world. It just seemed like something fun to do, but it's become for me a kind of public education.

DANA: Did *you* do all the editing after you came back to New York?

HALPERN: Paul didn't do any editing. He said, "This is *your* magazine. I will talk with you if you ask me questions, but you have to do the whole thing."

DANA: So you had to select all the fiction and poetry.

HALPERN: Well, it's always been that way. But I've always had a great deal of support from Ms. Heinz, as well as very good help.

DANA: Do you still do it?

HALPERN: I have readers now, because it's impossible for me to keep up with three thousand poems a month.

DANA: On the average, how many do you take for an issue?

HALPERN: I suppose in a regular issue we publish fifteen to twenty poets.

DANA: How many poems?

HALPERN: Oh, somewhere between twenty-five and sixty.

DANA: Would you say the quality of unsolicited manuscripts is high, generally, or erratic?

HALPERN: Most of it is competent and not bad, but uninteresting. Maybe it was always like this—a few people had interesting things to say and could say them well. If you have something important to say, the tragedy is not being able to say it, not having the language for it.

DANA: Well, I'm trying to decide whether you're saying that it's the content or . . .

HALPERN: Both.

DANA: Okay. So it's not a question of the form that somehow vivifies the material necessarily, or vice versa, it's some sort of balance between them.

HALPERN: Yes. I don't believe that form can make up for a lack of content. Perhaps there are a few exceptions. If you take a poet who really understands form, like Don Justice, for example, it is possible a poem that isn't one of his best poems can take on a kind of life of its own to create something worthwhile. It's interesting to read. It's interesting to me to see how form functions in a poem.

DANA: Do you think that most of the work, say, that Ecco turns down, or *Antaeus*, is rejected because its content is uninteresting? Or is it not formally interesting, or both?

HALPERN: Both. You're not being *told* the experience; it comes at you through the language. Really, the two things go hand in hand. If it's not an interesting idea, then the poem's not interestingly written. On the other hand, it's possible you'd publish a poem for its language and not its content. I'd publish that kind of a poem before I'd publish a poem with a really interesting idea but terribly written. The truth is, you get so many poems you could publish, but if you didn't, it's not going to break your heart. There are just not many poems you read as an editor and say, "I have to have this."

DANA: Do you think there's some point, then, at which you'll cease to edit *Antaeus*, or publish it, because poetry has become standardized and uninteresting?

HALPERN: I don't want to think that poetry *has* become that. Certainly Louise Glück's poems don't function that way, are never uninteresting. Sandy McPherson is like that. I think she's got such an odd and evocative sensibility. It often takes me four or five readings to understand what she's doing in a poem, but something wonderful is almost always there.

DANA: Louise Glück. Sandra McPherson. Who are some of the other writers you think provide a model of interest?

HALPERN: Obviously all of the people we publish at Ecco, Robert Hass's second book, *Praise*, is full of poems nobody else could have written. I think Dennis Schmitz is a remarkable poet who is, unfortunately, without the reputation he ought to have. He can be tough. Syntactically, he's difficult to follow at first, and then you get into his pacing. Once you're there, he's capable of amazing tricks, beautiful things turn over for you. And our other authors—Plumly, Pinsky, Jon Anderson, and of course Milosz, who's one of the greatest poets writing. There are a lot of people who write very beautiful books of poetry, and I would be happy to publish those books, but we're talking about people who seem to be moving in a direction nobody else is taking, directions of their own. It's distinctive, fresh territory. It's important to read a poem and not know where it's going by the third line. Too much poetry feels the need to signal and flash, grab you by the neck.

DANA: How did you move from *Antaeus* into the actual business of publishing books, into the Ecco Press operation?

HALPERN: It was one of Drue Heinz's goals to establish a literary publishing house, so she and I talked with Tom Guinzburg, the president of Viking. He asked me, "Do you know anything about publishing books?" I said I didn't, and he said, "Well, I'll give you the name of two of our people. They will explain to you how book publishing works, but you're going to have to do it yourself." So I went and talked to them. One of them was Michael Loeb. I was pleased that it was Viking, because they had already taken my first book of poetry. This was in 1971, and those were golden days at Viking. It was still a privately owned publishing house. It was small, intense—the perfect place to learn how books are taken from manuscript to bound books. Cork Smith was still there, publishing books by Pynchon and willing to talk to a novice about it. Alan Williams, who has recently left, was there, serving as an experienced, sympathetic, paternal presence. And Elisabeth Sifton, who now has her own imprint at Viking, was publishing authors such as Peter Matthiessen. I can't imagine a better introduction to book publishing.

In 1972 Ecco published its first book, Paul Bowles' *The Delicate Prey*. Like everything, you get started by doing it. Now Ecco books are selling pretty well. And the Neglected Books series, reprints, have all sold in second or third printings. At least five or six thousand copies.

DANA: Whose idea was the Neglected Books series?

HALPERN: Well, we started doing it before it *was* an "idea." Because a small press can't compete with trade publishers for new novels, it seemed that the best way to publish fiction was to print books that had gone out of print. *The Delicate Prey* was out of print. That seemed to me a very important book. *The Complete Works of Jane Bowles* was also unavailable. We did Sybil Bedford's *A Legacy*. So I just started reprinting the books I cared about that weren't available, and we did very well with them. *Then* we called these books the Neglected Books of the Twentieth Century.

DANA: You realized you'd done a number of them, and it was becoming a kind of series. Did you realize then that you had a continuing commitment to do it?

HALPERN: It realized it. It realized it and communicated that to me. More people should be doing it. It's appalling the number of books out of print in this country. *The Complete Poems of Marianne Moore* had been out of print for years until Viking finally decided they were going to do it.

DANA: There must be complexities associated with that. Somebody else, obviously, owns the copyright.

HALPERN: For that book, or just in general?

DANA: Well, for the Bowles books or . . .

HALPERN: You write to the publishers, or the authors (or their estates). Once the request has been made, a publisher has six months to reprint it. In six months the rights automatically revert to the author, who can then sell them to somebody else.

DANA: I see. So it's not as complex as it appears.

HALPERN: Oh, it can be very complex. I mean, look at Marianne Moore. That was a double imprint: Macmillan and Viking. Viking gave us permission right away; Macmillan took six months. And then Viking decided they were going to do it after all.

DANA: So Drue Heinz publishes both *Antaeus* and Ecco.

HALPERN: That's right.

DANA: She must be a very extraordinary person to want to do this.

HALPERN: She is. She's somebody who has always been involved with literature. Many of her friends are writers. In fact, she's one of the best-read people I know, and she's extremely smart about what she reads. She knows what's good and why. She often finds new writers for the magazine and press. Her range is extremely wide. For example, we are working on a travel reader by James Pope-Hennessy. She had access to his books, which are very interesting. She's always been involved in the magazine and the press—every aspect of it. And she's been incredibly supportive. Without her the magazine and the press would not have survived.

DANA: What would you say the effect of all of this publishing activity has been on your own work as a poet?

HALPERN: Well, my work habits are so strange . . .

DANA: I mean aside from the fact that obviously it takes time away from that.

HALPERN: I've got to be doing something, and Ecco and *Anteaus* are what I enjoy doing.

DANA: You're a gourmet cook. You could start your own restaurant. Daniel Halpern's Uptown Downtown.

HALPERN: That takes more time.

DANA: Does editing feed your work in some way? Does it change it?

HALPERN: Well, reading anything gives you new ideas, but it's also a way of defining things I'm working on. I imagine it sharpens certain ideas I have about writing. I don't think it interferes at all. In some ways it gives me a kind of confidence, being so involved with contemporary writing. I suppose this could be a hindrance and a way of making me self-conscious about what I'm doing. But it doesn't work like that for me. I write during concentrated periods of time. For example, last summer I went to Italy. Bill Mathews and I rented a house, and each afternoon he would go in his room and I would go in mine, and we'd spend three or four hours writing. Then we'd read each other what we wrote that day. It was a productive way to work.

DANA: You were instrumental in launching the National Poetry Series. I heard that you met Michener at a party and complained about the state of poetry publishing.

HALPERN: That's not the way it happened.

DANA: Can you straighten out the record on that?

HALPERN: All right. The Library of Congress had a conference five years ago, and everybody was talking about the same thing: Isn't it terrible nobody's publishing poetry. This and that. I thought, for my talk, I would propose something tangible. So I presented a plan called the National Poetry Series. I explained how it would be financed, how it would be judged, how it would be run, and why it would work. I said, "If there is anybody serious about really getting something done, I suggest you take up this plan and do it." Predictably, nobody did a thing. They all said, "Great idea. *Great* idea. Why don't you do it?"

DANA: It's always a great idea, if somebody else does it.

HALPERN: I said, "I'm not going to do it. I have my own press. I already publish poetry."

Five years later, nine o'clock on a Saturday morning, I get a phone call from somebody I don't know. I couldn't make out his name over the phone. I thought he wanted to get a book published. He said, "I saw your talk in a transcript from the Library of Congress." I hadn't seen it yet myself. I told the man I'd call him back. Saturday morning, I was too sleepy. So I called him back, and he said, "I'm willing to back your project on the condition that *you* do it, nobody else." I said, "Well, it's going to cost twelve thousand dollars a year to run the series." He said, "That's all right. I'll do that. I'll also guarantee it for ten years and give you the money up front." I said, "Who *is* this?" And he said, "James Michener." Once the money was in, then a lot of presses favored the idea.

DANA: Well, the first five books are out. How do you feel about it? Are you satisfied with the quality of the books?

HALPERN: I'm a little disappointed, actually. But one book I'm really pleased about publishing is Sterling Brown's *Selected Poems*. That's a very important book to have out. I'm really happy that it's being done. Next year's books have been picked as well, and there are some good ones.

DANA: So you think the series was a little rough the first time around, but that it will get better.

HALPERN: People aren't reliable. You pick somebody, and

you hope they'll pick a good book and not a friend's book. I guess that's expecting too much. But democratic procedure for publishing poetry does not produce good books.

DANA: Why not?

HALPERN: Great is not democratic. Everybody does not write great poetry. Everybody is not a great artist. Everbody is not smart. Everybody is not . . . the kinds of things that have to do with writing poetry. It's a very mean stance, I know. But the democratic way of doing it—the more the merrier, let everybody publish poetry, let everybody judge it—doesn't work. And there's no reason why it should, although that tends to be the general belief.

DANA: It's clear you think the NEA's way of going about it doesn't produce what it aims to produce.

HALPERN: Well, look, America is a democratic country, and the NEA is part of the government, and that's the "the more the merrier" philosophy. It seems to me it's a populist idea: Spread the money around. You cover every group, you cover every state, you do it geographically, by sex, I guess philosophically as well. It's not going to change. But the funds for the National Poetry Series are not public funds. That money was given to me to get five *good* books of poetry published.

DANA: What I hear throughout this interview is that, for you, publishing is a very personal business.

HALPERN: It has to be personal. I wouldn't do it otherwise. It's like drinking wine.

Tree Swenson and
Sam Hamill

Copper Canyon Press began as a collective in Denver, Colorado, in the fall of 1972. Two years later, it emerged as a partnership between poet Sam Hamill and book designer Tree Swenson and moved to its present location in a mothballed military barracks at Centrum, on the grounds of old Fort Worden in Port Townsend, Washington.

Mr. Hamill has been honored for his work as a poet, receiving both a National Endowment Fellowship in 1982 and a Guggenheim Fellowship in 1983. Ms. Swenson's design and printing have been honored by the American Institute of Graphic Arts and were included among other outstanding examples of the craft in the 1983 Western Books Exhibit.

Copper Canyon has published poetry by Kenneth Rexroth, Thomas McGrath, William Stafford, Denise Levertov, Olga Broumas, Madeline DeFrees, and Gary Snyder; and translations of Jean Kaplinski and Pablo Neruda.

HAMILL: All this began when I was a student at UC Santa Barbara, where Bill O'Daly and I edited the university literary magazine, *Spectrum*. I went down one day and sort of introduced myself to Graham Mackintosh, because I had known about him from a number of the poets there. In the course of all of this, I got interested in printing and working with another real good printer there, Gary Albers, who used to do the printing for Christopher's Books. He printed the magazine that we were putting together, so I worked a little bit with him and got a taste of it. I had no intention of becoming a printer, but if you intend to write a book, you've got to know what a book is. That was really all I expected to do, just develop a little bit more book sense. That was the sum total of my printing experience. I had worked for a few weeks as a printer's devil.

DANA: And Denver was chosen because . . . ?

SWENSON: We had to eat. We had to take jobs. We had already decided on Colorado; in Denver we could find work.

HAMILL: At that point—the fall of '72—I found myself with a group of West Coast exiles in a cockroach-infested tenement just off Seventeenth Avenue in Denver, a block off "adult arcades" and lunatic bars. We had planned to buy some land up in the high country. We figured that after a year or two in Denver we could probably do that.

SWENSON: Not while feeding printing presses paper. I think that we wasted as much paper as we printed on the first two books.

DANA: What *were* the first two books?

HAMILL: A little book of Gerry Costanzo's called *Badlands*, and I think Marianne Wolfe was second. A little book called *The Berrypicker*.

DANA: Why did you print those two to start with?

HAMILL: We liked the poems.

DANA: What did you like about them? Would you print them now?

HAMILL: Yeah, probably.

DANA: So there must be some quality about them that spoke to your particular taste. What was it?

HAMILL: Well, I think I'm clearer about that with Marianne than I am with that little chapbook of Gerry Costanzo's. Her poems are what I would call "body poetry." There is some sense of the human voice and the human body in the tone and texture of the poems. I think the humanness of her writing was very unusual. They're very quiet poems. She's not flamboyant. She's sincere, and that's a very remarkable kind of thing.

DANA: But you can be sincere and write bad poetry.

HAMILL: Sure. It's done all the time.

DANA: So you're really talking about a kind of kinetic quality in the language, or about the relationship between language and experience.

HAMILL: Yeah. A kind of grace. It's extraordinary, especially in women as young as she was. She was only twenty, twenty-one years old.

DANA: So out of the six of you who began the press in Denver, it's come down to two of you. What happened to the others?

HAMILL: Diaspora. I don't know.

DANA: Did they fade out of it because they lost interest in printing? What you're saying is that originally you had a printing collective. And out of that collective, Copper Canyon somehow emerged.

HAMILL: Yes. Various people drifted off in various different ways.

DANA: Leaving you and Tree.

HAMILL: Well, how all of this came about was we had just done a little book of Bill Ransom's, a book called *Finding True North & Critter*. He was one of the people who dreamed up the whole idea of Centrum. He was a poet-in-the-schools down in Tacoma, and Joe Wheeler, who is the director at Centrum, directed the music program in Tacoma. They got the idea to use this old fort up here, this idea for an arts organization, and Ransom became the first literature director for Centrum. He said, "Look, if you're going to have a serious writing program up here, you've got to have a printer/editor, because that's a real important part of it." What they had was space for somebody, but no money, no real guarantees for anything more than just a year's place to work. They invited all these different presses in the Northwest, and everybody told them they were crazy. So Ransom called me in Colorado to ask me if I knew of anybody.

DANA: By this time Copper Canyon was how old?

HAMILL: Two years.

DANA: What was it using for money?

SWENSON: I was working forty hours a week in an art store. Sam was working forty hours a week in a book distributorship.

DANA: Okay. Associated jobs?

HAMILL: Ran presses at night in the basement.

Well, when he called me I had just had it. I'd been a year and a half being straight guy for the largest distributor of pornography in the country, and it had just gotten real manic and real grim. I had quit, so I was technically unemployed. I had just been notified that because I'd quit I couldn't have unemployment compensation, so I said, "Shit. I'll come." I arrived three days later. No printing presses. I didn't know whether Tree was coming or not.

It was the first Centrum Poetry Symposium, and they had a former apprentice of Bill Everson's here. A guy named Tom Whitridge. He had a printing press over here across the street in a little room, and he had one type cabinet and that first platen press out there. When he left I convinced Joe Wheeler that it would be worthwhile for him to front me the money to buy that press. We had been printing offset, and I just hated the technology. I hated chemicals, I hated the machine. And once I got to diddling around with the platen press I said, "This is what I need to have."

SWENSON: Well, we also had one other person who had been with us in Denver who really liked the offset process and the possibilities of offset.

DANA: Did you work with large quantities?

SWENSON: Not so much that. In fact, the first few books that we did were printed in editions of a thousand on the letterpress. I don't think that back then we had ever considered doing an edition larger than a thousand copies.

DANA: So why did you hate offset?

HAMILL: I just don't have the temperament to deal with a lot of machinery.

SWENSON: Letterpress is such a direct process. It's so simple and exciting.

HAMILL: Once I got here and I knew I was going to be doing this all day every day, I just had no notion in the world at all that I wanted to get back there tinkering with a lot of this stuff that goes into a big offset machine.

DANA: So Centrum provided you space, and you bought the platen press from Whitridge. But it didn't pay your salary.

HAMILL: No.

DANA: Do they now?

HAMILL: No.

DANA: So what did you do with one press and one case of type?

HAMILL: Well, I spent the summer living in Bill Ransom's attic bedroom, and Tree came out before the end of that summer.

SWENSON: I stayed to sell the house in Denver.

HAMILL: We lived in town here behind a movie theater for about a year, in a house full of hippies and fishermen, loggers and tree planters and what have you. Then we bought a twenty-foot travel trailer and hauled it up to our property and lived in this dingy, grim, grimy, little trailer for a couple of years until we got to working on the house, and survived partly from selling books and largely from a lot of PITS [Poets-in-the-Schools, a program funded by the National Endowment for the Arts]. I taught PITS in Oklahoma, Montana, Wyoming, Idaho, Utah, Oregon, Washington, and Alaska. For about five years, I spent almost as much time living in motels as I did at home.

DANA: And what were you doing while he was PITting around the country?

SWENSON: Printing.

DANA: So you were printing full-time?

SWENSON: Yes. Well, we both printed full-time for at least a year before Sam started doing so much PITS. We generally worked seven days a week.

HAMILL: In fact, those first couple of years it wasn't at all unusual for us to put in fourteen, fifteen hours a day.

DANA: Did you do your own binding?

SWENSON: No, we've never done anything more than simple chapbook bindings.

HAMILL: That's a whole other kind of disposition. We just don't have what it takes to really want to do that a lot.

DANA: Well, that's another art in itself. Very few printers want to do their own.

HAMILL: And most of the printers that I know that *do* do bindings don't do them well.

DANA: Well, what's your professional relationship? How do you divide up the work?

HAMILL: Most of the time one or the other of us says, "Okay, I'm going to do this book . . ." Well, I'll give you a perfect example how this works. When I was about fifteen years old, Rexroth introduced me to this young English "poetess," as he used to say, whom he thought was astonishing. So I read Denise Levertov for about fifteen or twenty years. When she was out here a couple of years ago, I told her that I wanted to print some of her poems. So she gave us this lovely little manuscript, and Tree fell in love with it, and swiped it, and printed the book.

SWENSON: That's right. Sam was leaving to go do some PITS, so I had to start the book in his absence. It's really difficult to trade projects, to come into a project that Sam has started or vice versa, although we always talk to each other as we're working on books. Talk about what we're doing typographically, with layout, design . . .

DANA: There are differences in taste between you.

SWENSON: I don't know that it's even as much a matter of differences in taste as differences in the way we go about things. We're different people.

DANA: For example?

SWENSON: Absolute sensibility. Two people can't have the same sensibility. I don't know that there's a clear way of defining what the difference is.

HAMILL: When you say "differences in taste," it sounds like a bigger kind of division than what actually exists. Part of it is that I feel perfectly fine about leaving Tree alone and letting her go ahead and do her project. But when I'm working I always take everything to her and say, "Check this out, check this out, check this out," because she's done more homework along these lines than I have, and she has what I usually just call "better eyes." So before I do things, I want her approval. I want to know if this is going to be okay the way I'm working this.

SWENSON: Well, once a book is in production, you do have the visual considerations. You're trying to put the manuscript in a visual form that suits the work.

DANA: But his visual sense of the work is different from yours?

HAMILL: Oh, of course. But only slightly.

DANA: Did you ever disagree intensely over the way a book should be designed?

SWENSON: No. Because I think that the work indicates— the writing indicates—to a certain extent, what has to be done. We've never been very far off in how we would visually interpret a book. Sam might prefer slightly darker blue cloth. I might like a lighter blue. But the book is a blue book. That is, as we're discussing, if we're working that closely, we can both see why blue works for this manuscript.

DANA: Well, let's talk about a specific book. Sam just showed me that gorgeous new Stafford book, *Sometimes Like a Legend,* and he introduced it by saying he'd finally printed a book that he really liked almost everything about.

HAMILL: That I was satisfied.

DANA: Now, how did you decide what type to set that book in? How did you decide what kind of paper you were going to print that book on?

SWENSON: You get a feel for it.

DANA: But what are you keying in to?

SWENSON: I think it feels like Stafford in this particular Stafford manuscript.

DANA: What is there about that particular manuscript that makes that book a green book?

SWENSON: He sort of has his toes clenched in the Northwest soil in this book.

DANA: Alright, so it's a book that's somehow rooted in . . . But wouldn't you say that about almost all of his books?

SWENSON: Probably.

DANA: But you wouldn't do all his books this way.

HAMILL: Last stanza in the poem:

> We came to a lake so sudden that it
> held a sharp outline in it, upside down:
> the opposite shore offered us in the water.
> And we waded in trees, drowned in them, held
> there in the sky. I will never find
> enough of the open again. I walk with my
> family, carefully anonymous, hidden in trees.

It's gotta be green.

DANA: Well, how about type?

SWENSON: Type has character. Each typeface has a kind of personality. How do you define someone's personality? You get to know the type.

HAMILL: That type is Goudy's Italian Old Style.

SWENSON: When you get familiar, it's profoundly different. You learn to live with it. You learn its character and those traits.

DANA: Well, what do you think are the characteristics of Italian Old Style that make it just right for this book?

SWENSON: What is it about Bill Stafford's character that makes him so delightful?

DANA: Well, I suppose we could talk about that for a week.

SWENSON: Right. I think I can't say it. This is a visual language. It has a character, but I don't think . . .

DANA: But something beyond, "Well, this is a readable type."

SWENSON: Yes, definitely.

HAMILL: Well, there are all of those obvious concerns at the beginning. I would never print a book in a sans serif type—simple as that.

DANA: Why?

HAMILL: Because the serif leads the eye across the page. And the book is a text.

SWENSON: More than that. Serifs are the roots of the letters of the alphabet. It's parallel to having a sense of the etymology of a word. A serif makes some connection with the alphabet that shows where these letter forms came from. They're historically important. They root the letter forms.

Catich has a book on the origin of serifs, and there is some disagreement about whether the forms that we are familiar with in Roman typefaces are an imitation of the pen or the chisel. But it's, I think, generally believed that they are pen formed. And the early printing types were simple imitations of the current handwriting. Printing changed the western world. Sam always contradicts me when I start talking about printing beginning in 1447. The Chinese were printing in 800.

DANA: They were printing from blocks.

SWENSON: No, they had moveable types.

DANA: And when you came out of Santa Barbara you had little or no knowledge of type or printing presses?

SWENSON: Right. Somehow, I don't know, I was destined to take up books.

DANA: "Destined" is a big word.

SWENSON: I know. And I don't use it lightly. I've always had this love of books. I've always liked them as physical objects.

DANA: Where did you get this sense in a Montana town that had only two books of contemporary poetry in the public library?

SWENSON: I tried to read some contemporary poetry when I was in high school, and I found *A Coney Island of the Mind*, and I don't remember what the other one was. That was it, in the Great Falls Public Library. I don't know—some people love books. Why does one kid always prefer to take a book and go sit in the corner rather than run around outside playing cowboys and Indians? I liked books. And I liked books as physical objects, too. And when I begin to get depressed about the media, communications industries, and the future of book publishing, I remind myself that there will always be kids who love books.

DANA: Well, let's talk about that a little.

HAMILL: I have this recurring dream in which the Chinese come over here on their sampans in about a thousand years, and as they're sifting through all of this radioactive rubble and huge mountains of Styrofoam, they find, buried under all this shit, a few books. And all these books came from private printers, because they were not printed on dead trees, on highly acidic paper that dissolves in twenty years, and the Chinese say "What a strange culture this must have been. All of this radioactive rubble, all of this Styrofoam, and these wonderful books of poems."

Your average mass-market paperback now has a life expectancy of five weeks. So how many years do you invest writing this book that's going to have a life expectancy of five weeks?

SWENSON: I'm a lot more interested in things that will endure. And I have to keep reminding myself there will be kids who love books, and I don't know where they'll come from, what will happen, but there will still be a small audience for things that we care about because . . . because *I* care about them so intensely.

DANA: In other words, you want to convey this commitment.

SWENSON: Yes. I think that we've always had that sense

in making books, but you can tell as soon as you pick up a physical object whether or not the person who designed and produced that physical object . . . what inspired him, what's inside him.

DANA: But you are well aware that there are hundreds of thousands of people out there who pick up these books . . .

HAMILL: What are you going to do with them? You bring them the information and lay all this information at their feet and say, "The one thing I can't give you is care. I cannot teach you how to care. That has to come from within. I can give you all the rest of it. The rest of it's all right there, and it's all available, but I cannot teach you to have concern. I can show you my concern and hope that it's contagious. But I can't make you care. You've got to do that on your own."

DANA: But that's what obviously happened to both of you at some point. Somebody cared about something very intensely and . . .

SWENSON: I don't know. I don't know that I want to know where it came from.

DANA: Well, I'll buy that. Some things do begin in secret, grow in secret, make themselves known. So when did you really begin to study typefaces, the history of printing?

SWENSON: After we arrived here.

DANA: About '73, '74?

SWENSON: Yes. I'm now studying calligraphy as well as typography. Eventually you're studying letter forms, and you have to pick up a pen and imitate the letter forms, try to make the letters with your own hands.

DANA: So you're working backward.

SWENSON: I'm working backward.

DANA: Further and further backward. Starting with offset, going to letterpress, going to handmade letters.

SWENSON: Maybe in ten years I'll be able to make petroglyphs.

DANA: I think you'll do that. In fact, I think you've probably got a bunch of petroglyphs hidden around here somewhere.

SWENSON: Petroglyphs are very important to me. I've visited several good sites just to have a look at them. They are a *key* for me.

DANA: To what?

SWENSON: To why we take words and make them visual. The urge to speak and the urge to draw come from the same urge to communicate. At the level of petroglyphs there's that . . .

DANA: Merger?

SWENSON: Motion. They haven't become words; they haven't become understandable symbols yet, but they are chipped into *stuff*.

DANA: It's very curious that this subject should come up just now. I was very recently in the Valley of Fire in southern Utah, where there are petroglyphs. And you look at them, and at first you see nothing. All of a sudden you look at one and say, "It's a scorpion. There are scorpions in this valley. Watch where you walk."

SWENSON: If you spend much time around the sites, you do begin to learn to read the petroglyphs. I feel it's a kind of communication that becomes as direct as reading poetry. A direct communication. And if you read any books about petroglyphs . . . No one knows for sure anything about most of the petroglyph sites. Why, for instance. But why becomes obvious. You just look at the petroglyphs, and why they are located where they're located . . . The sites are visually very powerful places.

DANA: Well, this discussion's taking a very different turn from discussions with any of the other publishers—printers—I've interviewed.

HAMILL: Good.

SWENSON: Aren't they all different?

DANA: They're different, but they are also in some cases very similar.

HAMILL: Well, I guess we made a conscious choice somewhere along the line that we were not going to do untouchable books, and some of these books have gotten dangerously close to that.

DANA: What do you mean by untouchable books?

HAMILL: Well, you know these guys down in San Francisco just did a *Moby Dick*. It sells for a thousand dollars a copy. Now, if you buy that book, you're also going to buy your el cheapo unabridged *Moby Dick*. And your cheapo book is the book you'll read. The book you paid a thousand dollars for you'll keep behind glass doors.

DANA: So when you say "untouchable" you mean a book which is more an investment.

HAMILL: It isn't going to be read.

DANA: How would you characterize the books that you have printed?

HAMILL: Well, the supreme joy for me is a book like Lever-tov's book or Stafford's book, which is printed on damp, cotton rag paper and hand-bound. The care that we bring to the book, I think, is obvious in the physical object itself. It's a book that I'll treat very carefully. But it's also a book that I will read. I'll take it off the shelf and I'll read the poems in it. I'll use the book like the book is supposed to be used. But I will continue to treat that book with the kind of care that went into the making of it. So it's not something that I want behind glass doors for somebody to sell to a rare-book room in ten years for a great profit.

DANA: It will happen.

HAMILL: Of course it will.

DANA: How do you feel about that?

HAMILL: Well, I'm a little resentful of it. But in the long run, it's okay.

DANA: When Copper Canyon started out, it started by pub-lishing poets who were either less well known or not well known at all.

HAMILL: Mostly not well known at all. Mostly virtually anonymous.

DANA: Right. Are you still committed to that?

HAMILL: To a lesser degree. Part of this is an albatross. And that's that goddamn NEA thing. I feel like if you're going to take NEA money, you should spend that money on lesser-known people. People who might not otherwise get published. Tree and I sort of agreed on that. And we did a whole lot of that. Now, this year, we've got another NEA grant. And it's very likely to be our last grant. This year that money is going to get spent on Tom McGrath and on Madeline DeFrees and on a complete, bilingual Han Shan.

DANA: Tree, do you decide often what books to print?

SWENSON: When something comes under serious consideration, we both think about it for a while. Then it becomes obvious. Either we both care very intensely about a book, or one of us cares so intensely that the other is swayed. We don't have a system.

DANA: You don't have an absolute division of labor.

HAMILL: No. I tend to be the editor. Tree tends to be the printer.

SWENSON: But it's just about impossible—well, it's very difficult—to work on a book that you don't care a great deal about. Therefore, I don't think that it would work for Sam to be the editor and to accept books that I would have to design whether or not I cared about that book.

HAMILL: Not only that, but you don't have to make very many mistakes until you realize that those mistakes last forever. When you've got a book on your shelf that has your name on it, and you're not proud of the book . . . You don't have to do that very many times until you get real conscious. I'm not a corporation. I can't blame it on a board of directors. I can't blame it on the bottom line. All I can do is say, "I made this mistake. And if I had it all to do over again, I wouldn't do that book."

DANA: Do you think you've made some mistakes?

HAMILL: Doesn't everyone? If you don't make mistakes, damn it, you're not doing much work. It's like all these little, tidy grad school poets who trot out every three or four years their little book of writing program poetry. And they're all about this long and this wide and flawless. I call it clone poetry. I don't think we have any great poetry. There are a few that, I guess I could say, approach what I consider as grandness or greatness or whatever it is. And the remarkable thing about them is they're almost universally ignored. Tom McGrath is this incredible secret, and he is an astonishing poet.

DANA: Who else besides McGrath do you find . . . ?

HAMILL: Levertov is, I think, terribly important. An astonishing body of work.

DANA: Anybody else?

HAMILL: A lot of people I like, but not many that I feel I need.

DANA: Would you put Stafford in that class?

HAMILL: No. He's a wonderful man and a wonderful poet, but I don't hunger for him like I hunger for new work from Levertov and McGrath and Rexroth.

DANA: Well, a couple of more small questions. Copper Canyon—where does that name come from? Port Townsend certainly isn't canyon country.

HAMILL: Bingham Copper Mines. The Northern Utes—Piutes—used to dig copper up there for their medicine jewelry.

DANA: In Utah?

HAMILL: Utah. And, of course, the first thing Bingham did was tear down this mountain to get the copper out of it. When I was a kid, it was the largest open-pit mine in the world, and I grew up with this incredible rage. Part of my rage was directed at that particular mountain, which I would see year by year getting smaller and smaller because they hauled the mountain away.

DANA: So why did you name the *press* Copper Canyon? Are you putting back part of the mountain?

HAMILL: Yeah, maybe. Maybe. That's well put. Part of it is just this whole Gary Snyder-dharma-revolutionary-ecofreak-local-vocal stuff. I'll never get the desert out of my system, and I'll never as long as I live go back to the desert. So I live in this kind of schizophrenic world. I'm here. I'm going to stay in the Northwest. My ecological base is this political, economic, et cetera. I mean, we have given voice to this incredible number of people who are rooted in this place. For whom this place means something. All of that, I think, comes into play in Copper Canyon Press. And part of that marvelous sort of schizophrenic world that I endure.

DANA: Where are you on this ecological, political spectrum, Tree?

SWENSON: I think I'm not as political as Sam, although I share the same sort of views.

HAMILL: This is a Port Townsend art commissioner speaking, saying how she's not as political as I am.

SWENSON: Well, local politics . . .

HAMILL: Well, that's what all politics are.

SWENSON: I do my civic duty.

I try to pursue this craft of making books, which I do see as a craft, even when I am doing production management. I try to take it very personally and very directly and very immediately. And to always let my care, when I work, be reflected in the craft. I want it to look like *I* made the book, even if I am depending on cameras and machines and offset book manufacturers in Michigan to help me make that book. To take those poems and put them in a visual form. To make them available. To get them to facilitate the communication between the writer and the reader.

DANA: And the printer.

SWENSON: No, the printer should not be involved in that too much. The printer should just make it possible.

DANA: But that's being involved in it a lot.

SWENSON: Oh yes, it is. But the printer shouldn't show that much. The printer shouldn't get in the way of what the writer has to say.

DANA: How would you do that? Have you ever gotten in the way?

SWENSON: I think we've had writers who were not delighted with their books, but none that seriously complained that we got in the way.

DANA: Books turned out as they had not envisioned them?

SWENSON: When I read a book of poems that transports me, I am not particularly aware of the physical object. I read *that book*. I don't pay any attention to holding it. If a book demands that you pay attention to holding it because of some way that it was made . . . If the type is awkward . . .

DANA: Or the paper is too fine?

SWENSON: Or possibly if the paper is too fine . . . And, of course, there have been some wonderful essays and great controversy over whether or not producing fine editions isn't "getting in the way" of the work.

DANA: Are we talking about designing books in a way that makes them self-effacing?

SWENSON: Yes.

DANA: Or causes the poems to transcend the medium that printed them?

SWENSON: Allowing the poem to transcend the physical medium.

DANA: Yes. Well, certainly most commercial publishers aren't much interested in that. What are your future plans? Will you go on indefinitely?

HAMILL: Yeah. Or, as they say, for the foreseeable future.

DANA: Do you publish any prose, much prose?

HAMILL: No. The only prose we've ever done was a letter Jack Cady wrote to the IRS about why he wasn't paying his income taxes. No, I don't think we'll do any prose. At one time Bob Hass and I were going to edit an anthology of essays by poets of our generation. In the course of looking for material, we discovered that the poets of our generation are simply incapable of writing an essay.

DANA: Are you talking about literary essays or personal essays?

HAMILL: We were trying to keep it real loose. He had seen a couple of essays that he liked, and I'd seen a couple of his literary essays that I liked. And we thought, well, let's start here and we'll see what we can add to it, and then we can cut down later. Well, the whole thing just fizzled right there, because all we found in the course of looking that we both were enthusiastic about was Lewis Hyde's essay on "Poetry as Gift Economics," Bob Hass's stuff, and my stuff. Well, that's not a book. It wasn't there. I think it says a lot about our generation of competent poets.

DANA: Why do you think that's the case?

HAMILL: Well, I think a lot of it has to do with the institutionalizing of the poet. Most of these people come out of a grad school writing program in their twenties with an MFA degree, and they get a job in another college in an MFA program teaching undergraduates and graduates how to become certified poets. God knows, you know what it's like to have to endure that kind of artificial world. And I don't think that, generally, these people have a very good view of what in the hell is going on in the world and where they fit into it. Hence they have nothing to talk about, even if they did know how to write. And I haven't seen much evidence that they even know how to write. It's just this incredible kind of safety that's going on out there.

You know, when you start writing personal essays you become real vulnerable. Somebody can come along and pick up your book and say, "But you said thus and so." Well, I don't think that we're going to have more Edmund Wilsons. We don't have people who can write a personal, historical, literary essay anymore.

DANA: Is it that we don't have them, or that those people who could write the essay are writing different kinds of essays? People like Joan Didion or Edward Hoagland—*Walking the Dead Diamond River*.

HAMILL: Well, Joan Didion is older. She's in her fifties, isn't she? But among poets—we're talking about poets, remember. We'll use Rexroth, for instance. What we have is all these people who have become so specialized that they don't have his overview.

DANA: There's nothing else to talk about, you're saying, but poetry or literary matters.

HAMILL: Yeah.

DANA: How many titles have you published altogether?

HAMILL: About sixty.

DANA: Over the course of ten years? So you're producing roughly six books a year.

HAMILL: Well, the first couple or three years our output was real small. And, of course, when I say sixty titles, I mean including chapbooks and pamphlets. I don't even know, if I put together a package of all of our ephemera, what it would cover.

DANA: Well, it's probably time to do a bibliography. But actual books, starting with, say, chapbooks?

HAMILL: Probably about sixty.

DANA: And you publish more now than you did when you started?

SWENSON: I think we've cut down a little bit. We're probably printing about six books a year now.

HAMILL: We've steadied off at about six or seven books. We *are* going to reduce our output in the future.

DANA: Why?

SWENSON: Because we have spent most of our time, energy, and attention on producing books, rather than on marketing and distributing these books. And unless the press grows quite a bit—that is, more people become involved, . . . With the two of us, if we start spending more time advertising, promoting, distributing the books, that means that we have less time to produce the books.

HAMILL: And there are also other things that I want to do.

DANA: If you cut down production and put increased time into sales and advertising, where are you going to get the money for advertising?

HAMILL: Well, we're just going to have to generate it. We'll have cut way down on the number of younger poets. Whatever that means. I feel like we've done our duty, and now I'm more interested in being of service to Tom McGrath and Madeline

DeFrees. I expect to keep Tom McGrath in print for as long as I live. I've already committed us to do volume two of *The Collected Poems*. There will eventually be a volume three, which we will do. We will do the final *Letter to an Imaginary Friend*.

DANA: Is there any chance you can get the other titles under one roof?

HAMILL: Well, no. They had *The Movie at the End of the World* in cloth forever. Then it went out of print. They kept putting him off six months at a time all during the fall, and the spring, then the fall. Finally, I wrote him a letter and I said, "I will publish *Movie at the End of the World* in cloth and paper. I will keep it in paper in print for the life of the press, and I will pay you ten percent." Then I put a note on that, saying, "Show this to Swallow. Tell them you're going to give them three months, and if they don't do something about the book, we're going to do it. If they don't like it, they can sue us." And three months later, almost to the day, that book came out in paperback. If it goes out of print, we'll pick it up. At least we've got the book available, one way or another.

DANA: Well, that's really what should have happened for him, a long time ago. I think it'll do good things for Copper Canyon and for him.

HAMILL: I also have in mind eventually to reissue some Rexroth stuff. His *One Hundred Poems from the French* is out of print, and I have a great deal of respect for what he's done with those poems. There's a little book by O. V. Milosz, a Polish Lithuanian expatriate who lived and worked in France and wrote in French. A little book of marvelous poems. Kenneth picked up a couple of them for *One Hundred Poems from the French*. But I would like to eventually reissue that whole book. So I guess what I'm saying is that I think that what we should do is be serious. And do less, but do it better.

DANA: Are there books, Tree, that you'd like to do sometime? Is there something you would like to do with a book next year, five years from now, that you cannot at the moment do?

SWENSON: No, I intend to do things that I cannot foresee, that will become apparent as I work.

DANA: The mystic and the politician?

SWENSON: The craftsperson Tree. A simple craftsperson.

DANA: You or him?

SWENSON: Me. I don't mind if you call *him* a politician.

DANA: That combination is clearly the ground on which your whole relationship with people and the press rests.

HAMILL: That isn't really true, either. That assumes (a) that Tree is not political, and (b) that I'm not a mystic. Neither of those assumptions is correct.

DANA: Well, it's interesting to see how two people can adjust as closely as you two seem to have adjusted. All the small presses I've dealt with so far are basically one-person operations that reflect that person's taste and no other's.

HAMILL: Both of us are, I think, extremely eclectic. Sometimes I go out there and just kind of stand there and look at the shelf and think about all of these people who we've published, and it's bizarre. It's really incredible, the diversity of kinds of poetry. And it extends to everything. I can go home and be equally happy watching a football game on the tube or studying the Confucian classics or listening to Beethoven's Pastoral or playing George Jones. And I get from all those things something that is somehow the same thing. An energy.

DANA: And you see your publishing record as reflecting a similar kind of eclecticism and energy?

HAMILL: Yes.

Jonathan Williams

Jonathan Williams is part poet and graphic artist, part printer and publisher. He is also part yarn-spinner, a respecter of the "homemade," and among small publishers, a genuine American exotic. His press, the Jargon Society, has been an important presence on the margins of American letters for thirty-five years. In his own words, "those are the people I go for . . . the guys on the edges."

Among Jargon's noteworthy achievements, none is more significant than the publication of Charles Olson's The Maximus Poems. *But Jargon's list also includes Kenneth Patchen, Robert Creeley, Louis Zukofsky, Russell Edson, Guy Davenport, revivals of the work of Mina Loy and Lorine Niedecker, and photography by Ralph Eugene Meatyard, Lyle Bonge, and Doris Ulmann.*

Mr. Williams' career began when he dropped out of Princeton to study etching at Atelier 17 with Stanley

William Hayter and graphics at the Institute of Design in Chicago. Jargon Press was born in 1951 in San Francisco and was associated for a time with Black Mountain College.

After a year of fugitive correspondence in preparation for this interview, I finally met Jonathan Williams in 1984 on a fine, mountain spring day at the family house in Highlands, North Carolina. It was to be an afternoon memorable for its candor and good humor.

DANA: Well, let's go back to the very beginning for a moment—Buncombe County, North Carolina. You once said you suffered from "Buncombe County afflatus." Did you grow up there?

WILLIAMS: I didn't, actually. Most of my connection with Buncombe County, after getting born there, was coming back to go to Black Mountain College. I didn't actually grow up in Asheville, where I was born. My parents lived over in Hendersonville, twenty miles away, where my father had a stationery store that went bust during the Depression.

There wasn't much else to do. Ben Williams was a man interested in filing systems, visible-index systems, and he designed these things. So he went up to Washington, D.C., and got lucky. The war was very good for him. All of his equipment was used by the army and the navy and the government. So he did well. He was the class poet at Fruitland Academy in Henderson County. I have a tradition going.

DANA: So there was a kind of literary tradition in your family to begin with?

WILLIAMS: Of a very simple order. Ben Williams liked dialect poetry, and he was a friend of DuBose Heyward, who used to summer up in Hendersonville. My father was a great reader of things like *Uncle Remus* and *Porgy*. There was a dialect poet in North Carolina back early in the century named John Charles McNeill. He's the best-selling poet that's ever been in North Carolina. *Lyrics from Cottonland* was one of his titles. He was an alcoholic reporter for the Charlotte paper and wrote black dialect poems, which were tremendously successful. Chapel Hill has sold more of that than any other book of poetry, hundreds of thousands of copies. My father was very good at this dialect, so I was brought up on it. Not bad. And Joel Chandler Harris—my mother's family lived about three or four blocks from Joel Chandler Harris's Wren's Nest in Atlanta. Thus, on both sides of the family there were these funny, Southern, . . .

DANA: Funny, but powerful.

WILLIAMS: Yes. Well, I'm glad I got to listen to all that stuff when I was a boy. It must have had its effect, because, in my own way, I finally turned back and became very acutely interested in what southern mountain speech was all about.

DANA: You call yourself "a seeker of the homemade." Are we talking here about the roots of that interest in the homemade?

WILLIAMS: I think having heard and been exposed to those Southern genre and imitation-black writers must have had its effect. I would never have admitted this until I got to be about forty, I'm sure. Suddenly I realized, well, hell, it's where it came from, really.

DANA: What do you think are the virtues of the homemade?

WILLIAMS: It's the only kind of virtue I know about.

DANA: How would you describe it?

WILLIAMS: I mean, I'm only interested in homemade people and homemade writers. Out of the main stream. Nonacademic. Nonurban. Really, when you look at the Jargon list, that's almost exclusively what it is. And this is not to say that I'm not also interested in endless kinds of refinements, because I am. But, as a way of life, . . . That's why we are sitting on a hillside in a very remote county in North Carolina. Or why I live in Cumbria. Why I don't have lunch with Ashbery or Stanley Kunitz or Mark Strand three times a week. All that stuff. I could, I guess, but I don't want to.

DANA: What would you say the qualities of the homemade are that are attractive to you and seem to have value, as over against the urbane, or urban?

WILLIAMS: I don't know. It's not to preach the great gospel

of democracy. But it seems to me this country is so local and so particular and so ordinary that I like people who start from there and then, of course, change it and become extraordinary. But they have to be ordinary first. Country people seem to reveal it a little quicker to my ear and eye than the urbans. I'm not used to the city life much anymore. I've lived in plenty of them, but I like the attention and the time the people in the country are so willing to give to creating these things that they make, and the time they'll give to you. I find it so hard to go to cities and talk to people in the cities now, because they don't have any attention. Their minds are somewhere else. You know, you can't get them on the telephone. They won't answer their letters, and when they do they miss the boat. What you wrote to them is not what they're writing back.

DANA: I hear you. They didn't read the letter.

WILLIAMS: They didn't read the letter. The secretary told them what it was about, and she never heard of you before. To get into communication with these people is too difficult. You go to New York and you have an appointment, and you call up that day and they say "Oh, sorry, he's been called out of town." You know, you've had this thing set up for three weeks—and he's had to go out of town. So you might as well just forget it. That's my experience.

Attention is probably the main point. It takes me longer and longer to do anything, I guess it's like throwing the fastball, or whatever. It ain't as fast as it was. It just sort of flutters up there. I have to live out here in order to keep days open when I can work and not be bothered and not be distracted.

DANA: Could you pick a writer from your list, aside from yourself, who seems to demonstrate the virtues of the homemade?

WILLIAMS: Well, what I might do is skim the Jargon Society list and just comment.

Of course, one of the people that I was first interested in was Kenneth Patchen. You might say our first real book was a book of Patchen's fables that I had had a lot to do with in its inception, because when I was in Princeton I read something by Henry Miller about Patchen. Did you ever see that pamphlet, *Patchen, Man of Anger and Light*? Saying how bad his back was, how he found it so difficult to write, all that kind of thing. I wrote Patchen a letter, in fact, and said, "If I could be of any use, I would come and type for you," something like that. Just one of those letters you write, but he took me up on it. He had a book of fables he wanted to write. I could come and stay with them. It was about 1949.

So I went up to Old Lyme, Connecticut, and Kenneth and Miriam took me in as part of the household. I stayed maybe five or six weeks and took dictation. Again, very homemade stuff. You know, turn on the tap and start spouting it was Patchen's way. I just typed, and he would correct. Not very much. He was a very spontaneous writer, an almost automatic writer. So for six weeks I sat there in the house and ate and talked to the Patchens and typed four or five hours a day. That was the book later on, when I had the opportunity to go into publishing, we decided was the natural thing to publish.

DANA: So homemade means something spontaneous.

WILLIAMS: Well, cottage industry sort of thing. He was being published by Laughlin, but Kenneth wrote two or three times more than anybody could accommodate.

Charles Olson was the next one. Here again homemade, meaning "excluded by the official publishing world." The only firm that had ever published him, Reynal and Hitchcock, had done the *Call Me Ishmael* book, and I forget the circumstances. I think that Robert Giroux had something to do with that book. And that was his only commercial book. Caresse Crosby had done *Y & X*, which was a little collection of six poems. One of the last publications of Black Sun Press.

DANA: Olson must have been pretty young then.

WILLIAMS: Youngish. Let's see, 1910. We're talking about 1950. His first poems were published when he was about thirty-five, and *Call Me Ishmael* was published in about 1946, '47. So he was, how old? In his late thirties. He'd been diverted by politics. He spent a lot of time in the New Deal. He worked for the Roosevelt Brain Trust.

DANA: Doing what?

WILLIAMS: He worked for the Office of War Information, Foreign Nationalities Division. He wanted into either the Treasury—that would follow his Poundian proclivities—or State. I think he was angling for a big job in the State Department. Then Harry Truman was rumored to have said something like, "Get that goddamned intellectual out of here!" He didn't go for Olson at all. So the government career suddenly came to an end and he was looking for a job, and I think Dahlberg got him something at Black Mountain.

DANA: Where did he get his degree?

WILLIAMS: Clark College in Worcester, Massachusetts, where he was born. And then he did graduate work at Harvard in the American Civilization program. He was one of the first candidates for a degree. I'm not sure he ever got that degree. That I can't tell you, but he was there. Then the war came along. And so he was maybe ten years later in his publishing career than he might have been. He had done a year or two down in Mexico, in Lerma, Campeche, studying Mayan stuff. There's that work of his called *Mayan Letters*, letters between himself and Robert Creeley. And so he turned up in 1951 back at Black Mountain to teach, and nobody seemed to be very interested in what he was doing. I think J Laughlin had printed one or two things in the New Directions annuals. And a little press called the Golden Goose Press—Frederick Eckman, and his partner was Richard Wirtz Emerson, who lived out on the West Coast. Golden Goose published Robert Creeley's first book and were going to publish an Olson book, but then they went bust. And so, as I say, there was nobody, as far as we could determine, who was going to publish any Olson. Being new to the cause, as well as full of adolescent fervor, I decided I was going to do it. The reason, really, why Jargon started was to publish Olson.

Funny. Patchen and Olson were really quite antagonistic to each other. I've discovered most of the people I publish despise each other. There's really very little community of sympathy. As Mr. Goodman used to say, the avant-garde was nothing if it was not that, you know. Well, there ain't much, I've discovered. Everybody wants his piece of the action. His three-quarters of the pie.

DANA: That's because the pie is so small.

WILLIAMS: The pie is small. Hard to get any. But boy, there is little tolerance or generosity from one writer to the next.

DANA: It's a variation of Hutchins' Law: "The reason the politics of poetry are so vicious is that the stakes are so low."

WILLIAMS: Exactly.

DANA: And apparently, from what you're saying, they've been low for quite some time.

WILLIAMS: Well, yes. Again, it was Olson living in relative poverty in Buncombe County, North Carolina, writing *The Maximus Poems*. In this crummy, beat-up summer camp that the college occupied. One had the experience of writing or working "at home," outside the known world. Creeley, somewhat the same story. They needed support from their friends and their students.

Then Zukofsky came next. A poet who, because of the difficulty of his works, had almost no commercial possibilities and at that point had almost disappeared. The only person who knew about him . . . well, there were two. Rexroth talked a lot about Zukofsky, and Duncan did too. Those were people I had known from going out to California. They had nothing, at that point, to do with Black Mountain.

But, really, the people who started me out on this whole business were L. Frank Baum, J. R. R. Tolkien, Hugh Loftis (Dr. Doolittle), and Kenneth Grahame.

DANA: What do you mean, they "started you out"?

WILLIAMS: They made me read their books. They made me buy their books. They made me put them on shelves and treat them as sacred objects. The unique books of childhood.

DANA: But a lot of people get attached to childhood books. They don't become publishers.

WILLIAMS: Well, I wanted to make more childhood books.

DANA: How did St. Albans School figure in this?

WILLIAMS: Well, perhaps as a sort of upper-class diversion.

DANA: An upper-class diversion?

WILLIAMS: You know, "proper" education. The family were anxious for me to be extremely well educated. Better myself.

DANA: Well, you did, in fact, win a prize for Latin.

WILLIAMS: The American way. Better education than the parents. All that. Which I was very happy to have, because I had John Davis as a teacher. John Davis was just one of those astonishing people that you find rarely in prep schools. I found him at St. Albans. Actually, I studied very little with him. I think he tried to teach me Spanish, and Sacred Studies, as they called them. It was just the fact that he was living in the school and was always available to interest you in music, or art history, or literature.

DANA: What was his specialty?

WILLIAMS: Well, he came there to teach Spanish originally, and French. He was a Union College, and then Princeton, graduate before the war.

DANA: Is he why you went to Princeton a couple of years?

WILLIAMS: No, I don't think so. But he introduced me . . . he not only introduced me, but he finished me off as an opera and theater enthusiast, and the first time I went to opera and theater was almost the last time I went to opera and theater. He took three of us up to New York at Thanksgiving. You know, when I was about fourteen. He says, "Well, we're going to go to the opera, and we're going to go to the theater. Something really good." The afternoon was *Tristan und Isolde*, one until six. Then we got to eat a quick sandwich at Longchamps. At seven or seven thirty, we were back at the theater to see *The Iceman Cometh*, another six hours. So I never have recovered. I also had a difficult but interesting English master by the name of Ferdinand E. Ruge, a man from Dahlonega, Georgia. Of German origins. A real martinet. A real wacko. But he made you spell and he made you punctuate and he made you write syntax and grammar and descriptive simple prose. I have to thank him. He was also the faculty advisor for the newspaper at St. Albans. And I learned a hell of a lot from him. You know, how to write headlines, how to write copy that fit, and all these things . . . how to get it right, so to speak, within its limits.

DANA: Did your mother have literary aspirations?

WILLIAMS: No.

DANA: But she knew Joel Chandler Harris, or grew up in his neighborhood.

WILLIAMS: Yes. The parents exposed me to some good children's books, but after the first six months of reading, I started finding my own books. I mean, I'd go to the library. But they did read to me. My father's reading aloud was excellent. And I've still got those books. I've got all the Oz books. I've still got my copy of *The Hobbit*.

I went down to the local department store, Woodward and Lothrop's, and for forty-nine cents, remaindered, there was the first American edition of *The Hobbit*. And I became absolutely enamored, entranced, by wonder-book writers—Baum particularly, and Tolkien. And these led to an interest in fantasy, and so I went through all those English writers that few Americans know about. People like H. G. Wells, all the science fiction side of things, and then the fantastic side of things, people like M. P. Shiel, Algernon Blackwood, M. R. James, and Lord Dunsany.

DANA: Well, that doesn't sound very preppy, not very Latin studentish.

WILLIAMS: No, not at all. But we had a very conservative and very boring English program at St. Albans. In the sixth form, when you were like seventeen or eighteen years old, they were still having you read things like *What Every Woman Knows*, by Sir James Barrie. You know, Walter Scott and all that.

DANA: So you were driven to seek some more . . .

WILLIAMS: I got very involved with H. P. Lovecraft. And, of course, then I got to corresponding with August Derleth, who was running that wonderful press in Sauk City, Wisconsin: Arkham House. Arkham House was taken from a fabled village in western Massachusetts, and that's the site of several of the Lovecraft stories. Things like *The Rats in the Walls*, post–Edgar Allan Poe like *The Vale of Arnheim*, up-the-river stuff. And so I was very involved with Lovecraft, and Lovecraft sent me, by chance, to a bookshop where I bought Patchen. The Argus Book Shop, which was one of the great bookshops of its time, run by a man by the name of Ben Abramson, who was a friend of people like Christopher Morley and the Baker Street Irregulars. And Tiffany Thayer. People who wrote "strangely" strange . . . the books of Charles Fort. Then I went there one day, probably the day of the terrible experience of *Tristan* and *The Iceman Cometh*, probably that same weekend, and I saw these curious books on the shelf. Kenneth Patchen books, you know. Hand-painted books. *The Journal of Albion Moonlight, Sleepers Awake*, et al. So I started buying them.

Then I started buying Henry Miller books. Because Ben Abramson had all these things. I went from H. P. Lovecraft to Patchen and Miller like overnight, when I was about sixteen. And then picked up Robinson Jeffers, who also had nice-looking books.

So the book as a kind of a childhood desire, childhood object, has always been . . . I mean the books I do now, . . . they still must have that feeling about them. I want them to be as good as that. I want them to be as entrancing as those. I don't think I'd bother if I didn't feel that way about them. Why else would one? You know, they cost you time and money and lots of work, and nobody pays much attention to them, they don't sell, and all that.

DANA: The love of the book is an exotic subject.

WILLIAMS: It came from those childhood fantasies. People like Robert Duncan, I think, feel very much the same. He kept all of his kid's books. You just go to certain poets' houses, certain writers' houses, and you see those things. And you say, "Ah, he's one, he's one." It's something like that.

DANA: As I was thinking over my questions for you, an interesting coincidence came up. On the one hand, you have the mostly self-made publisher: Halpern at Ecco, John Martin at

Black Sparrow, Sam Hamill at Copper Canyon. On the other hand, Laughlin, Harry Duncan, you, David Godine all come from prep schools. Is there something about prep school life that makes for publishers . . . that makes for the impulse to publish books, to edit books, to build a list of books, to distribute books?

WILLIAMS: I wonder. I believe that's what Ronald Firbank said about everything, "I wonder."

It didn't occur to me, at the time, to do this. That came a bit later, but I certainly was exposed, by going to libraries, by going to bookshops at a very young age. I started building a library when I was seven or eight years old. I guess the fact that I had an allowance and had a sheltered, upper-class education, . . . I suppose it allowed the time. On the other hand, I spent most of my prep school years editing the newspaper, being captain of the tennis team, being captain of the soccer team, being a prefect. I was very social in those days.

DANA: So you wouldn't call yourself bookish.

WILLIAMS: Yes and no. Well, I remember giving—not to Ruge, who didn't read modern things—but another of my English masters, when I was like seventeen or eighteen, a copy of *The Portable Thomas Wolfe,* and he'd never heard of Thomas Wolfe. Edith Wharton was as far as they got.

DANA: So it was probably a combination of factors: your family, certain contacts, prep school.

WILLIAMS: I had very few friends who read any of this stuff. This was private—a personal, private obsession. I guess it was the opportunity afforded by living in a place like Washington, where there are wonderful museums. You know, all the art and book shops that one could hope for. That was lucky.

One obvious thing you should say about these books is that they were books of the imagination, and they were books that were—not forbidden, in that sense, but I mean they were private. The ones father and mother wouldn't particularly like, or you'd think that they wouldn't, books that nobody at school would have read. There's the whole fact that they were your own, and this is a world of imagination which I think any budding poet would have gone for.

DANA: Closer to the private life.

WILLIAMS: Yes. It was out of traditions. And then when you got older, into adolescence, seventeen, eighteen, then you began to get into the other areas—antiauthoritarian, anti-government, anti–Episcopal church even. I mean, you'd get into people like, well, Patchen and Miller, of course, and Rexroth, and then Paul Goodman, and then all of a sudden you have to make a decision about what are you going to do about the war, about whether you were going to be inducted into the army and all that sort of thing.

DANA: Now this is before you went to Princeton?

WILLIAMS: Yes.

DANA: What made you decide to go to Princeton?

WILLIAMS: Well, there again, it more or less followed.

DANA: Why didn't you stay there?

WILLIAMS: St. Albans was a school that fed two or three of its graduating class to Princeton every year. There was no family tradition. My father had spent a little time at the University of Colorado, I think, back about the time of the first war, but didn't graduate because he had to go into the navy. And so, as I say, it had been the first time there had been any money in the family, and the first time there had been any opportunity for any of us to go to someplace like Princeton. So they were all for it. And I think that the hope was that I would do something like get a degree in art history. And if I *had* to write or do something like that, maybe I'd be an art critic and write for the *New Yorker*. Which would have been a way of having a job and enjoying the arts. That was the understanding. I'm not saying I was particularly right about dropping out of Princeton, but it seemed at the time very important that I do so.

DANA: Now, you stayed at Princeton three semesters?

WILLIAMS: Three semesters. And it was basically the attitude of the *being*, and the attitude of the Princeton undergraduate, that I didn't like. There were a tremendous number of people who were sleeping their way through four years, including the faculty. You know, underachieving like mad. You know, bored. They had no reason to do anything, because they were going to go in as junior members of the firm and start off at fifty thousand a year, or whatever. They seemed to be arrogant, boring, just "twits," as the English would say. Most of them. And very anti-intellectual. I'd never had that problem. You know, in school, where you were surrounded by maybe ten or fifteen people like that, there's no problem. But when you get hundreds of them . . . I felt like I was in some zoo. I didn't see the point of spending the money, frankly. It seemed to me I could do most of the classes there in about the three days before the final exam. And even if I hadn't done anything the whole semester, it was fairly easy to crank it out.

DANA: Now this was 1947–48?

WILLIAMS: Yes. It was a funny time to go to Princeton, because the veterans were a big factor. Who were a bit older, and more serious. And then the Choate-Deerfield lot.

DANA: Had you just missed Delmore Schwartz and John Berryman and Bellow when they were teaching in the English department there?

WILLIAMS: Yes. I don't know who was around when I was around. I think Galway Kinnell would have been an undergraduate about the same time I was. I didn't run into him for years after that, however. I don't know. I only knew three people in the class that I spent any time with. No literary people. Most of my friends were art historians. I had a vision of spending my life in the basement of the Morgan Library. You know, studying Byzantine iconography, which was all right, but it didn't sort of seem like the world of Kenneth Rexroth or Paul Goodman or Henry David Thoreau, which was more and more to my taste. Like I say, refinement's never been a problem, but I just didn't seem to fit into that kind of academic milieu very well.

And then everything shifted—again, led by people like Patchen, with their interest in William Blake—into graphic arts, and then I began to write poems. It was the idea of their presentation on the page that was important to me. Blake was somebody I looked at a lot. Then I set about trying to learn how to do some of these processes like etching and engraving, which I studied with Stanley William Hayter in New York for a year. Then it seemed necessary to know even more. So then I went to Chicago to the Institute of Design and studied typography, briefly, and various kinds of graphic arts.

DANA: Now, by this time, when you were studying typography, were you studying typography as an art form or were you beginning to think about print?

WILLIAMS: Beginning to, yes. Like I say, nothing had happened quite yet, but I was getting a few tools in the shed for the time when it would happen.

DANA: Had you thought of becoming a publisher by that time?

WILLIAMS: It happened when I was in Chicago. There was a fellow student, a painter, named Paul Ellsworth. We spent a lot of time talking about the idea of making books and making broadsides, putting art next to words. This is all in the spring of 1951. It all happened very quickly, all prior to Black Mountain. So I stayed one semester at the Institute of Design, and again I found it . . . I don't know who was giving me all these ideas . . . I guess Patchen and Paul Goodman and Thoreau. They were all saying, "Don't get involved in this kind of commercial stuff." It was a blow to the family, because that was exactly what they wanted me *to* do. Not waste my fine Eastern education by becoming some poet or . . .

DANA: Something that wouldn't make a "success."

WILLIAMS: Something awful. That's right. Something that would have to be housed and fed the rest of its life. You know, on *their* money. Difficult. Because, as you can see from this house, they were people of taste, but on the other hand, they came out of a shirt-sleeve business, and they were the first people that ever went off to the city and knew more than the country things that their parents and brothers and sisters had known. It was a great blow.

DANA: How did you hear about Black Mountain? What brought you from Chicago? And there's a stint in the army.

WILLIAMS: That's a little later. Everything was happening very fast. I was in Chicago the spring of 1951, beginning to theorize about printing, and studying with a very good German. The Institute of Design was full of German refugees, Jewish refugees, European refugees. And Moholy-Nagy, who had been at the Bauhaus, was the director. Lorna Zerner, I think her name was, was terribly good talking about typography. I learned a certain amount, quickly, from her. She had been the student of a man who was very important, a man named Jan Tschichold, a German Swiss who was really one of the great modern typographers. Many books. He had been at the Bauhaus. He is the man that laid the basis for all the Penguin Books. That very simple, nice design that Penguin took on. Anyway, I studied with Lorna Zerner. And then M. C. Richards, who was a teacher who had been at Black Mountain, came up. She would make the rounds and go to all the schools that might have interested students who'd like to come to the Black Mountain program. She turned up in Chicago in the spring of '51 and started talking about Black Mountain. I only knew it by its evil reputation in Highlands.

DANA: What *was* its reputation in Highlands?

WILLIAMS: Free love, communism, and nigger-lovers. The usual. Several Black Mountain founders had had summer houses here, oddly enough. They had a very unsavory reputation with Southern aristocrats and conservatives in places like Highlands.

It never occurred to me to want to go there particularly. But Harry Callahan, the photographer whom I wanted to study with, said one afternoon, "I'm going to be down in North Carolina this summer. Why don't you sign up at Black Mountain College." "Well," I said, "I just heard about Black Mountain yesterday." And he said, "There's a terrific guy named Aaron Siskind, friend of mine from New York, who's going to come down too." So it sounded perfect. And I didn't know who Charles Olson was. He just happened to be on the place, as I say, when I got there. So I went to Black Mountain basically to study photography.

DANA: Where did the interest in photography come from?

WILLIAMS: It just came. I don't know.

DANA: The natural outgrowth of experimenting with a lot of graphics?

WILLIAMS: Yes, because I'd done some of the other stuff: etching, silk screen, engraving. And I had seen Callahan's work, and there were other people around there—Art Sinsabaugh. I can remember, also, going in to see Stieglitz's place slightly earlier than this. An American Place, or 291, I forget what it was called in those days—291 Madison, I think. So I had looked at things but surely didn't know much about photography. It just seemed like one of the things *to* know about. After all, I was only about twenty. There weren't many people then interested in photography, when you come right down to it. It wasn't like it is now. The art photographers were still an unknown quantity. Edward Weston had a show at the Museum of Modern Art about that time, so one knew a little bit about Weston and Adams.

DANA: Then you actually went to Black Mountain to study photography.

WILLIAMS: I believe that's true. I certainly have convinced myself of it, because I didn't really know who Charles Olson was.

I'd also done a lot of painting back in school. And that didn't seem to be getting anywhere, the painting side didn't. But I still was interested in designing things, making images of some sort. So the camera suddenly seemed a very plausible substitute for drawing, which I couldn't do very well. Anyway, I left the Institute of Design in May 1951, then went to San Francisco for a brief visit in order to meet all the people that I'd been corresponding with. Patchen had just moved out there, I think. At any rate, Rexroth was certainly there, because I went immediately to see him. And a couple of friends of the Patchens, a young engraver named David Ruff. He had worked with Hayter, and I knew him from New York. And

Henry Miller was down the coast. I rented a car and went down and spent a day or two talking to him. And out of nowhere David said, "Oh, let's do something. You've got some poems." So he engraved a tiny copper plate with a Blakean image and then set type, and we printed off fifty copies of it—fifty copies of Jargon Number 1.

DANA: That's . . . ?

WILLIAMS: Yes, the thing to clarify is that actually by two weeks or a week, Jargon Number 1 predates Black Mountain.

DANA: I don't think that's recorded anywhere.

WILLIAMS: Well, it's certainly not been very clear, and it's probably my fault. You know, it's easier to say that, essentially, Jargon did come out of Black Mountain. But Jargon Number 1 . . .

DANA: . . . really came off the Coast. San Francisco.

WILLIAMS: Yes. The only place you can see that is up at the Buffalo archives. They've got a couple of copies.

DANA: What year was that?

WILLIAMS: 1951. It's June '51. It's an awful Patchenesque poem of mine. And a very nice engraving by David Ruff.

DANA: And how did you decide on Jargon as a name for the press?

WILLIAMS: It was this guy, Paul Ellsworth, fellow student, painter, at the Institute of Design. He was barely articulate at all. He would throw words around, and he kept talking about jargon. "Life's jargon. Jargon." I said, "What do you mean?" and he'd say—he did have it right, in a way—he said, "I mean in my own speech. My language, as opposed to the tribe's language." Actually, that is one definition. But then I liked the irony of the word. And then I happened to be checking in a big dictionary, and there was the word "jargonelle," a kind of spring pear in France. And jargon in psychiatric jargon is the language of the infant before it learns social conventions. And, also, in French *jargon* means twittering of birds. So when you add all these things up, it seems just fine. But the twittering of birds is about the best definition. People who need to be put off, it does put them off—the Jargon Society.

DANA: But why Society? Anyone else would have said the Jargon Press.

WILLIAMS: In the beginning it wasn't called the Jargon Society, but as the thing got more and more structured, and more and more people were involved, it became . . . Like I say, it's not just me, it's a lot of people helping me, you know, advisors, people writing letters, viz Gilbert Sorrentino will send me a manuscript by somebody, or Guy Davenport will have a suggestion. Always been kind of a group or community aspect of it. It's not a one-man band, it's a backwoods symphony.

DANA: When did you decide to add the word Society to the Jargon idea?

WILLIAMS: I think it was in the sixties when it became necessary to become a nonprofit, tax-exempt foundation, and to set up a structure, and have a board—all these things. It seemed people would not give money unless they had particular tax benefits. Also, to get money out of the National Endowment or any of the foundations, you had to do this. So that made us become more social, then, than perhaps we had been before.

DANA: Black Mountain brings up the question of Olson's direct influence on your publishing life. Some people have given the impression that Olson really started you in publishing, but that doesn't appear to be the case.

WILLIAMS: I think that he convinced me that it was something one could do and should do and perhaps could make part of one's life for a long time. I think that's fair to say. He certainly didn't pick the books or anything of that sort. For instance, in his class were people like Joel Oppenheimer, who had had training as a printer. And there was a small Kluge job press on the property. And it just occurred to us that we should take advantage of the stuff we had on the place and use it. One of Olson's great lines, which I've probably said before in talking about all this, he says, "The artist is his own instrument." I don't know whether that's something John Dewey said or . . . it might have been Lenin, who knows? "The artist is his own instrument."

And Olson's point was that why the hell should you expect

New York publishers, or *anybody*, to have any particular interest in what people who were student age had to say. If you felt that strongly about it, go to the press. Print it yourself. Print your work and your friend's work for the community that you lived in, or for the better community which I have always hoped was there, and I guess sometimes I feel like it is: the world of letters which exists courtesy of the post office. So if you wanted Patchen to have a copy of your new poem, you printed it and put it in an envelope and sent it to him. And then you got a letter back. That was reason enough to do these things. Oppenheimer had the facility, had the training, to make these things possible. So Jargon Number 2 was a poem of his, illustrated by Rauschenberg, dedicated to and about the dancer Katherine Litz, who happened to be at the college that summer. It was called *The Dancer: For Katy*, or something like that. As I say, Rauschenberg did some drawings, we picked out one, went into Asheville, had a zinc plate made, brought it back to the press, and Joel ran the thing off. Edition of one hundred and fifty, as I recall. He had fifty, Rauschenberg had fifty, I had fifty.

DANA: Were you then committed to the idea of publishing?

WILLIAMS: I think so. That was about August. And then that autumn I asked Ellsworth, the artist at Chicago, for some drawings and printed up six poems of mine that I had written during the summer with Olson. Six drawings, six poems. Very much like the format of Olson's *Y & X* that the Black Sun Press had done. Except that our drawings were on coated paper, and they were tipped onto the paper with evil rubber cement. Which has ruined all of our copies, of which there might have been a hundred, plus a few hand bound. I'd taken a course at BMC in hand binding, so I made up a few specials.

DANA: What was Olson like in those days?

WILLIAMS: Irish and Swedish, full of the blarney. But very impressive, extremely impressive, and amazingly energetic. You felt you'd never quite experienced anybody like this before. He made his mark; there's no question about it. Well, let's see. How old was he? He was forty-one, in full vigor, writing *The Maximus Poems* like mad and cranking them out. Full of himself, as he always was. Full of himself, full of *it*, but great, you know. I mean after the laid-back, bored Ivy League professors I'd had at Princeton, he seemed like a new world. A man who really cared about what was going on and cared about his students. Give you more time than you wanted, you know, day after day, night after night. No let up.

DANA: Energy on the hoof. Or on the wing.

WILLIAMS: Yep. And as I say, totally available. It must have been exhausting for him. I don't know how he did it. Wife and young child and no money. Trying to take care of the college, more or less. I don't know if he was the so-called rector by that time or not, but it certainly wasn't long after. So he had all that to do, plus writing all the time, and the endless demands of the students, who thought they could confront you, grab you, day or night. Black Mountain was a very tough place in that way, a very hard school.

DANA: Did he change your ideas about literature at all?

WILLIAMS: I don't know. I guess he must have. Yet, the things that absorbed me before continue to do so. He didn't stop me reading Ronald Firbank, or Stephen King, for that matter. I still read widely and stupidly. I like to read anything. Olson was not casual.

DANA: Did he turn you in the direction of different *kinds* of writers?

WILLIAMS: Well, he did expose me to people that I certainly wouldn't have got to for a long time. But he couldn't wash out the Rexroth, the Paul Goodman, the Patchen, all that "crap," as he would have called it.

DANA: What didn't he like about Rexroth?

WILLIAMS: I think he probably mistrusted his homemade education. And also Rexroth was very much like Edward Dahlberg. Olson had turned against Dahlberg at this point and found him a great *poseur*, full of cranky, useless information and bad ideas and who didn't really know about the real world of politics and power. Olson, you know, was a very po-

litical guy. He liked to wield power, which he had. Just physically, he was gargantuan. Anybody had to pay attention to
Charles Olson, and you were always intimidated by him. Just
like playing basketball against Watusi princes at seven foot
two, you know. Akeem the Dream. Olson the Whatever. Well,
Olson was a guy *like* that. He was a monster. And even if it
didn't make any sense at all, that didn't matter too much. He
was a real dazzler, and most people were there prepared to be
dazzled. Not everybody. I remember Francine du Plessix
thought he was a total crock. And he said, "I don't feel I have
to teach girls as ignorant as you. You shouldn't be in my class."
After all her fancy education, and she was practically writing
for the *New Yorker* already. They were great antagonists.

DANA: Who else was in your class? Joel Oppenheimer.
Francine du Plessix Gray, you, . . .

WILLIAMS: Fielding Dawson. There were several people
who didn't go on, but who were very capable. And other
people came later, like John Wieners. I think Ed Dorn was
around, but he had some special kind of scholarship, and he
was in charge of the farm. Helped the farmer. I don't know if
he came to Olson's classes or not at that time. But he was
around. So this class was maybe ten or twelve people, of
whom six or seven are still doing it, which speaks well.

What happened after that was I had finally to confront the
conscientious objector business. This was going on in the autumn of '51, going to see federal hearing officers and trying to
explain what right you had claiming that you were not going
to fight the war when you weren't a member of a peace church,
et cetera.

DANA: Now, we're talking about the Korean War?

WILLIAMS: I guess it was going on, as a matter of fact. But
I'd been fighting that fight since I got out of St. Albans. I
mean, I'd been saying I wasn't going to, no way at any time.

I was counseled by Olson, by Rexroth, by Patchen, and by
Paul Goodman. They all said, in my case, they thought I
should go in. But I refused to be inducted at one point, so I
was faced with either a five-year jail term in Virginia or with

going into the medics. Anyway, we were trying to figure that one out, and Olson was very helpful to me on that level. I finally went into the army and had a hell of a time getting into the medics, it turned out. The first thing they did was put me in a rifle company in Fort Knox, Kentucky. So then came the day when I said, "I don't know why we're having all this trouble, you know. I'm not supposed to be here. I'm supposed to be down in Camp Pickett, Virginia, in the medics. I'm not going to pick that thing up. And we're just going to cause a lot of trouble. It's going to cost you money. I'll just go to the nuthouse rather than mess with this thing." Finally, I got a Jewish chaplain. Sat down and talked for a few minutes. Gave him a book or two, and he said, "Get this guy out of here." Picked up the phone and said, "You know, this is ridiculous. Send him to the medics. He's either going to go to the stockade or get a Section 8," or whatever they called it. So they sent me to the medics.

The next thing I know, I'm in Stuttgart, and I remembered from some New Directions books I had that there was a printer in Stuttgart named Dr. Walter Cantz. Dr. Cantz'sche Buchdrucherei, Bad Carnstatt am Neckar, bei Stuttgart. So within a few days I'm down at the printshop meeting Dr. Cantz and saying I wanted to do some publishing. Just then, a friend of mine from Georgia, Charles Neal, died of a kidney disorder, and his widow, Dorothy, wrote me and said "Here's two thousand dollars." Maybe it was only fifteen hundred. "Do with it what you like, but Charles liked the idea of your publishing." So it was a choice of three things. Either buying a Porsche, which all the dudes in Germany were doing, two thousand in those days would nearly have bought a Porsche. I also had my eye on a Max Beckmann portrait that could have been had for two thousand dollars. Or starting to print some books. So, being a good Southern boy, I printed some books. The ones that were printed were *The Maximus Poems*, one to ten, with Dr. Cantz, one of the best printers in Germany. He was a five-minute walk from the hospital where I was working.

DANA: You had a stroke of luck.

WILLIAMS: Absolutely. Another printer across town printed my *Four Stoppages*. He could accommodate the big format, a big machine press. And I had yet another printer over in Karlsruhe that was like an hour and a half on the train. So here I was, working as a "neuro-psychiatric technician," subduing and pacifying malingerers and psychopaths and really mean folks in the locked ward in the Fifth General Hospital. They gave us a lot of time off because we were under pressure. I had funny hours where I could zip up to Karlsruhe and do business and come back on duty at three o'clock or at eleven at night, that kind of thing. I had a hell of a lot of free time. So I went through the army staying up at night correcting proofs, pasting up the books. Doing my stint, but having a very good time learning about marvelous German printing. The books looked good because I was in the hands of some of the best printers in Europe. They taught me a lot.

DANA: Can we go back for a minute to your relationship with Rexroth? You said that Rexroth had a lot of influence on you. How did you come to meet him? How did your relationship develop?

WILLIAMS: I started reading him, I suppose, about the time I started reading Robinson Jeffers, which would be about 1943, '44. He only had a couple of books out, but I got hold of those. And I wrote him, you know, after reading *The Signature of All Things*, which I felt was one of his best. And he answered. We exchanged letters back and forth, and then he invited me to come see him when I went to San Francisco. When I got to meet him in 1951, we went hiking in Marin County, up in that state park. I forget the name of it. Where he used to keep his Japanese-style cabin in the twenties and thirties. I had never met anybody who knew the names of all the plants, knew the names of the rocks, knew the names of the trees, knew the names of the birds. He knew what was out there. I was very impressed by that, because American intellectuals just don't know the natural world like that. Most of them don't.

DANA: I know. I'm always shocked by that fact.

WILLIAMS: And literary people don't know. Olson knew there was something called "rhododendron" and something called "grass," and he had trouble even telling those two things apart. One was bigger than the other, but that was about it. He had no eye for nature, whereas Rexroth was wonderful. He was like a refined Englishman. Somebody rare, like Geoffrey Grigson, who has that command of the things that you are in. Rexroth was wonderful on that level. I mean, you could talk to him about anything. And, also, he was extremely funny. He acted like he was your age, as opposed to you being a kind of disciple, that kind of thing. Which is rare. Most of the sages always treat you as though the generational deference is important. You know how that is. Olson was particularly bad that way.

DANA: The voice from the top of the mountain.

WILLIAMS: Yes. You could get Olson to unbend and be very jolly on occasion, but Rexroth was a very different sort of person. I always did like him better than any of the rest, although I had more to do with people like Dahlberg and Zukofsky. But they were prickly, thorny sort of people and, as I say, most of the writers that you publish are endlessly demanding. You never get it right. You can't do enough for them. I never did actually end up doing a Rexroth book. I couldn't raise the money, which was unfortunate.

DANA: That's amazing, because he's very important.

WILLIAMS: But it was hard to. In those days, anyway. Laughlin was printing him, and I don't think he was making any money off of it.

DANA: Did Rexroth influence your decision to publish any particular writers?

WILLIAMS: I would say Zukofsky. Certainly Mina Loy. He was the only person for a whole generation who said anything about her.

DANA: Did he turn you on to Levertov? She was an early favorite of his.

WILLIAMS: Yes, he did do that. I don't think he'd been able

to convince Laughlin about her. At that point, we said it'd be great if we could do one. He said if there's a book, then that makes more impact, which is true. A lot of times you can't see people until you see them in a book. I can't, and I think most people are like that. That's partly what the book *Overland to the Islands* was about. To get her on to somebody's attention, perhaps J's. Which happened, of course.

Patchen I was already involved with, and then Robert Duncan began talking Zukofsky. And then Zukofsky would talk Lorine Niedecker. So that's the way it works, or worked.

DANA: Most of Niedecker's work was surely out of print.

WILLIAMS: There really hadn't been very much ever printed. There'd been the little book that she had paid for herself, *New Goose*. The press of James A. Decker, that small press in the Midwest. Prairie City, I think.

DANA: Would you comment on the way your list looks when I try to make sense of it? There's the Black Mountain group, of course. Oppenheimer, Olson, and I guess Creeley fits in there by way of Olson. And Robert Duncan.

WILLIAMS: Let's see, how would it work? Creeley was in Majorca when I was in the army in Stuttgart. So the contact was made through Olson, who had never met Creeley at this point, but they corresponded like mad. And Cid Corman had printed them both in *Origin* magazine. So I started writing letters to Creeley and said, you know, I'm going to start this publishing operation, and do you have anything that you might like to have in it? So he sent me this—it's only eight or ten poems—*The Immoral Proposition*, and we made a very nice thing of it. Then I took a furlough and went to see him in Majorca. Then, later on, he went back to New England and then came down to Black Mountain and taught awhile. That's about 1954, when the *Black Mountain Review* started. It was printed in Majorca.

DANA: Did you have anything officially to do with the *Black Mountain Review*?

WILLIAMS: Until the college actually closed down, Olson had aspirations of me coming in and having the Jargon Society of *my* thing, and then becoming publisher to the college and printing a program of books he was interested in, i.e., *his* list. So I think I'm listed as publisher of the *Black Mountain Review* in the last issue. But that just meant that I was left with, you know, a garage full of it. Nobody wanted it. I wonder if I was a contributing editor? There were four or five contributing editors. Rexroth withdrew over an article he didn't like. I think Dylan Thomas was attacked. I know I did some things on photographers—Siskind, I think, maybe Callahan. I wrote a piece on New Orleans music. So I was feeding visual stuff and doing small articles for the magazine in that way.

DANA: So Oppenheimer, Olson, Creeley, Duncan. Now, where do Sorrentino and McClure fit into that? McClure didn't go to Black Mountain.

WILLIAMS: Well, Sorrentino was very much in that orbit, just like Denise Levertov was, and Paul Blackburn, and Hubert Selby. They were New Yorkers who simply were interested in what was going on in Black Mountain and became great friends of people like Oppenheimer and Dawson. The only thing of Sorrentino's I did was his first book of poems. But that's a bit later, about '60.

DANA: Then you did several people who were out of print— Zukofsky, Niedecker, Mina Loy.

WILLIAMS: Yes. This would be largely through Rexroth and Duncan.

DANA: Then there's a group I'd call the eccentrics, the "culls" you once called them. In this group I put Davenport, Alfred Starr Hamilton, Mason Jordan Mason, Douglas Woolf, Russell Edson. Would that be a fair grouping?

WILLIAMS: Absolutely.

DANA: Then you also have a group of British poets: Simon Cutts, Edwin Morgan, and the Scottish poet . . .

WILLIAMS: Thomas A. Clark. He's a kind of minimalist poet. And then Ian Finlay. Stuart Perkoff was a poet whom Olson liked, who had been published occasionally by *Origin* magazine. Nobody knew much about Stuart except he lived in California. So I made it my business to see him in Venice.

Even in those days he was very involved with drugs, which killed him, years later. He was interested in the jazz world and the drug world. He wrote some good poems. So that was another book that was done in 1956, *Karlsruhe*. Michael Mc-Clure? That came out of my days in California, 1954, '55. We got to be good friends. So I printed his first book, *Passage*.

DANA: What would you say these out-of-print poets, like Mina Loy and Zukofsky, on the one hand, had in common with people like McClure and Levertov on the other hand, or the English poets you were publishing? Is there a coherence?

WILLIAMS: Is there a coherence? I'm not sure. No, I don't think so. I often harken back to that pleasantly simple-minded thing that Pound once said: "I now divide poetry into what I *can* read and what I cannot." And so, if I can read it, and if I like it, I always figured that was all the coherence that's required. If I want to do it.

DANA: I noticed Lowenfels is also on your list. Another sort of odd choice.

WILLIAMS: Yes, perhaps it is. He's in there because of Bob Brown. And Bob Brown is there because of visual poetry. Did you ever see that thing: *1450–1950*?

DANA: No. But it's clear you do have an interest in visual poetry, probably the only publisher in the country who does.

WILLIAMS: I guess this interest starts with Patchen, cummings, Lear, Lewis Carroll. Then if you want to get high-falutin, there's Mallarmé and Blake. And if you lived in the South, one of the things that was so wonderful about living down here in those days was the signs that you saw. Not just the Burma Shave signs, but the things that Walker Evans would take photographs of, or that you just saw and felt. Great signs. If you had *eyes*! The quality of seeing these extraordinary messages. Which had to affect you. It just did.

DANA: So you don't think that poetry is simply a bunch of lines and stanzas. It can take other shapes. More sculptural shapes or designed shapes.

WILLIAMS: There's certainly a kind of poetry that doesn't require . . . that doesn't have any necessary basis in what you hear. It's not connected to the ear. And it certainly can be connected to the eye. Mostly somewhere betwixt and between, elements of both. But I had a lot of correspondence with Ian Hamilton Finlay. Having been brought up by Olson, whose first line in *Maximus* was "By ear, he sd," you can also compose by eye. It'll work. I still continue to make postcards and poems that only function in a silent, emblematic way. Of course, there was a lot of that in England, in the old days, the metaphysical days, but Finlay was the man who revived my interest in it.

DANA: Let's talk about the financing of Jargon, which is a subject we haven't touched on. What was the original financing of Jargon, and how has the financing changed over the years?

WILLIAMS: I suppose everybody ultimately must consider it a tediously poor-mouth operation. It had to come from somewhere else, because I didn't have it.

DANA: So it wasn't family money that went into the press.

WILLIAMS: No. The only money that went in was the two thousand dollars, or whatever it was, from the man in Georgia, Charles Neal. That little bequest. There wasn't any other money. In Germany that paid for Patchen, and it paid for *The Maximus Poems*, and it paid for Robert Creeley, and it paid for my little *Four Stoppages*. And then, when I came back over here, books had to be subscribed. So I had to figure out a way to pay for one title after another.

DANA: So you sold them in advance?

WILLIAMS: Tried to. I'd have a list of a hundred people to whom I might be able to send a letter about Louis Zukofsky, suggesting they either might want to be a patron and have their name in the back for twenty-five dollars, or did they want to subscribe for just the three-dollar regular edition, or five dollar, or whatever. The second volume of *Maximus* was subscribed, and Zukofsky's *Sometime*, which is one of our prettiest and finest books. That was again printed by Cantz, who did the *Maximus* in Stuttgart. In those days, the production money was not excessive. Those books would only cost five hundred to seven hundred and fifty dollars, about two dollars per copy. That wasn't so bad. Unfortunately, patronage hasn't kept pace. We still have people who are prepared to give fifty dollars and twenty-five dollars, but that's really not very interesting. Now we need thousand-dollar contributions.

DANA: So you're still selling books by subscription to a certain degree.

WILLIAMS: Basically. In other words, you have to go out and find the money to pay the printer before you undertake to do the book. They have every right to expect to be paid, and nothing is worse than holding them up. It's not fair. One has to cover the printer.

DANA: So then you went into a period of foundation financing?

WILLIAMS: There have been some lulls in this thing. In the late fifties, I was living in New York for a year or two. We were doing some Irving Layton books. And then people like Larry Eigner. Again, sort of an adjunct of Black Mountain. Russell Edson, and now we're getting into the late sixties. Most of that stuff had to be paid for by me begging contributions from all over. From individuals and small foundations. And then, of course, the NEA came along about 1968, '69 and gave ten thousand dollars for a few years to help a great deal. You could pay for things like the Russell Edson book, or Richard Emil Braun, or Alfred Starr Hamilton. The first of my "village idiots." The village idiot is becoming a specialty of the Jargon Society. To the extent now that I'm going to do a folk-art book just about village idiots, who are out there in deep left field, very wacko, all on their own, idiosyncratic, autochthonous, whatever you want to call it. They are strictly their own people. This is an interest that has been built-in all along.

DANA: Do you still average four books a year?

WILLIAMS: We overdid it a couple of years ago, did about six books. Then last year we were down to two. This year, with any luck, we'll do two or three. It's slowed down. But the reason they've slowed down is because they're getting to cost twenty-five thousand dollars a book. Well, the last Paul Metcalf cost fifteen thousand; the Mina Loy cost closer to thirty thousand. *The Photographs of Lyle Bonge* cost a good twenty-five thousand. He's a remarkable eccentric from Biloxi, Mississippi. Black Mountain, but before my time. I didn't encounter him until the late fifties. And representative again of people who are out of the ordinary. Bonge's images are just stuff on the highway in Mississippi. Everything is built out of the ordinary, but it's the people who become "out of the ordinary" who interest me. God knows, we have enough ordinary.

So that's why we've had to slow down. The contributors do not keep pace with the production costs. On the other hand, there's another reason to slow down. Because, more and more, I write more of my own stuff, and that takes more time. So I split the time. Half, perhaps more than half, is devoted to Jargon, and the rest is devoted to my own reading and writing. I mean, after all, you have to go and walk. You can't be writing another dozen letters to try to get money for Jargon Society on that particular day. It's amazing how much effort it does take to raise any money. I don't know whether everybody has this experience or not.

DANA: Was it the finances that led you to a cooperative venture with Corinth?

WILLIAMS: Yes. Well, again, they had some dough, they were generous, and it would speed things up. The books were somewhat journeyman productions. Not so good as they might have been, but they were perfectly okay.

DANA: How did you get in touch with Corinth?

WILLIAMS: I worked at the Eighth Street Bookshop. I had a job wrapping books, in the fifties. I liked to wrap books. In those days, I did anyway. I used to take pleasure in wrapping books nicely. Well, you know the feeling when you get one and it comes with the corners all beat up—nothing worse. So I liked to be able to wrap a book and get it out to the customer so that it arrived looking like something. A lot of bookstores in New York are awful that way, these days. Even good bookstores. They put a staple in the end of a jiffy bag and think they've done something. Anyway, I knew Ted Wilentz and his brother Eli, the best kind of old-fashioned bookmen, who liked writers and enjoyed having a literary shop and trained people to work there. You had practically to have a Guggenheim or a Fulbright to work in the Eighth Street Bookshop. It was very funny. For the pleasure of forty-two fifty a week. And you could sell books to . . . hey, there's PeeWee Russell, or Geraldine Page.

So Jargon's been an impecunious operation, but, on the other hand, it's just about been possible to do it.

DANA: Now, is that partnership still operative?

WILLIAMS: No. They went separate. We did, I think, three or four things together. We did the Creeley, we did the Bob Brown, and we did the one-volume Olson *Maximus*. The first time it had been collected into one substantial book of about the first, whatever it was, thirty letters or thirty-five letters. The Stuttgart editions plus another third. And that was the standard text for about ten years.

DANA: That may have been the first time I'd heard of Jargon.

WILLIAMS: Corinth had better distribution. Of course, we've had about ten different distributors. The people I picked as distributors are about as bad as I am. You know, the proverbial blind leading the blind. We got Jim Lowell out in Burton, Ohio. Well, Jim is even more sardonic than I am. A lot of things he just doesn't like. He likes Robert Duncan, and he likes most of the Black Mountain people.

David Wilk at Inland is the best we've ever had.

DANA: Is he the same David Wilk who used to be with the National Endowment for the Arts?

WILLIAMS: Yes. He used to have Truck Press before that. David is great. He loves to try to sell books. It's not "beneath" him, and he's young enough not to be tired of all that detail. And, thank God, he does a job.

There are three or four operations like this. There's Writers and Books up in Rochester; Bookslinger, or whatever they call it—David started that thing in Minneapolis and then sold it. And then there are the people out in California—Serendipity.

DANA: So you're really using more or less small outlets?

WILLIAMS: Various jobbers and distributors, they get Jargon from David. The books don't sell in any quantity. The only book that has ever paid for itself is *The Appalachian Photographs* of Doris Ulmann. We printed two or three editions of that and have sold about fifteen thousand copies of it. But there ain't a poem in it, like they say. Not one. Not a poem. That helps. We've done five or six photographic books. Then there's Paul Metcalf. We've done five prose books of his. And *cannot* sell them. I don't know why. *Nobody* buys them. He doesn't understand it either.

DANA: Do you get your books reviewed?

WILLIAMS: Not much. We try. I think our review list is about the list that anybody else would use. About sixty-five to seventy-five review copies of everything are always sent out.

DANA: Are there any small-press reviews that could help you at all?

WILLIAMS: I don't know. I know there is that new one, *Small Press*. It's a Bowker publication. They must have some notion of what we're doing. I mean, they certainly have all the library contacts we need. There was an article in it on Inland Book Company's distribution early on. I think David's uncle is one of the heads of Bowker. All these things help, I guess.

I used to try all these alternative ways of doing things. In the fifties, I used to travel around the country with a station wagon full of stuff, and just sell it as I went. You'd go to the one bookstore in Houston and you'd sell them a few things and leave an invoice. Half the time, of course, you never got paid— which is the nature of "literary" bookstores. The biggest places are the last to pay you, usually.

DANA: Do your books sell well in England?

WILLIAMS: No. We've tried two different distributors over there. They both went bust carrying this kind of stuff. New Directions is about the only thing you can sell over there in any quantity. And City Lights.

DANA: Do they know you exist?

WILLIAMS: They know very little about this kind of thing. The only people that teach it, I suppose, are a few poets.

There are people like Charles Tomlinson, who's been here, you know, and can preach William Carlos Williams at Bristol University. Eric Mottram knows. Donald Davies knows. Gael Turnbull. And there's a middle generation who teach American Studies, Roy Fisher comes to mind. But once you get outside the university in England, you're practically in the midst of, well, I don't know, something like Neanderthal times. Nobody is educated. You know, only six percent of the English are university or technical-college trained. Six. Six percent. I don't know what it is here, but I would venture a guess it's somewhere between twenty and thirty percent at least. So you wonder how anybody is functioning over there? There is no little band of eccentrics or people who know about literature. You're either working class or you're university. And the English do not particularly welcome foreign influence. A few of them do, but the English are the English. They're island people. They don't like people from other places.

DANA: Very insular?

WILLIAMS: Very, very. I was more active over there in the early sixties. There was much more interest in American things then than there is now. You go and give a reading, and if you read Olson or somebody like that, or yourself, or whoever, people like Christopher Middleton would show up. Good people. Christopher Logue. But most of them don't want to know. They're quite content.

Then, of course, the people I publish over there the English don't like either. I've done Simon Cutts, who is of no interest to the English because he's influenced by the French. Thomas A. Clark is, in part, influenced by William Carlos Williams. Ian Hamilton Finlay is a bit wee and twee for their tastes. A little too whimsical. No, they're meat and tater people. They know what they like, and they don't like very much. And that's that. I'm sure nobody in England knows who Simon Cutts is. We printed a jolly book of his, *Pianostool Footnotes*, one of our nicest books lately, and blimey, it's had one review in England. One review.

I don't go out of my way to be that way, but I'm just not

interested in a lot of things that are "mainstream." And this holds true for literature and music and art and so on. Maybe it's because I feel I don't have to pay attention to the well known. For instance, I don't like listening to Beethoven (that boring old monkey) very much. Mozart, if I may be so bold, is something I can almost do without. Let me hear some Balakirev or some Jelly Roll Morton. So I resist people like Philip Larkin, although, in fact, Philip Larkin is pretty good. I wouldn't say I am marginal, in terms of quality, but I'm peripheral in my vision. I'm looking for the edges. I'm looking for the stuff on the outside. So Bunting was very much to my taste, and David Jones, people like that, not that I read them very well or always intelligently, but still, I'm interested in it. Those are people I go for, the guys on the edges.

The program is just me, for better or worse. Consider Ronald Johnson; we've done three books of his. While he comes out of a tradition that involves people like Williams and Olson and Duncan, his work is very much on its own. And so is Davenport's.

DANA: Yes, how did you come up with Davenport? He seems like a real original.

WILLIAMS: Originally, he'd come to a poetry reading I gave back in the sixties at Haverford College, when he taught there. We got to talking about Ezra Pound and this and that, started corresponding, and the next thing you know he wanted to know if I might be interested in one of his long poems, which I looked at and thought, well, you know, it ain't Charles Olson, but on the other hand it's very intelligent and it's interesting. So why not? If I can print Alfred Starr Hamilton, I can print Guy Davenport.

Once in a while you want to print somebody you have doubts about or don't really understand. For example, we have Peyton Houston on the list. Peyton Houston is extremely conservative, I suppose you might say. He's a very philosophic poet, and he's all the things that maybe the Jargon Society isn't about. But I'm always impressed by his intelligence. I don't

quite get it. But a lot of people like it. A lot of people that I
talk to, and they write me letters about it. So why not, you
know, why not, why not? Maybe I'll *get* it one of these days.
So we've done three books of Peyton's. I'm glad to have him on
the list, although he's a kind of mystery man for me. I don't
see anything wrong with that. I don't want to be too sure
about these things. And I'm not. I'm trusting my ears and my
eyes. I don't really try to approach the thing in a very brainy
fashion.

DANA: Well, that's certainly an attitude you wouldn't find in
New York.

WILLIAMS: Well, I suppose not. But we don't care whether
we sell books or not, in a way. We're covered, more or less,
before we start. The printers are more or less paid. We do the
best we can. We give readings, we travel about, we talk, we
write letters, we do this and that, and we do all we can think
of to do. And hope there's an audience out there equally interested. At times, it seems as though there perhaps is, but I
don't know.

Another thing that I think might be said is that a press like
New Directions or a press like mine, I think, is so much de-
pendent upon the taste of Laughlin or my taste, being acted
on by all these other people, of course, as he had Rexroth and
so-and-so to suggest things to him. I think a press does have a
kind of shelf life, as they say. I don't think you're right on top
of things, but maybe fifteen or twenty years, in terms of what
other people are thinking. And then, suddenly, you get to a
certain point, and well, I don't much care what people in their
twenties are doing at the moment. I reckon that's up to somebody else to figure out. I don't want to have to take that on,
because I'm still interested in making sure that Lorine Niedecker is going to be around for people. That seems more important to me than to be worrying about the latest hotshot. So
I make no effort to keep up with those things. In a way, that's
good, and in a way, it could be better. I don't care about the
music they listen to. It's a different sort of culture, that's all.

DANA: Well, perhaps it's as Robbe-Grillet says of writers, that one must consent to bear the imprint of one's own historical period, the limits of one's own time.

WILLIAMS: Well, I would say that's true. And some work of the Jargon Society is coming to a conclusion. I mean, most of the poets that I've wanted to print, I've printed. If they have a next book, and we can afford to publish it, fine. Thomas A. Clark has had three. I would like to do more, except that I've gotten cross with him, and he's gotten cross with me, so there may not be another book. Ronald Johnson, if necessary. He's really not been taken up by anybody. You know, Norton reprinted *The Green Man* from England, and then they did one other book. That was that. And then Jack Shoemaker did one book of his at North Point, but North Point seems to be going in a much more . . . what's the word? I don't think "commercial" is quite fair, but they're not going to be printing many books like that. They seem now more interested in protecting their pocket than in protecting excellent writers from *Boobus americanus*. So, it may become necessary to print more Ronald Johnson. We've done four or five of Tom Meyer's books. Of course, that's fine. Maybe other publishers feel like, oh well, Jargon will do those, so there's no necessity. But it would be nice if some other press came along and wanted to do a nice big book. He is very special.

DANA: Do you see any fresh direction for Jargon in the next, say, ten years?

WILLIAMS: There are more photographers I feel strongly about, that I would like to do. We're going to do a couple of picture books. Two people down in Georgia, visionary environmentalists, we are going to do sort of picture books on their places. One of them is a man called Saint Eom of the Land of Pasagnan near Buena Vista, Georgia. EOM. It's an acronym of Eddie Owens Martin. He's the only official in his religion, which he gets from Mu and Atlantis. The spirits tell him to do this, that, and the other thing. Build temples, dance floors, pagodas, and stuff out in the woods. Eddie is a sight and a half. And then there's the Reverend Howard Finster, an old Baptist preacher and carnie man up in Penville, Georgia, who's building a Paradise Garden and the World Church of Folk Art, a sixteen-sided thing. Looks like a big wedding cake with towers all over it. They're both very interesting figures and accomplished artists in their own way.

DANA: Are there other possibilities?

WILLIAMS: If I can find some funding, I'm going to do this book on, well, I don't know, it's called "A Wild Book of Southern Non-Folk Folk Art." Obviously that can't be the title, but that's what it's about. And, again, it's the Alfred Starr Hamiltons and the Guy Davenports of the visual world. Not "naive" necessarily, but mostly. The people who are tucked away in the tall trees, who need a spokesman for them, I think, just to be identified, some of them. And that interests me, to do that. So I've been working on that fitfully for the last three or four months. It'll be about maybe fifty people, maybe a hundred places.

Let's see, one of the books that we have never finished, ever, is "The Poems of Mason Jordon Mason." That is still on my mind after twenty-five years. But have you ever tried to deal with Judson Crews? He's a very exotic character. He probably *is* Mason Jordon Mason, but won't admit it. There are numerous personae in his head, with all the attendant psychic mysteries. Anyway, we're edging toward being able to produce that manuscript. I've gotten Jorge Fick to do wonderful drawings for it. There's another book, called "Notches Along the Bible Belt," which will be a collage of found material, mostly from Baptist bookstores down South. Put together by a master finder of extraordinary things. You wouldn't believe the things he finds. There are already evangelical billboards in North Carolina, for instance, that say, "Jesus is the beef." How can you believe it? But it's there. Richard Craven is the collagist, with a keen eye and a strong stomach.

Did you ever see *Bible Stories*?

DANA: I don't think so.

WILLIAMS: I'm very keen on cartoons. This is our version of the Old Testament by Bill Anthony, who, happily, was a student of Joseph Albers at Yale for about a half hour. He says he tries to draw as well as any psychotic eleven-year-old creep. I love his stuff. It's pleasantly wacko. We're going to do a book of his called "Drawings of Truth and Beauty" which will astound and offend everybody. So that's in the works.

And John Menapace. A book of photographs, very formal, austere photographs that nobody, probably, will buy. I don't know why. Where *are* people? Do we still have an audience? Are they still out there? These are questions you don't dare ask yourself some days.

DANA: Well, most of them are buying their books in Walden and B. Dalton.

WILLIAMS: Most of them are probably sniffing nose candy and watching videos. Or listening to Michael Jackson or Culture Club. Well, that's fine. I don't care what they do. I just hope there are fourteen hundred and fifty-seven people as curious as we are.

DANA: That leads to an interesting question. What advice would you give to someone going into the small-press business today?

WILLIAMS: The numbers racket being the numbers racket, maybe the best way to do it is to become technologically competent and maybe do like students of Harry Duncan's who have set up printshops. Just thinking about the people in your book—I mean the approach is so variable, and so various. Ferlinghetti's attitude about the book as an object versus Harry Duncan's.

DANA: Miles apart.

WILLIAMS: They're worlds apart. Lawrence always used to say, "Well, I sell it for a buck. Anybody will waste a buck." And that's fair enough. You can't argue with him because, god, look at the sales. On the other hand, Ginsberg once offered me a shot at *Howl*, or a book along those lines. I could have printed that. I think I met him before Lawrence Ferlinghetti did. At any rate, he was very interested in the idea of a book. When I think back, what a terrible thing it would have been for him, you know, because we would have sold maybe three or four hundred copies. Our approach is high culture and exclusive, I suppose. It doesn't make any sense.

DANA: Are you more interested in producing the books than selling them?

WILLIAMS: Well, of course, yes. The day the thing is there, that's the great moment. How much can you expect out of the world? It's easier to go to bed with a thousand people than make them buy a thousand copies of a book. It'd be much easier to get them to do that than to get them to read what you'd written. Interest is so "marginal," that word again. It's not nothing, but the numbers involved are very small. How many people does it take to get Lorine Niedecker recognized as a really important poet? I just don't know, but if you've got a couple thousand of the thing, or of Mina Loy or Basil Bunting . . . Have you seen his *Collected Poems*? Oxford does it, off-print, the English edition. He got his royalty check last year, 1983. Four pounds. *Four pounds.* You know, people write whole books about Bunting. But you cannot find the book in a bookstore in England. Even in Newcastle, where he's based, you can't find the book. This is something to do with the attitude of the publisher. And this is a *major* serious publisher. *We* might have some excuse, because we can't find a distributor, or the bookstore just doesn't think they have an audience. But from Oxford you might expect something more.

DANA: Do you advertise your books?

WILLIAMS: Occasionally. We let David Wilk decide that. He takes out a few ads. And we have mailing pieces. We don't have to think about bookstores as the only possibility. In fact, we would like to circumvent bookstores, since there are so few that really want what we have. There are only fifty. So you service them, fine. Then you deal directly with people.

Again, it was easier when people were used to sitting down, writing a letter, asking for a book. Now a lot of people have forgotten that you can do that. You don't get the mail that you did. It used to be that every week five or six people would like to buy a book or have a catalog. That's slowed down, like all correspondence has slowed down. So it may be that we are in just some funny point in time in which this is old-fashioned stuff and something new is coming along. I don't know. But I'm very obstinate—I don't think "obsessed" is quite the word—and I'm very stubborn, and I want to do a certain kind of book, devoted to certain kinds of people. And I do them. Their fate in the public world is not very outstanding, but I don't know how else to do it. I'm stuck with my own tastes, my own limitations. I can only do what I can do. I can do a certain few things rather well. Other things I don't have any head for.

DANA: So you think that publishing is still a viable life for somebody just starting out.

WILLIAMS: Yes. I started to say I think you want to make yourself technically proficient, competent, and then figure out whether it's going to be offset, using the facilities of one of these big print centers, or whether you want to really keep it small and do it letterpress and do fine editions, like Walter Hamady or his disciples, who've set up in New York the Red Osier Press. They do very handsome work. Of course, it's editions of two hundred at most, and they cost a lot of dough.

I don't think anybody should do this unless they're very determined and just cannot imagine *not* doing it. You've got to be very fierce about it, and then it's a crime of passion to get on with it. "Get hot or get out," like the man said.

David Godine

*David R. Godine issued its first books in
1970, mostly handsome printings of classics like Whitman's*
Specimen Days *and* The Collected Songs of Thomas
Campion, *and museum books like* The Sculpture of Rodin.
*Policy, however, quickly shifted Godine's emphasis to origi-
nal works, and over the next fifteen years its list expanded
to include books in history, art and architecture, typography, photography, books of poetry, fiction, and even children's books.*

*Godine's authors include William Gass, Andre Dubus,
Stanley Elkin, and George Starbuck. Its Nonpareil series
has reissued the letters of William James, scholarship by
Francis Steegmuller, fiction by José Donoso, and poetry by
Greek poet George Seferis.*

*The following conversation actually took place on two dif-
ferent occasions two years apart. The first meeting occurred*

*on a hectic Friday afternoon in June 1980 in the publisher's
Dartmouth Street offices in Boston. The second meeting occurred in the house of a friend, late in the evening, in Iowa
City. Each interview was singularly plagued: sections of
tape inexplicably blank, statements muzzled by background
noise, lost threads. Often it seemed that David Godine, like
the unphotographable Crazy Horse, had the power to defeat
both technology and history.*

DANA: You once said the army was a better experience than
Harvard Ed. Do you want to elaborate on that?

GODINE: Nobody believes me who hasn't been in the army,
and anyone who's been in the army understands exactly what
I mean. It's a leavening experience. You meet people in the
army whom you will never meet again in your life. Whereas
you meet people at the Harvard Ed school whom you will continue to meet for the rest of your life.

DANA: Did you meet anyone in the army who moved your
career in the direction of publishing?

GODINE: No, but there were some very good writers. I was
in basic military journalism, and we had to write every day.

DANA: Anybody who has since turned up on your list?

GODINE: No, these were career people. These were people
in the army teaching people to write camp newspapers.

DANA: Did you work on a base newspaper?

GODINE: Yes. I worked on the one at Fort Benjamin Harrison in Indianapolis. It was a very good newspaper.

DANA: Was that your first editing experience?

GODINE: I guess officially. You had to edit for brevity, sense,
and comprehension. The readers ranged from high school
graduates to Ph.D.'s. It was a very mixed bag, and the experience demanded a mixture of good syntax and great humility.

DANA: Can we review the Dartmouth period? You began
setting type there as an undergrad?

GODINE: With Professor Ray Nash. He just died two years
ago. I was in two of his courses: Prints and Printmaking, and
Books and Bookmaking.

DANA: How did you happen to take his courses?

GODINE: I'd heard good things about them from people who'd taken them. It was the way so many decisions evolved in those days. These were the days before published curriculums were available, so you really relied on word of mouth. Also, Dartmouth was a small school and had very few extracurricular activities. So I would spend half of my time practicing music—playing, usually every night from seven to nine—and then I'd go and set type until eleven, or whenever I'd finish. There weren't many of us in the course, twelve people max. Nash taught an advanced course, which I took my junior year. This was a very interesting combination of purely academic study and practical application. Namely, when was this book published, who did it, how can you tell, what materials was it made of, what was the style involved? That was to develop, I think, your visual sense. A lot of reading in the history of books—and for printmaking, prints—along with the workshop, so that you weren't just learning typesetting in the abstract. You had to go set type and then print it. You had to wet the paper and print it damp. And that, to my knowledge, was unique in the Ivy League, although it was becoming common in the West and Midwest at that time.

DANA: What year was that?

GODINE: 1963–64. Because my senior year I had a senior fellowship, and that absolved me of all coursework to print a book called *Lyric Verse* and to study bibliography and bookmaking in London, Oxford, Paris, Antwerp—as well as printmaking.

DANA: This seems a pretty unusual commitment for an undergraduate.

GODINE: Well, the senior fellowship program is very similar to the scholar-of-the-house at Yale. It took—I think it still does take—between ten and thirteen seniors who had crazy things they wanted to do that did not fit at all into any schema which could be officially sanctioned or even encouraged. I remember vividly that, of the eleven of us that year who got it, two of us got it for fairly wild projects. Mine was one, and another kid was studying French theater design of the eighteenth and nineteenth centuries.

I remember Professor Jensen, the head of the project, saying when he announced this award, "I don't know what you're going to do in life, but there are two of you here I'm convinced will never do anything remotely like your senior fellowship programs." He looked at me and this kid Hargraves and said, "You two." You know, everyone else was going to be a lawyer or a doctor, and the irony is that only three of us did anything in later life remotely connected with our senior projects. Hargraves went on to be a pretty important and very good theater designer. I went on to become a printer and a publisher. And Jensen, to this day, is very contrite on the issue. Because all the doctors turned out to be lawyers, and all the lawyers turned out to be accountants, and all the accountants turned out to be teachers in South America, and so on. There was no relationship except in three cases.

But it was a great thing for Dartmouth to do that, to take a certain critical mass of seniors and just say, "Do as you like. Just show up in June for graduation." That's basically what we did. We took no courses, no exams. They just let us do what we wanted. And you felt a supreme sense of responsibility to the school and to the program for putting that amount of trust in you to really come through with the goods. Much more so than you would under a more rigorously supervised program, the typical course for seniors.

DANA: I see. So Ray Nash got you started. Among the publishers I've been interviewing, the mentor's role seems especially important. Laughlin was a protégé of Pound; Halpern met Bowles in Morocco, and Bowles helped him start *Antaeus*. Is there someone who plays a similar role in your own development?

GODINE: I think Leonard Baskin was a similar influence. A man of immense intelligence. A man of complete understanding of the history of the book. Not only of the book qua object, but of the book qua recorder and transmitter of information. People like Meynell, Geoffrey Keynes, and Stanley

Morison—the great English triumvirate—certainly influenced the way I view printing and publishing. Particularly Meynell, who was my hero as a publisher. Morison was a consummate scholar of typography, and Geoffrey Keynes was an editor and a doctor, a real man of mind and action.

DANA: Had you had any prior printing experience before you went to Dartmouth?

GODINE: None. No one in my family had printed. And I didn't know that much about printing when I left Dartmouth, either, by the way. I was very bad. I didn't learn printing until I really worked with Harold McGrath and with Leonard Baskin. Harold was a great printer. Leonard knew what he wanted the printing to look like, but he wasn't sure, technically, how to get it. Harold was a great technician, but a technician of limited taste. Whereas Baskin was a designer of great taste, with limited technical ability. But that's insignificant. He knew what he wanted and how he wanted to get it. He had design in his fingertips. A genuine genius.

I think that's a place where Nash and the program fell down, because I didn't learn how to print commercially or even artistically until I worked with the Stinehour Press and the Gehenna Press. I made terrible mistakes. I mean nobody told me when I printed my first book that I should obtain copyright releases. And I was printing people like William Carlos Williams and e. e. cummings and Robert Frost and William Butler Yeats. I remember sending these books off to people like J Laughlin and Alfred Knopf—the book was called *Lyric Verse: A Printer's Choice*—and getting these marvelous letters back. And at least a third of the book was in copyright—absolutely, clearly in copyright. I was selling this book for, I think, ten dollars. I only printed five hundred copies, so it wasn't an enormous amount of money, but nonetheless the law is the law. Then I got a letter back from Knopf saying, "Dear Mr. Godine, I was very gratified to receive your book, and I think it's beautifully printed, but before you proceed too much further in the profession of your choice, I strongly urge you to observe one of the small conventions of the trade known

as copyright, and I enclose a small booklet for your edifica-
tion, which I heartily endorse your reading." And I got a nice
letter from J Laughlin, because many of the poets—Williams,
Pound, Dylan Thomas—were all in copyright. And I'd never
written J or anyone at New Directions, who I'm sure would
have said, "Sure. Go ahead, kid. It's okay." Then I got a letter
back from Macmillan saying, "Forget it. You've got two poems
by Yeats in there. It's fifteen hundred dollars."

DANA: How old were you at this time?

GODINE: I was a very chastened twenty-one-year-old at
that time. Twenty-two, maybe. But they stuck to their guns. I
wrote back one of my more obsequious letters of all time, ver-
bally falling on my knees and slobbering with guilt. I said,
"My whole inheritance is tied up in this book, and if I don't sell
these copies, I will never be able to publish another book."
They said, "Sorry, kid. It's a tough lesson to learn, but you
can't sell them." I can't sell them to this day, because of those
Yeats poems. I give them away. They didn't make me destroy
them, thank God. But it was a hard first lesson. A good first
lesson.

DANA: So no one in your family had ever been involved with
books or printing or art. What was your background?

GODINE: Well, my father got his Ph.D. from Harvard in political science, published a very good book with Harvard University Press on labor negotiation in the public sector, was an
assistant professor at Harvard until 1948 or '49, when my
grandfather died. My grandfather had started a wonderful
business fabricating stainless steel, called the Market Forge
Company. During the Second World War it was run by my
uncle, who was my grandfather's son, and his sister was my
mother. When my grandfather died, it was a family-owned
business. Since there was no one really to help my uncle run
it, he asked my father if he would. So my father ran that company, with my uncle, for a good twenty-five years.

DANA: About Oxford and your time with Baskin.

GODINE: Well, Nash was asked to go over there that year to
teach bibliography, and I attended some of his classes. I found

them frightfully boring. This was really technical bibliography. What I was really interested in doing, and what I did, was looking at the books. And looking at art. I spent a lot of time looking at art. It was just really a *Travelsjahr*, I guess. A taste of how you build up your eye.

Oxford was very cold, but it was very obliging. At the Bodleian I could see whatever I wanted. I'd start at the Italian sixteenth century and work my way through the nineteenth. Just having them bring out books. The middle of every morning, I'd fill out little slips of paper, and they'd send them out one by one, and I'd look at them for maybe ten or fifteen minutes each then send them back. That's all I did. Just look. But that was a year of very good looking.

DANA: So England had some influence on you.

GODINE: Yes. First, I was really staggered by how better-educated the English were. There was no comparison. I was a two-year classics major. I'd had Latin and Greek in high school. It was my major, along with English. The senior fellowship had made that decision unnecessary. But I didn't know anything about classics. I was in roughly the ninth grade in terms of what they knew in the ninth grade and what I knew as a senior in college.

Secondly, I thought you really got the feeling of what scholarly books and scholarly publishing were. I spent considerable time at the Clarendon Press, which was still actively involved in letterpress printing then, still teaching their apprentices how to set type. It was a very serious scholarly press. So I think my attitudes toward scholarly presses took shape in those months at Oxford.

Also, there's a tradition in Europe, and particularly in England, at least there was then, of fine bookmaking, the machinery, the attention to minutiae, which was absent even among the rare-book lovers I knew. These people really knew books, knew printing. The history of printing and publishing were in fact one. We had nothing like that at Dartmouth, and there was no one like that at Harvard after Bill Jackson died. The Houghton had a great collection of these sixteenth- and seventeenth-century books, but they were inaccessible. Ruth Mortimer, who published the monumental bibliographies of these sixteenth-century Italian and French holdings, was basically a bibliographer. There was no one in America to whom you could talk, to whom I could talk, except Leonard Baskin, about the history of the book qua object, qua art, not the book as a potential Shakespeare text, but the book as it presented the history or process of printing, of illustration, of typesetting, et cetera. I didn't meet people like Joseph Blumenthal or James Fraser or Hermann Zapf or Alex Lawson until much later.

DANA: How long did you spend at Oxford?

GODINE: December through March or April. Then in April I left, because Dana Atchley had been a senior fellow the previous year, and he was finishing a movie at the Plantin-Moretus Museum in Antwerp on the making of the Renaissance book. So I lived with Dana for about a week and a half, helping him with that movie. It was a lot of fun, because the Plantin-Moretus Museum is really an unchanged printing shop that has materials going back into the sixteenth century, and it has all the really great cuts by Rubens and Holbein. An amazing repository of sixteenth-, seventeenth-, and eighteenth-century material that was given to the city intact during the nineteenth century. It's the oldest printing museum of its kind in the world. And Dana's movie showed how sixteenth-century books were made. Sixteenth-century books are the greatest books in the history of printing, especially the French.

DANA: And after you returned from abroad, you worked for Baskin?

GODINE: No. In 1966, we had a hot war, and I was 1A all the way. I enlisted in the reserves, I went through basic training, then I went to Fort Benjamin Harrison. After the army, I went to Harvard and got a master's in Education for General Purposes. It was for people who thought they might want to go into education but didn't want to be teachers. It was a great year; you could take courses anywhere at Harvard. After that, I went to work for Baskin.

DANA: Had you known Baskin before?

GODINE: Yes, Nash had introduced us. I think Lenny asked me, or maybe I asked Leonard after I got out of Harvard, if I would come and house-sit for him for that summer, in Northampton. The whole entourage would go to Maine every summer: Lisa, Toby, Esther, Lenny, everyone would clear out of the house. And that house was a real *Wunderkammer* in the seventeenth-century Dutch sense. There was an incredible collection of books, coins, stamps, medals, drawings, etchings, paintings. You name it, Lenny had some of it. It was a small museum. He was appropriately nervous that someone might break into it, so he very generously gave me the keys to the house for that summer, and then when he came back . . .

DANA: What year was this?

GODINE: 1968. That's when Lance Hidy had come up from Yale, too, to study with Leonard. And that's when Leonard had the idea, which I thought was idiotic then and consider idiotic now, of reprinting all thirty-eight of Shakespeare's plays. Instead of approaching this from a practical point of view—namely, of having the metal set in a machine—Leonard insisted on setting the books in thirty-point Centaur by hand. That's a hell of a lot of typesetting. It quadrupled the costs, and Leonard was not assiduous in paying his bills. I said that we needed a new edition of Shakespeare the way a Buick needs a fifth hole. Editorially, there was absolutely no justification for this project at all, except as a showcase for Leonard's art.

DANA: He was financing this project?

GODINE: He was financing it, or maybe there was some other angel behind it. But it was primarily Leonard's credit, or lack thereof, which was on the line. And I knew this would never get beyond maybe two or three plays at the most. It was just an insane idea. Starting with certainly one of the least attractive plays in the Shakespeare corpus, *Titus Andronicus*. It's not a work that people buy and put on their coffee tables. It's a play of great morbidity, violence, and death. And perhaps not even by Shakespeare in its entirety.

Leonard thought, perhaps rightly, that Harold might need

help, because the metal would come in in this truck from California, and there would be galley after galley that would have to be made up into pages, and the sheet was enormous. It was made by machine by Strathmore, but it was still an all-rag sheet. And we could only print one-up. Well, two-up, but one side was usually used for illustration, the other was for the text, so it was an incredible process, printing this huge sheet, because the format was an elephant folio. It was eighteen by thirty-four, or something like that. Harold and I spent the better part of the year trying to get this thing printed.

DANA: Where was your shop at this time?

GODINE: We had just been given a barn in Brookline. It was an enormous amount of work, but we had been given it rent-free for ten years by a very generous Bostonian by the name of James Lawrence, who was just a sweetheart and liked what we did. But we had to install heat, lighting, plumbing, the works. Of course, the cows had just left. So I was spending my weekends there *and* working with Leonard. It just had to end. And Leonard was probably more than generous letting me stay as long as I did, doing as little as I did. But there wasn't much work to do.

I think by April or May of '69 it was clear that someone had to make a move. We'd come to a parting of the ways where he couldn't afford me, and we understood this. It was clear that he was not going ahead with his thirty-eight plays as planned, and Harold was becoming increasingly upset with the whole thing, and resentful, and rightly so. I mean he was such a great talent.

So Lance Hidy and myself and Martha Rockwell began the press in 1969. Lance had come up from Yale, where he had printed and designed and illustrated three or four extraordinary little books. And Martha was essentially a cross-country skier from Putney, Vermont, who was a marvelous typesetter and binder. And we didn't need much more than that. We had enough money to buy a Kelly Number 3, which was a flatbed cylinder press. We had to get a phase changer, 220 and all that, but we then had a big book press to print on, and we produced a lot of very good, finished work right away. We were the only letterpress people with design sense at that time who were doing commercial work. So we did books for the Bostonian Society, the Massachusetts Historical Society, the Grolier Club of New York, the Metropolitan Museum. I think, looking back, it was an amazing period, because we had no money. I think we made sixty-five, seventy-five dollars a week. That was our salary. None of us was married. We were all in our twenties. But we had a lot of time, and the time to do anything we wanted. And looking back at those books, they were extraordinary. Between 1969 and '73 or '74 we were still doing most of our books letterpress. We were not publishing anything of any great literary significance, certainly not anything of contemporary literary significance, but the books were beautiful. Unsaleable, but beautiful.

DANA: How did you capitalize the press to begin with?

GODINE: I had a trust fund which really was more than I needed. I had a very long-suffering, generous trustee, and for some reason which is to this day impossible for me to define, he had the feeling that this just might work out if he stuck it out. He gave me enough rope to hang myself and then some.

You know, I often wonder what would have happened if I hadn't used that capital then. Could I have used it to better purpose later? Was he right in giving it to me? It's not that we ever used it for anything frivolous, but we went through . . . well, not an extraordinary amount of money. You couldn't start a publishing house today for the amount of money we put into the press, which was well under $600,000 over a period of years.

DANA: Over how many years?

GODINE: Oh, that's total. I mean the total capitalization never exceeded $680,000. At any time. We had loans, of course, which we paid back. Capitalization was always kept very, very low. My trust would loan me the money, and I always loaned the money to the press to be paid back when we could afford it.

DANA: Do you have other investors?

GODINE: We have one other investor. A lovely guy by the

name of Robert Richardson, who owns eleven percent of the company. But I still own eighty-eight or eighty-nine percent. That money was there. Of course, the money advanced at that time could buy anything you wanted in terms of equipment, except offset equipment. We weren't interested in offset; we were interested in letterpress. People were getting out of letterpress like there was no tomorrow, so we could pick up presses, type, cases, cuts, et cetera. People would give us the stuff just to get rid of it. Our timing was perfect. We put together wonderful type, paper, and an even more wonderful collection of people, many, many of whom are still in publishing in one way or another.

DANA: So the original staff was three people.

GODINE: The original staff quickly went to about eight or nine.

DANA: What's your present staff?

GODINE: Well, the highest we ever were was sixteen. But remember, that's when we were doing everything: all the shipping, the invoicing, the printing, et cetera. It didn't make any sense. We're now around twelve. Harper and Row does all of our distribution, shipping, warehousing, and collections. We pay Harper and Row close to $300,000 a year for that service, so you can figure out what we would have to have to take care of what we pay for in outside services. That would be at least another ten people. In the early days, we were really printers first and publishers second. It wasn't really until I came back from Book-of-the-Month Club in 1976 that I perceived our role as being publishers first and printers second. I think it had gone through my mind, in 1973 and 1974, that we could really shut down the printing operation.

DANA: Now, when you say "printing," you're really talking about the actual process of printing, and not just choosing types and so on.

GODINE: That's correct. That's the difference between a builder and an architect. You had to decide whether you wanted to be a contractor, wanted to build the books, or did you want

to design the specifications and job the building out to someone else. It was clear by '74 that if you were going to go into
the market, even on a fine-printing basis, you had to get into
offset printing, and offset printing meant major investment of
capital. Which I wasn't willing to do at that time. We were looking at $250,000, $350,000, which is about minimal for the equipment we would need if we were to set up as offset printers. We
didn't know anything about offset printing. Printing is the
most competitive industry in America. There were a lot of
people out there who were doing good offset printing, so we
basically said, "What do we want to be printers for? You can
find them around Boston." And we decided at that point to be
publishers. Of course, I knew nothing about publishing.

DANA: So this was a major shift in emphasis.

GODINE: Quite conscious, I must say, but not instantaneous.
It wasn't as though one afternoon we stopped being printers
and became publishers. But two things were clear. First of
all, we couldn't continue to print *and* publish. And, secondly,
if we were going to become publishers, we could not make a
company survive doing basically public domain material. We
had to find original manuscripts. We had to publish authors as
well as books, find authors as well as titles. And I didn't know
much about that.

DANA: A second major shift in your program.

GODINE: Yes, because our books, although they were beautiful—I'm talking about books like *The Collected Songs of
Thomas Campion* and *Deaths Duell* and *Letter to a Friend*,
by Thomas Browne, and even *Specimen Days*, which was a
great book—were all public domain. They were all beautiful
books. Really, we could not have done better books, ever, than
those books. I still look back at them with great pride, but I
also still have a basement full of most of them. If not literally,
at least metaphorically. They hung around for a long, long
time. You couldn't give some of those books away.

And the investment was really quite high. We're talking, in
those days, between three and four dollars a book. You could

have published a novel for a quarter, for a third, of that. The return on a novel, as we found out later, or on a good children's book, was much, much higher.

DANA: You're saying you were fairly naive about . . .

GODINE: It *was* naive, and it was also stupid. What someone should have told me was, "Why don't you go work for a classy New York publisher for a few years. Work for Roger Straus or Viking and find out what goes on in publishing." J Laughlin had a lot of good advice from people; I mean editorial advice. He always, I think, approached it from the point of view of an editor first and a printer second. Knopf approached it first as a production manager, but he also had great editorial taste. He came at it really much more nearly the way I did; he was interested in the design and production of the books, and then became savvy as an editor. But, yes, I had to learn publishing, and there was, believe me, no one in Boston who could teach me.

DANA: When you finally made up your mind that you were a publisher, what standards did you apply to your choice of books? A couple of years ago, you said a publisher had essentially two choices: to publish what he thought everyone else liked, or to publish what he liked.

GODINE: I still stand by that statement. I still think we operate very much along those levels. My taste and the taste of the people working for us then were very . . . I don't mean to say eclectic . . . We were very recherché. It's not as though we were a side eddy to the mainstream. We weren't even on the same continent. It was clear by '75 that we were substantively on our own. Maybe we wouldn't break even, but the objective was certainly to make money. We did some great books in that period, but a lot of the editorial choices were just not very well informed.

DANA: What are some of your favorite books from that period?

GODINE: Well, I think the great books we did, we did in association with museums, like *The Art of the Printed Book*, which we did with the Morgan Library, which is still in print. It's going back for its fifth printing, in fact, this month. *Two Hundred Years of American Sculpture*, which we did with the Whitney Museum. *The Sculpture of Rodin* we did with the Philadelphia Museum. We did a lot of very good co-publishing, and we did pick up a lot of authors who are still with us. But we certainly were not an author-oriented house. It was a book-oriented house. The distinction, in my mind, was very clear. We were not publishing authors, we were, by and large, publishing books. But we were not always very clever in choosing authors either, even when they were very distinguished and even well known.

DANA: Are you referring to books like the Seferis, or the chapbook series?

GODINE: Yes, the poetry, as one example, never made money for the company.

DANA: How many copies did you publish?

GODINE: Three or four thousand. It was crazy. We should have been doing fifteen hundred. Remember, between '69 and '72 you could have published anything and gotten away with it, because the library budgets during that period were still intact. Libraries had money. All you needed was a decent review in *Library Journal*; you didn't have to hit the *New York Times*. Just *LJ*, and maybe *Kirkus* if you were lucky, and you'd sell two or three thousand copies of a book. And it was stupid that we didn't get into children's books earlier. It was something eminently suited to our list. We were graphically sensitive; we had a good sense of design and color. And despite what everyone told us, we should have been into fiction much earlier than we were. Fiction was then, and remains, where the big money is made. It's true for us as well. It's not that we're selling subsidiary rights today for $100,000, but we do sell many titles to reprinters for serious money. Serious money to us is $10,000 or over. But we were paying for paper, printing, and binding, instead of for authors. It was a big waste or leak of capital opportunity from 1972 to '75. Then the

Book-of-the-Month Club really changed me. I got a look from the inside into how New York publishing works and what it took to make a publishing operation work.

DANA: How did you happen to go to work for the Book-of-the-Month Club?

GODINE: Oh, I just got a call one day from Al Silverman, saying come down and talk with us. To this day, I don't know why he picked me.

DANA: Who was he?

GODINE: He was the editorial director. He's now chairman of Book-of-the-Month Club. A very, very sweet guy. He probably saw that we were in a little bit of trouble, didn't know whether the press would last. *I* wasn't sure whether the press would last. Offered me a whopping big salary—not in New York terms, but it was certainly better than the eight thousand a year I was making being president of Godine.

DANA: What year was that?

GODINE: '74. Or was it '75, '76? It was a miracle Godine survived during that time. I wasn't there more than two or three days a week, and sometimes I wouldn't be there for a month. It was very hard dealing with two different jobs. Then, when they were bought by Time, Incorporated, he rightfully came to me and said, "I think you have got to do one thing or the other, because you can't continue to do both." I was offered a very good salary to stay, but I just had to say no. I've never regretted that, although at the time it was a very tough decision to make, because there was no assurance in the least that going back to Godine would improve things. He was very fair with me.

DANA: What sort of decisions did you make at Book-of-the-Month?

GODINE: Well, I ran a book club called Quality Paperback Book Club. When I came there, it had about thirty thousand members, and when I left, about a hundred thousand. It was Ed Fitzgerald's idea. I take very little credit for the idea. Ed Fitzgerald was the president—wonderful man, smarter than anyone I've ever met in the world of publishing, including all the publishers I've mentioned. I mean, he was just a natural genius. He was a great administrator, he had a great editorial nose, he had a flair for running a company and getting people to work for him, and I would do anything for Ed. Al, too. They were all like that. It was a very nice company to work for.

They were absolutely honest, they treated their people fairly, and I think by virtue of working there you had antennae out to everything. You got a real sense of how media publishing operates, and the differences between, let's say, Farrar, Straus and E. P. Dutton, or Alfred Knopf and Random House, who were actually in the same building but had very, very different styles. Or Doubleday—you know, the world's greatest disaster area. You were aware of what the small presses like Ecco were doing, not just the megagiants like Simon and Schuster.

And we were buying very interesting books for Quality Paperback Book Club, from a literary point of view. *Terra Nostra*, by Carlos Fuentes, was, I think, the first name selection that I chose. We did everything from Lewis Carroll to *The Tao of Physics*. It was a great education. And I will say publicly that there would be no Godine today if I had not worked there. It changed my whole conception of what our job was, of what we had to do to make the company survive.

DANA: Are you saying it changed you from a printer into a publisher?

GODINE: Well, that decision had already been made, and it was the right decision, but there was no expertise on my part, no knowledge of how to implement it. It was as if you were making raw pine furniture and you suddenly decided you wanted to become a cabinetmaker, but you didn't even know what tools to buy to start to learn your job. Or you'd played ragtime piano and you suddenly decided you wanted to become a classical pianist, and who do you take lessons from? I was really lucky because I had free lessons. I could do a good job for them, and I think I did do a pretty good job for them, but at the same time I was really helping myself define much more clearly and precisely what it was that I wanted, and how I could do it. And this process of definition still goes on.

DANA: So how *do* you decide what to publish? Where does your list originate?

GODINE: In the minds of the people here. Not just the editors, everyone in the company.

DANA: Well, how do they go about selecting a particular writer or book?

GODINE: I don't know. That's their problem. I just think anyone who's in publishing should have at least four or five good book ideas a week, or they shouldn't be in the business. Some of them may be not practical. Many will be impractical. Some of them may not be the kinds of books this company should do, but they still may be good ideas. I think these ideas are always looking at you.

DANA: You once said you'd know a true classic if it fell into your lap.

GODINE: I don't think that's true. I probably said I would not know. *On Being Blue* is a true classic, but nobody had a clue that book would sell more than twenty-five hundred copies. We printed twenty-five hundred copies letterpress with our heart in our mouth. You know what you like. You publish what you like or what you believe in. You hope that other people share your taste. There are only two ways to publish. One is to try to figure out what everyone else will like, which I've generally found to be totally unsuccessful, because nobody knows. And the other is to know what you like. So what I like is what I publish. There may be a lot of other things I haven't published that I like, but that's because a good book on the subject hasn't come in. I like photography, poetry, graphic arts, fiction. I like books on music, even of art criticism, books on fishing, although I've never published a book on fishing.

I think you're betting on either a subject or an author. Those are the two ways you publish if you publish by your own taste. If it's a subject, you try to determine whether this author knows more about it, or can do a better job on that subject, than any other author. And you're the best judge. If it's an author you're betting on, you're basically betting on the future of the author as a writer and on his qualities as a human being.

DANA: How would you necessarily know these personal qualities from a manuscript?

GODINE: You wouldn't. But then you would never publish an author on the basis of a manuscript alone. You would always meet the author.

DANA: You would?

GODINE: I'd never publish an author without meeting him or her.

DANA: You're not saying you just publish people you like.

GODINE: No, not as a principle. But I wouldn't publish someone in whom I did not have confidence that that person would, if we did our job properly as publishers, stick with this company. I mean I believe in loyalty. Just the way I would be loyal to an author through thick and thin, through good books and bad books. The way Roger Straus has been loyal to Malamud or been loyal to McPhee. They lost money on many of their books, even though they did all their first eight or ten books. You expect that loyalty to be reciprocated. And it isn't generally, in the industry. That's a big problem with the industry.

DANA: You mean that publishers, in general, aren't loyal to their authors?

GODINE: No, the author is not generally loyal to the publisher, or the author's agent isn't. The agent will go where he can get the most money for the author, and that puts you as a publisher in a very untenable position. Because only three things can happen with a published book. One, it's a failure. Two, it's a success. And, three, it goes to a middle ground. In two out of those three options, you're in trouble. If it's a failure, the author's going to be unhappy with you, generally, or at least the agent will be. He'll take the next book from that author somewhere else, so you've invested a fair amount of time promoting a book or an author, and you don't get a second chance. And each time you publish an author, if you do a good job, you do it better and better. Secondly, with success the same thing happens. "You've done so well with this book, Mr. Godine, that we think we can get fifty thousand dollars from Doubleday. 'Bye." The third thing that happens is you run a middle ground. You do an okay job. By doing an okay job, just a satisfactory job, you have a better chance of keeping an author. By doing a terrifically successful job, you run the risk of losing the author.

DANA: To a bigger firm.

GODINE: To a bigger firm or a richer firm. It doesn't even have to be a bigger firm. I don't think Joseph Heller left Knopf because Simon and Schuster was bigger or better. I just think they offered him more money.

DANA: Authors often have the opposite view of the situation.

GODINE: Sure. Never forget it's often an adversary relationship.

DANA: The author-publisher relationship.

GODINE: Yes. Where there's an agent in between.

DANA: But if you deal with the author directly . . . ?

GODINE: Then you're much more his ally, because you're very conscious of your responsibility toward the author, and you're very, very rigorous about not doing anything that in any way could be interpreted as taking advantage of the author. Whereas, when there's an agent involved, you basically say, "That agent should know his business. I'm going to get away with everything I possibly can." And, by God, you try to, because you know the agent is trying to. Not every agent.

DANA: In a sense, you're talking about the old relationship in which the publisher acted as the author's agent.

GODINE: Yes. But that *was* the situation in publishing twenty years ago. That's why Knopf had a terrific, as they say today, "stable." Knopf would say "collection." He had authors who were loyal to him because he was loyal to them. Agent or no agent. Same thing with Roger Straus today.

DANA: Speaking as a writer, that seems an ideal relationship.

GODINE: It is. I like to think ours is not an adversary relationship with our authors. But I know in New York you're kidding yourself if you don't think it's an adversary relationship. It is. The agents are out to get as much as they humanly can from the publishers. And there are no contracts that say that in perpetuity such and such an author will publish with such and such a publisher. I think it's a terrible situation. I think it has done more to hurt publishing than anything else.

DANA: There's probably no way to restore the old situation.

GODINE: No, not without offering the kind of money that most publishers just don't have to offer. I mean Time-Life can offer Norman Mailer a million dollars for a three-book contract, but there's no way Godine can offer Andre Dubus or Janet Malcolm or any number of other people we publish even $25,000 for a three-book contract. Can't do it. We have trouble signing a one-book contract.

DANA: It raises an interesting question. Should a writer take less money in order to have a better relationship with a publisher?

GODINE: Absolutely, because in the long run, if the publisher pays the royalties, he's going to do better. What's an advance anyway? It's a guarantee. But if the publisher sells more copies of the book . . .

DANA: Well, most advances turn out to be debts.

GODINE: That's right. Which is why publishing is in trouble. Authors bemoan the fact that there are fewer and fewer publishers publishing new fiction, quality fiction, or experimental fiction. It's easy to answer that. Authors and agents have driven most publishers into debt. If you look at the number of unearned advances at a house like Harper and Row or McGraw-Hill or even Random House, you understand why publishers are reluctant to invest money in an untried author. Because they've been burned too often, and because they owe established authors so much money already.

DANA: Let me put something of myself on the line here. I'm a poet. I've had two publishers. I started with W. W. Norton, and Denise Levertov was my editor. As long as she was there, things went fine. But when she left, my work was orphaned, along with that of a number of other writers—Ronald Johnson, Margaret Avison, Jim Harrison. I later had a similar experience with Swallow. I feel betrayed by publishers who failed to support my work, and I'm sure my story isn't unique. It's an oft-repeated one. What does this side of it indicate?

GODINE: I think, power. You have a relationship with either a publisher or an editor within a house, and you expect that person to read your manuscripts, to comment on them, to promote them within the house. The advantage of someone like Halpern, me, or Laughlin, or Scott Walker, or whoever, is that you've got the best of all worlds. As the heads of the house publishing, it is we who are putting our taste and our asses on the line.

DANA: But today any editor can come to a writer and say, "Well, you know, your book wasn't moving, so until we sell all the copies of the first edition, we're not going to do another book." That might be two years, five years, or ten. Not much loyalty there.

GODINE: Well, that's right. No poetry would be published in the United States, probably, if that were the case. But we have the same problem with our chapbooks here. That's clearly a one-shot deal. I mean we make it clear: we want one book of yours. You can go anywhere else after this. The purpose of the chapbook series is to give a good poet a chance to be published and reviewed seriously.

DANA: I hear in what you're saying the voice of the pragmatic publisher, and it's probably true that even poets wonder sometimes why publishers bother to publish any poetry at all, since they infrequently break even, let alone make any money on it.

GODINE: It's a moral responsibility.

DANA: Then let me play the devil's advocate and say, "Well, that's crazy."

GODINE: Yes, it *is* crazy, absolutely crazy.

DANA: Why do you feel, then, that you have a moral responsibility to do it?

GODINE: I probably shouldn't feel that way, but I just don't think you're a serious publisher if you don't publish some poetry—good poetry. I think that's intellectually indefensible. But the first job I have is keeping the company in business, not defending morality in America. On the other hand, I do believe that if you do it carefully, if you try to cut your losses, if you promote it well, if you're careful about who you choose, you make your expenses. You shouldn't lose your shirt, just lose a sleeve on the deal or a shirttail. It's very, very tough. Getting tougher all the time.

DANA: It's interesting that you and the publishers I've been interviewing for this book have all, in a sense, staked your taste and money in a gamble on quality.

GODINE: What we perceive as quality. As I've said before, personality moves the age more than principles. Doubleday's principles would be the same as ours. I'm sure they think they publish a quality list. I'm sure, by the lights of the editors at Doubleday—some of them are very intelligent and good people—they are publishing quality books. To some degree, they are. You know, in terms of total books published, they probably publish more of what I would call quality books than Godine does. As a percentage of their list it may not be, but it's the personalities at Doubleday who are making that determination, just as it's the personalities here. The same with Gottlieb today at Knopf, or Straus, or Elizabeth Sifton, or Cork Smith. Now, Laughlin happened to be a great genius at it. Either that or he had to be listening to very good advice.

DANA: Well, that's what he claims, that he listened to what Pound and Rexroth and others told him.

GODINE: But I don't believe that entirely. You know, Laughlin was obviously a man of terrific taste and great initiative and ingenuity. But there are other publishers who have been equally blessed with money and opportunities, and years, who have not been entirely successful, who have wasted enormous amounts of money. So Laughlin, or the other people you've mentioned, obviously came to it with something different than, or something more than, money. Although the money enabled Laughlin—or, God knows, me—to do what we're doing.

DANA: Earlier you called your publishing house "eclectic." I think I'd agree with that. You publish an interesting, odd variety—books on gardening, two books on whales—does a book like *The Democratic Art: Chromolithography from 1840 to 1900* really pay for itself?

GODINE: No. We got creamed on that.

DANA: Why did you publish it?

GODINE: Well, first of all, because the author has wonderful feeling for his subject and is capable of expressing himself eloquently. I liked the subject of that book, because it wasn't a technical book; it wasn't even an art book. It was a social history book. It was about the democratization of art in America. That's what chromolithography did: it made art available to the masses. And talking about chromolithography and art is like talking about mass paperback publishing and literature, except that one happened a hundred years after the other. I don't regret publishing it. I mean, lots of books you could publish could do disastrously, but you'd publish them again in a minute, and that's certainly true of a book like *The Democratic Art*. A lot of other books, looking back you'd say, "I never should have done that." But that is the best book on the subject. There will never be a better book on chromolithography, an art which is still seen as cheap, tawdry, or garish. But this one will be looked at, I'm really convinced, in thirty or forty years, as the seminal book. A few reviewers, God bless them, picked up on that. But most of them—it went right by them. It would be like devoting a major book to mass paperback publishing—which a major book should be devoted to. There are other art books or photography books where you say, "We just never should have put the money into that one. It was a big mistake." But not this one.

DANA: Your list exhibits a really intense commitment to art, typography, and photography. Where does that emphasis originate?

GODINE: Well, I think there have to be some publishers besides New York Graphics, and Aperture to some degree, who really tackle art and architecture. And there are four or five.

There's us, Braziller, New York Graphics, Abrams, and the university presses, particularly Yale and Princeton—very strong—and then California. We've always been a graphically oriented house, particularly in typography. And when I see good, solid books about photography, I try to buy them.

DANA: Does that come from you?

GODINE: Yes, I think that's my scholarly side. I would hate to think of the day that we'd have to be so commercial we could not do a serious, scholarly book by Peter Marzio, that we were too poor. But the cash drain of those books is incredible; I mean, you're looking at—for a book like Peter's or the one we just did on the architecture of Russia—forty or sixty thousand dollars. You could publish four books of fiction for that. So there's enormous investment and equal risk.

DANA: So you publish the book, really, because you feel a commitment to the subject.

GODINE: Yes. I also think it's a subject that people have come to trust to us. They know that the book as a book is going to be a lovely thing, lovely to look at, and they're willing to take one or two copies. Last year we did *Great Camps of the Adirondacks*. Great "camps" not as in summer camps, but great houses. We did seventy-five hundred copies of that book, and, by God, we sold sixty-five hundred copies, which is damn good. Now there's a success story no one, including me, would ever have anticipated. And at forty-five dollars a pop, which is what that book cost, it was a major source of income for us last year. So when they work, they work in a very major way, providing new cash. When they fail, they are cash drains of the first order. So that risk is the price you pay for opportunity. Or, rather, you pay a high price for that opportunity.

DANA: Speaking of risks, let's talk about William Gass for a minute. How did Gass come into your list? You've now published four books of his by my count.

GODINE: Let's see. *In the Heart of the Heart of the Country, On Being Blue, World Within the Word,* and *Fiction and the Figures of Life,* number four, and we're trying to get more. Well, I think Gass is a very interesting writer. I don't pretend to understand everything he writes, but I'm always interested by what he writes. He's basically a philosopher who can write beautifully.

DANA: Yes, I find him a very interesting critic. He may be wrong, but he's never dull.

GODINE: That's right. I agree with you completely. He may be wrong, but you're always interested in what he has to say.

DANA: Did you bring him into your list, or did some other of your editors?

GODINE: I think I did. We completely, again, miscalculated on *On Being Blue.*

DANA: That got picked up by the *Times*, didn't it?

GODINE: Oh yes, it got a very good review. Our first printing on that, to give you an idea of how off we were, was twenty-five hundred copies. I think Knopf had turned it down because they thought it was too special or something. I had heard him read a section of *On Being Blue* somewhere, and I had written him about it. Knopf had said, "We don't want it." So I called Bob Gottlieb and said "Would you mind if we did it?" And he said, "Be my guest." We did up twenty-five hundred copies, at ten dollars a book, beautifully printed, and sold out immediately. Then we went back and did another twenty-five, another twenty-five, another twenty-five. Then we did it in paperback. Then his other books came up. They were going out of print, and Knopf very kindly called us and said, "Well, you did one. Are you interested in doing the others?" We said, "Sure." And then when *In the Heart of the Heart of the Country* went out of print—that had been done by Harper and Row—we picked that one up.

DANA: What percentage of your list is fiction and poetry right now, and what percentage would you say was nonfiction?

GODINE: I'd say twenty-five to thirty percent is fiction, and the rest is nonfiction.

DANA: To shift the subject for a moment, the purpose of your Nonpareil series . . .

GODINE: Oh, I'm very excited about that. I'm hotter on that than anything else we do, except maybe children's books. Its purpose is very clearly stated—it's to bring back into print, in some cases, or to keep in print, major works of fiction, poetry, criticism which are just disappearing—they're going out of print.

DANA: How would you characterize the difference between your series and Ecco's Neglected Books of the Twentieth Century?

GODINE: Our tastes aren't identical, but the idea is very, very similar. Listen, everyone's getting into the act now. Random House is doing it now, and the whole Obelisk series with Dutton.

DANA: And Black Sparrow is reissuing all of Wyndham Lewis.

GODINE: Yes, so I don't think the idea is so original. It's an idea that's being picked up more and more. What's incredible to me is how many great books are available for reprint. Because either the publishers can't justify keeping them in print or . . . Look at the books we've done in that series: Edmund Wilson's *Memoirs of Hecate County*, Warren Chappell's *A Short History of the Printed Word*, the Gass books, Stanley Elkin's *The Franchiser*.

DANA: How many copies of these titles do you publish? Does it vary?

GODINE: Sure it varies, but of all of those, we've sold well over five or six thousand copies over the life of the book. We took an old Knopf book on how to write by Sidney Cox, sold over eight thousand copies, and paid Knopf over two thousand dollars in royalties. We're doing a lot of modern work; we do José Donoso in that series. Almost everything he's done we will bring out in the Nonpareil series, so we're trying to build around a writer as well. William Maxwell's books have done extremely well; we're doing them all. We pay fair royalties. The authors are very happy because their books are back in print. The publishers are happy because they're making money on books they hadn't been able to sell.

DANA: How many books a year are you doing now, and what sort of future do you see for Godine?

GODINE: I spend an inordinate amount of time, lately, thinking about that. I guess in the last year we just paid much more money for writers and books than we ever considered doing. A few years ago, paying twenty-five thousand dollars a year for advances would have been considered impossible. This year we've spent twenty-five thousand in the last couple of months; it's our investment in the future. Even with the Nonpareil list, books that you were getting three or four years ago for five hundred or seven hundred and fifty, you're now paying two or three thousand for. So we have much more money tied up in rights or advances than we ever did.

Next year we'll publish close to thirty books. That includes the children's books, the Nonpareil list, and our original list. I think the optimum size for us would be close to fifty books a year. Remember, we're on a three-list system and not a two-list system, so we could do fifteen, sixteen books a season, I think, and do them quite well.

I think we have to be much more . . . well, I think everyone has to be much more savvy about what they publish and how they promote it. The balance between the amount of money you can put into hype and promotion and advertising versus the return you would expect. We have to invest in more people. I've been very lucky with the people who have worked for the company. I mean, the editors we've got now—Bill Goodman, myself, and Deanne Smeltzer—are all people who've been with the company four or five years, so they know their way around, and they're all very good.

The price of being very good is that you get more submissions and more good submissions than you can possibly handle. I tend to be an expansionist in this, and everyone else has to be terrified, because you can't expect forever to expand until you publish twenty percent more books every year than you did the previous year, or even ten percent more. So I think it's that balance between what's desirable and what's possible, which is always a publishing dilemma. What's practical versus what's aesthetically desirable—it's becoming increasingly difficult to make that judgment. I have a hard time adjusting that balance. How the list should be balanced between children's books and the Nonpareil books, the Nonpareil books versus Godine books, how the list should be balanced between really quirky, risky books versus "mainstream" commercial books, how the list manages to maintain a certain independence and distinction and "look" while competing on the shelf with everybody else's books. Remember, no bookstore—and bookstores are, by and large, our main outlet for our sales—separates a Godine book from other books. I mean you're in there competing with Knopf and Viking and Penguin and everyone else. That means they have to be designed with that "look" in mind.

DANA: What is the Godine "look"?

GODINE: Well, I can't say anymore that Godine's books *have* a look, except to say that each book, I hope, looks pretty good for what it is. It's designed for what it is. A first novel, you probably help it with a sexy jacket, but it's not produced as beautifully as someone like Andre Dubus, who's done five or six books now. We know pretty much what we're doing with Andre by now.

DANA: On the subject of small presses and the NEA—last time I talked to you, you felt that the National Endowment for the Arts "supported the wrong constituents." Do you still feel the same way?

GODINE: Oh, I feel that just as strongly as ever. I'm on the NEA now, so I'm in a better position to comment.

DANA: At that time, you felt it would be better to give the money to libraries or writers, to let libraries purchase from small presses of their choice, or let the writers take their thousand-dollar chip to a small press and say, "Here, . . ."

GODINE: I would still like to see some of the money used that way, because I still think a lot of our money gets spent in two nonproductive ways. The first is subsidizing presses who do beautiful printing and print books of absolutely no intellectual merit whatever, mostly poetry. Even if they were publishing Anthony Hecht and the entire Atheneum list, they would still not be able to sell more than two thousand copies. But they're publishing people who are totally unknown, and they're totally overproducing the books. I know from experience it's just money down a rathole. It may be a worthwhile rathole, but it's still a rathole.

The second place we throw away money is in not trying to figure out how to solve two major problems. The first is distribution itself. How do you get the books out of their basements and into the stores and into the distributors who might be effective with these kinds of books? How to publicize them? The second problem is how do you collect money? I mean, once you've sold the books, how do you get the bookstore to pay the money? I can guarantee that the bigger these people get, the worse problem they're going to have collecting their money, because they're going to be at the very, very bottom of a very, very tall totem pole. And they are the last, last, last people any major chain-store distributor is going to pay.

It just seems to me crazy that we have now six hundred little presses, or whatever, all of whom want to be commercial to some degree, trying to sell their books in an extremely competitive, volatile distribution system which is notorious for not paying its bills, which is equally notorious for returning books, or losing them, or damaging them, or otherwise mutilating or destroying them or having them disappear. It's like they're producing beautiful Lalique glass and sending it to the five-and-dime store. Or they're doing DeLorean cars, and they're selling them to the Chevy dealer. There's a disparity between the product and the methods whereby it's distributed, and I'd like the NEA to address that.

On the other hand, I am extremely impressed by the panel headed by Frank Conroy, with how assiduous they are in reviewing the material, how fair-minded and generous they are in sending out the money. There is no politics that I can figure out involved in this. The guy who runs NEA and Mary MacArthur, who's sort of the top sergeant there, try to be fair to everyone. They are the perfect people to run that program on the federal level, and they're getting more money, not less money, which is a very good sign. They keep waiting for the bottom to fall out of the ship, but the ship just keeps getting bigger and faster, and the feds keep putting more money into it, which is a surprise to everyone. Every year they say, "This year the shit is going to hit the fan." And this year they got more money than last year.

So I guess I still believe strongly in the free-market economy. I think what's happened is that, because of people like myself and a few other people on that board who are looking at how the money is being used and what return it's getting, the people whose sales were not keeping pace with the infusion of capital are being cut ruthlessly. If I see their sales were ten thousand dollars and we put twenty thousand dollars into them, there's something really wrong. It's crazy; we're subsidizing a negative, net loss situation. If I see we put in five thousand dollars, and their sales went up fifteen thousand dollars, that's money well spent. It's like when the forest gets hit by gypsy moths—the strong trees survive, and the weak trees just die three years earlier than they normally would. They were sick to begin with. So I say, "Let the sick trees die. Support the healthy trees."

DANA: So your position is essentially the same.

GODINE: Yeah, it is fundamentally the same. The money, in many cases, has been very well spent. I don't look at it as a black-and-white issue, but there are people getting money who should have shut down ten years ago. I look at the cumulative amount of money they've gotten—you're talking about sixty, seventy, eighty thousand dollars. I won't name names, but you know there are presses whose sales are still twelve thousand dollars a year, and they've collected eighty thousand. It's an annuity. It's like they're on the dole. Every year they can count on it.

DANA: But does that have anything to do with the quality of what they're producing? I mean, I can imagine printing poets who are really very good who will not sell enough to make, even subsidized by the Endowment, your figure for increase in growth.

GODINE: Oh no, no. I think it *is* quality. First of all. Like Persea Books or Sun Books or something like that. Give them money. They publish very difficult books. Translations. It's a very tough list.

DANA: You're arguing that you become good at selling books when somebody wants to buy your books.

GODINE: That's right. It would mean that a press would have to be selective about what it took and what it thought it could market. If small-press people had to compete in the marketplace for NEA funds, whether the funds were to come from the writers on one side or the libraries on the other, that would encourage a certain expertise, a certain—forgive me for saying it—commerciality, commercial instinct, a quality many of these presses don't have. After all, if the money is guaranteed, if they know they're going to get the money, what is the incentive to sell books? There is none. Now, don't get me wrong. There are good small presses, but some little-press people are dilettantes, and I don't think the NEA should be in the business of encouraging, promoting, or sponsoring dilettantes.

I've worked ten years for this company. I still think we have a lot to learn, but we're not dilettantes. I'm saying that a firm like Godine has an incentive to survive because, as Johnson observed, nothing so concentrates the mind as the possibility of an imminent hanging. And the possibility of hanging has to be in the air every day.